What can economics tell us about work? To answer this question, David Spencer has investigated the role that work has played in economic theory, from the time of the industrial revolution till the present day. With the surprising range of perspectives he uncovers he delivers a sharp critique to modern-day neoclassical orthodoxy, and to recent theories of happiness at work. This is a deeply insightful book that should oblige labour economists and sociologists to think further about their most basic assumptions.

Francis Green, University of Kent

This book raises fundamental issues around the political economy of work. It does so through comprehensive command of, and yet judicious critical selection from, appropriate contributions from the history of economic thought and radical political economy. As such, it offers an invaluable contribution to the study of work, going beyond current alternatives in both mainstream economics and other subjects such as human resource management

Ben Fine, University of London

In *The Political Economy of Work*, David Spencer uniquely accomplishes three things that are difficult to do in a single text: he introduces economists to important aspects of work that have been neglected in the mainstream economics literature; introduces non-economists to important aspects of work that have been neglected in the literature on the sociology of work (broadly defined); and uses historical analysis to critically assess important examples of contemporary theory (e.g. happiness research). The result is a concise and very readable, interdisciplinary approach to the political economy of work.

Steve Fleetwood, University of the West of England

Work matters! A timely and highly engaging intervention into contemporary debates on the nature of work and the so-called 'economics of happiness' (why we're not as contented as we could be), Spencer shows us that another conception of work is possible.

David Harvie, University of Leicester

The Political Economy of Work

Against the background of increasing interest in the changing nature and quality of work, *The Political Economy of Work* offers a new and unique assessment of the theoretical analysis of work. The author challenges some common preconceptions about work and promotes an original approach to the field, contemplating the nature and development of ideas on work and its impact on human well-being.

Spencer approaches the subject through a careful examination of the history of thought on work over the last three hundred years. A key focus is the development of ideas on work in mainstream economics, starting with the mercantilists and the classical economists, and continuing with neoclassical economists (e.g. Jevons, Marshall). The contributions of modern approaches including the new 'information-theoretic' economics and the new 'economics of happiness' are also discussed. The author sees flaws in the depiction of work in mainstream economics and instead draws insight from the writings of critics of the mainstream paradigm, such as the nineteenth-century 'utopian' writers (Godwin, Fourier, Carlyle, Ruskin, Morris), Marx, and the old institutional economists (Commons, Veblen). The alternative approach outlined in the book stresses the barriers to rewarding work under capitalism and develops a case for radical change in the organisation of work.

The book cuts across different disciplinary boundaries and is likely to appeal to researchers in a number of different fields, including labour economics, labour history, the sociology of work, industrial relations, and human resource management. It will appeal to all those who wish to promote a more critical understanding of the role that work can and ought to play in society.

David A. Spencer is Senior Lecturer in Economics at Leeds University Business School.

Routledge frontiers of political economy

The Political Economy of Work

David A. Spencer

Routledge
Taylor & Francis Group

LONDON AND NEW YORK

First published 2009
by Routledge
2 Park Square, Milton Park, Abingdon, Oxon, OX14 4RN

Simultaneously published in the USA and Canada
by Routledge
270 Madison Avenue, New York, NY 10016

Routledge is an imprint of the Taylor & Francis Group, an informa business

Typeset in Times New Roman by
Taylor & Francis Books
Printed and bound in Great Britain by
Biddles Digital Ltd, King's Lynn

British Library Cataloguing in Publication Data
A catalogue record for this book is available from the British Library

Library of Congress Cataloging in Publication Data
Spencer, David A.
  The political economy of work / David A. Spencer.
    p. cm. – (Routledge frontiers of political economy)
  Includes bibliographical references and index.
  1. Work. 2. Industrial sociology. I. Title.
  HD4904.S696 2008
  331–dc22
                                        2008014913

ISBN: 978-0-415-45793-4 (hbk)
ISBN: 978-0-203-88997-8 (ebk)

For Deborah, Polly, and Florence

Contents

Preface

This book is concerned with the subject of work. Work is something that most of us do on a regular basis. However, there is a tendency to see work as merely a functional activity. Work is what we do to earn a living. An influential idea is that work is a chore or distraction. Work gets in the way of doing what we *really* want to do. Given the space and freedom, hence, it is supposed that we would all opt for a work-free existence.

This book seeks to challenge some common preconceptions about work, drawing on some three hundred years of scholarship in the area. It is argued that while there are costs attached to work, these costs in many cases emanate from the way in which work is actually organised. It is further stated that work can be, and indeed ought to be, fulfilling in itself. There is much reward in doing work, not simply for the sake of monetary gain, but also for the sake of realising and developing human creative capacities. Doing a job well is important to people's sense of personal worth and is also essential in establishing good social relations. To understand work in purely instrumental terms, in short, is to misconstrue its role and importance in human life.

The book aims, specifically, to present critically the historical development and contemporary state of the analysis of work in the economics literature. This reflects on my own background in economics, as well as my interest in the history of ideas. However, this book also adopts an interdisciplinary perspective by dealing with concepts and themes that fall outside the economics discipline. Hence, for example, I address the ideas of some prominent social critics, such as John Ruskin and William Morris. I also offer an account and appraisal of Karl Marx's conception of work. The book, thus, is likely to appeal to researchers interested in work issues across a range of subject areas, including sociology and industrial relations.

I realise that there are varied and vibrant literatures on work in the other social sciences. I would argue, however, that economics has remained important to debates on work. Hostility to the views of economists on work can be seen to have played a part in the development of ideas in other subjects: hence, the subject of industrial relations initially developed as a counterpoint to the impersonal view of work held by classical and neoclassical economists. Further, among contemporary academic disciplines, the most influential theorisation of work, at a policy level, is to be found within the discipline of economics. Current debates surrounding 'welfare to work' programmes (Layard *et al.* 1991) and changes in job quality (Green 2006; Goos and Manning 2007) thus have been shaped by the ideas and concepts of economists. Yet, to date, there has been no systematic explanation and critique of the contribution of economics to the conception of work. A central task of this book is to fill this lacuna.

I am aware that at the time of writing mainstream economics has changed (and is changing). Recently, a growing number of modern mainstream economists have sought to occupy previously uncharted terrain in the other social sciences. At the same time, other social sciences have witnessed a partial retreat from the excesses of post-modernism and an increasing engagement of social scientists with economic phenomena, for example in debates on 'globalisation' (see Fine 2002). In consequence, new space has been opened up for dialogue between economics and the other social sciences. These developments are nowhere more apparent than in the study of work and labour. To take just one example, some mainstream labour economists have recently shown an interest in subjective measures of job quality that have been of longstanding concern to researchers in sociology and psychology (e.g. Clark and Oswald 1996; Clark 2005). The focus on such measures forms a part of the burgeoning literature on the 'economics of happiness' (see Layard 2005). I reflect critically on these developments in the latter part of the book, pointing out weaknesses in the new research within mainstream economics on work and its impact on human well-being.

One aspect of mainstream economics, however, has remained unaltered. In spite of seeking to address issues of concern to the other social sciences, most mainstream economists have remained reluctant to engage with ideas and theories offered by non-mainstream economists. The contributions of Marxian economists and 'old' institutional economists (e.g. Thorstein Veblen, John R. Commons) have continued to be marginalised in mainstream economic debates. Non-mainstream economics has not fared much better outside economics. I refer, for example, to the recent transformation of industrial relations into human resource management. Where previously the subject of industrial relations drew some insight from the institutional tradition in economics, its rebirth as human resource management has tended to push it further away from institutional economics and political economy more generally.

My argument in this book is that the isolation of non-mainstream economics and political economy has been harmful not only to the development of ideas about the economy but also more specifically to the understanding of the nature and importance of work in the real world. I contend that there are certain fundamental ideas on work to be taken from non-mainstream economics. These include the idea that work has importance not merely as a means to consumption but also as an end in itself. I make the point that people have a need for creative work and that the promotion of human well-being ought to extend to the achievement of intrinsically rewarding work.

On the other hand, I stress (again following non-mainstream economics) that there are acute barriers to securing 'good work' under present circumstances. Capitalism as an economic system has no inbuilt tendency to promote the well-being of producers. Indeed, it has made the creation of increased profit an imperative that is prior to improving work quality. I argue in this book that fundamental social changes are needed to enhance the quality of working life.

The book overlaps with the work of scholars in other disciplines. The sociologist Richard Sennett (2008), for example, is one modern author to highlight the potential intrinsic worth of work and to criticise the modern form of working. My argument in this book is to some extent complementary to that of Sennett and others. However, I take as my starting point the economics literature, inclusive of non-mainstream economics. I argue that non-mainstream economics can make an important contribution to the study of work, especially in orientating the researcher towards examination of the system-wide aspects of work. It is clear that, while work includes important non-economic features, its links to the economic system as a whole cannot be discounted or ignored. Ultimately, thus, I am led to argue for a 'political economy of work'.

The changing nature of work is an increasingly prominent economic and political issue, underlying, for example, modern debates about the quality of work life. There is a widespread belief (convincingly supported by available evidence) that work has become more demanding and less satisfying in Western economies over recent years (see Green 2006). I aim to contribute to these debates, specifically by exploring the history of ideas on work. Hence I seek to offer context and depth to the understanding of the forms that work has taken and could potentially take in the future.

I hope, in summary, that the book will be of interest to a wide audience. For historians of economic thought as well as labour historians, it provides a unique insight into the development of ideas on work in economic enquiry. An earlier work by Ugo Pagano (1985) offered very useful insights into the nature and evolution of the economics of work. However, it left certain debates and theories unexamined and I aim in this book to offer a more comprehensive and up-to-date examination and appraisal of the economic analysis of work. For non-economists, including sociologists as well as industrial relations and human resource management specialists, the book offers an account of the contribution of political economy to the study of work. It is hoped that it will encourage researchers outside economics to take seriously contributions made in the political economy tradition. Finally, for economists as well as other social scientists with interests in work related issues, the book points the way to a potentially more insightful approach to the analysis of work than currently exists outside non-mainstream economics. My sincere hope is that the book will help to stimulate and sustain a critical debate about the role that work can and should play in society, now and in the future.

Acknowledgements

This book has proved something of a labour of love. Some of the ideas stem from my PhD thesis, completed at the University of Leeds in 1998. However, the idea to write the book only developed after my PhD, as I took my research into new areas. At each stage, I have been fortunate to draw on the support of a number of people. Andrew Brown provided vital encouragement and advice in the development of the ideas contained in the book. I owe him an enormous intellectual and personal debt. Others have read and commented on various drafts, including Ben Fine, John King, and Gary Slater. For their input, I am truly grateful. I am indebted to others for conversations and written comments on earlier versions of the ideas developed here. They include Peter Nolan, Malcolm Sawyer, Ian Steedman, Tom Walker, and Michael White. I have also benefited greatly from working with Andy Charlwood and Chris Forde on the topic of job quality.

I would also like to thank the students who took my third year undergraduate module, 'The Political Economy of Work', at Leeds University Business School. I very much appreciated their engagement with the ideas and themes on the module and learned much from their comments and questions. I am also grateful to my work colleagues for creating an environment where I was able to develop a module based on my research. I would like to thank Quentin Outram, who originally suggested that I put on a new module.

I am grateful for the permission to reproduce some material from the following two articles:

'From Pain Cost to Opportunity Cost: The Eclipse of the Quality of Work as a Factor in Economic Theory', *History of Political Economy*, vol. 36, no. 2, pp.387–400. Copyright 2004, Duke University Press. All rights reserved.

'Work in Utopia: Pro-Work Sentiments in the Writings of Four Critics of Classical Economics', *The European Journal of the History of Economic Thought*, 2009, vol. 16, no. 1.

Finally, I would like to thank Deborah, Polly, and Florence, who have endured the trials and tribulations of this book at first hand. I would not have completed it without their unconditional love and support.

1 Introduction

The real price of every thing, what every thing really costs to the man who wants to acquire it, is the toil and trouble of acquiring it. What every thing is really worth to the man who has acquired it, and who wants to dispose of it or exchange it for something else, is the toil and trouble which it can save to himself, and which it can impose upon other people.

(Adam Smith 1976b)

All in a day's work

Work is an activity that dominates most of our time, and which occupies many of our thoughts. Work matters in an economic sense, because of its contribution to wealth creation. It also provides an important source of social interaction, and can be a means to develop skills and competences. Although under capitalism work is mainly performed out of necessity, the non-pecuniary aspects of work remain essential influences upon the life experiences of people. Work has a crucial bearing upon the material as well as affective well-being of those who perform it.

This book is concerned, at root, with the nature and evolution of ideas on work in the economics literature. The concept of work, as the following chapters will make clear, has been defined in a remarkably consistent way in the history of economic thought. Thus, one can find in the major periods of economic thought – mercantilist, classical, and neoclassical – a clear emphasis on the negative features of work. The prevailing opinion in mainstream economics has been that work is an inherent 'bad' or 'disutility' that must be bribed from workers.[1]

This opinion, to be sure, has been challenged by critics. In the nineteenth century, writers such as Thomas Carlyle, John Ruskin, and William Morris highlighted the potential benefits of work, and proposed various measures to realise the goodness of work. Marxian writers, on the other hand, have argued that work is only avoided because of the way that it is organised under capitalism and have pointed to the possibility for converting work into a source of fulfilment in a future communist society (Fine 1998; Sayers

2005). Institutional as well as social economists, finally, have drawn attention to the intrinsic qualities of work and have been supportive of moves to improve the quality of work (see Lutz and Lux 1979; Kaufman 2000).

Yet, such views have failed to alter in any significant way the conception of work in mainstream economics. Institutional economics, in the early twentieth century, exerted a powerful influence over the field of 'labour economics'; however, its influence declined sharply in the post-war period (see McNulty 1980; Boyer and Smith 2001). From the mid-1950s to the present, the neoclassical approach to labour economics has risen in importance and has largely succeeded in marginalising the contribution of institutional labour economics. One result of this has been to consolidate the 'work as bad' thesis in mainstream economics.

This is not to suggest that the analysis of work undertaken by mainstream economists has remained unchanged in all respects. On the contrary, such analysis has evolved quite significantly over the last thirty years. Researchers have looked to explore a new set of topics that previously fell outside the mainstream paradigm. Notably, research has been conducted into the internal organisation of work. Important contributions include transaction costs economics (Williamson 1975, 1985), efficiency wage theory (Akerlof and Yellen 1986), and personnel economics (Lazear 2000a, 2000b). Yet, each of these theories continues to build from the same basic axiom that work is a disutility and so they all assume that employers must intervene in production to prevent workers from avoiding work.

Much more recently, there has also emerged a new literature on the 'economics of happiness' (Frey and Stutzer 2002; Blanchflower and Oswald 2004; Layard 2005). The economics of happiness goes against established thinking in mainstream economics in arguing that the utility or happiness of individuals can be measured directly (and cardinally) using social survey data. Within this line of research, work itself is sometimes recognised as a direct source of 'happiness' and measures of job satisfaction are taken to offer a reliable and meaningful proxy for 'happiness at work' (e.g. Clark 2005).

The new economics of happiness has further expanded the study of work in modern mainstream economics. However, as is argued below, the individualism of the economics of happiness (embodied in its central concept of utility), in keeping with that of mainstream economics in general, obscures and distorts the essential social, cultural, and historical aspects of work and ultimately imposes severe limits on the development of new knowledge. It is argued here that progress in the understanding of work necessitates going beyond the concepts and method of mainstream economics.

The book supports an approach to the study of work that is rooted in non-mainstream economics or political economy. Political economy has been sidelined not only in mainstream economics but also in the other social sciences. In industrial sociology, for example, there has been a relative neglect of the material and economic dimensions of work and production.

The important and insightful 'labour process debate' that grew up in response Harry Braverman's path-breaking *Labor and Monopoly Capitalism* (1974) promised for a time to restate the place of political economy in work and labour research. However, its contemporary evolution has been marred by a preoccupation with the application of post-modern ideas and themes (see Spencer 2000a). As a result, political economy has not been able to gain a firm foothold in the labour process debate. Other notable developments include the conversion of industrial relations into human resource management. Industrial relations, traditionally, has been a haven for critics of mainstream economic theory and has been a place for critical scholarship on work and labour issues. Its replacement with human resource management – a subject with connections to both management theory and practice – can be seen to threaten this tradition. What, then, does the political economy of work entail?

Nice work if you can get it: an introduction to the political economy of work

Work can be characterised as merely a means of earning a living. However, it can also be viewed as a potential source of personal achievement and self-fulfilment. A central argument of this book is that work can be something more than a mere means, so long as it is organised in a manner that accords with the interests of workers. From a political economy perspective, work can have important creative aspects and is not necessarily a burden. Although the words 'work' and 'labour' have become synonymous with drudgery and toil these meanings in part reflect on the ways that work and labour have been organised, especially under capitalism.[2] There remains the possibility for 'good work' by reorganising and restructuring work in society.

An underlying theme that runs throughout the book is that the human ideal is not a life of freedom from work. This particular conception is to be found in mainstream economics. To some degree, it has a ring of truth: there are many millions of workers in the real world who loathe the jobs they do and who would love to give up paid work for a life of leisure. But the problem with the mainstream economists' conception of work is that it universalises the badness of work. There is no sense of the historical trajectory of work: hence, for example, the form of work under capitalism is very different from the form of work under earlier socioeconomic systems such as feudalism. Further, there are wide differences in the quality of work across workplaces, occupations, and nations. Such heterogeneity is not accommodated in mainstream economics that paints *all* work as a bad.

There is a fundamental issue here about how human nature is defined, for at the heart of the mainstream paradigm in economics is the view that human happiness is increased only by the consumption of additional goods, including 'leisure'. The position of political economy, in contrast, is that there are definite (non-financial) benefits to productive activities. These benefits take a number of different forms. For example, they include the social contacts forged in the work sphere. Work, unlike most consumption activities, is largely a cooperative venture and helps to build important personal ties between people that can potentially add to the quality of life. Further, work can be a way for people to realise and express their potential to be creative. Indeed, a mark of meaningful work is that it enables people to experience self-development and self-actualisation. Think how much more rewarding life would be if the work people did offered not just a means to consume but also a way to realise and develop their own individuality.

The issue here is not simply whether work is 'good' or 'bad'. One might derive some benefit from work under quite oppressive conditions, say in the context of working cooperatively in a chain gang, but this need not be taken to imply that such work is necessarily a 'good thing'. Indeed, on objective grounds, it can be argued that work under certain specific social conditions, as in the case of a chain gang, is low quality and ought to be curtailed. Beyond individual feelings about work, the quality of work and its impact on worker well-being must be judged objectively, by reference to the way in which it is actually organised and structured. The positive contribution of the following chapters will be, in part, to specify how representatives of the political economy tradition have placed emphasis on the role of the objective conditions of production as a primary influence on work quality and hence on well-being at work.

Essentially, the book argues that work can be, and should be, a source of intrinsic benefit to workers. It contends that the quality of work is an important issue to consider in its own right and promotes the case for change in the organisation of work to make work into a positive and satisfying activity. In the course of developing this argument, it is seen as necessary to transcend mainstream economics and to develop an alternative political economy of work.

Structure and outline

The book is organised as follows. Chapter 2 considers the views on work of the mercantilists and the classical economists. During the late seventeenth and early eighteenth centuries, the mercantilists censured the labouring classes for their sloth, and recommended low wages to maintain the discipline of work. After 1750, with the transition to classical economics, there emerged greater awareness of the possible positive impact of wages on labour supply and some (though by no means unqualified) support was given to the principle of a high wage economy. This much is well known. The chapter makes a new contribution by arguing that the view of work in the periods of mercantilism and classical economics did not undergo any fundamental change. That is, there remained an underlying belief that work was by its very nature a pain and that idleness was associated with pleasure. There was a general failure in both periods to recognise the possibility for work to become an end in itself. Indeed, the focus on the inevitability of the painfulness of work became a barrier to work reform, insofar as it suggested that nothing could be done to resolve or overcome the human costs of work.

Chapter 3 examines the writings of five authors who challenged the classical economists' conception of work as intrinsically irksome. These authors are William Godwin, Charles Fourier, Thomas Carlyle, John Ruskin, and William Morris. All five believed that work was, or could potentially be, a rewarding activity in itself. Yet, according to them, industrial capitalism had turned work into a loathsome activity. In their view, radical change was needed in the system of production to combat the hardships of work. These authors, it is contended, dispelled the myth promulgated by classical economics that work was to be accepted by workers as a painful necessity and opened the way for an alternative vision of society in which work could be pursued in its own right and not merely as a means to income and consumption.

Karl Marx's analysis of work is considered in Chapter 4. Marx's views on the centrality of work in human life are outlined, including his idea that work ought to consist of free creative activity. This is followed by a discussion of Marx's important concept of 'alienation'. On the one hand, Marx believed that work could be potentially uplifting and fulfilling. Yet, on the other hand, he argued that capitalism had resulted in the alienation of workers from their work. From Marx's perspective, the achievement of non-alienating work required the abolition of capitalism. The chapter discusses Marx's vision of work in the ideal society of the future and also examines some contemporary debates regarding Marx's analysis of work, including the influential work of Braverman.

Chapter 5 considers the early debates in neoclassical economics regarding the relation between cost and utility, and examines their implications for the conception of work. W.S. Jevons, as one of the founders of the neoclassical school, took seriously the intrinsic costs and benefits of work as an influence on the supply of labour. Yet, his views were rejected by early Austrian economists, who argued in support of the notion of 'opportunity cost' that took no direct account of the qualitative content of work time. The Austrian-led critique and rejection of Jevons's notion of disutility, it is argued, culminated in the acceptance in neoclassical economics of a 'work-less' theory of labour supply. The chapter also discusses the contribution of Alfred Marshall. In contrast to Austrian economists of his day, Marshall stressed the qualitative features of work and their effects on the motivation as well as 'character' of workers. Marshall's ability to develop an analysis of these features, however, was ultimately thwarted by his subscription to utility theory.

Chapter 6 examines perspectives on work and labour within American institutional economics. The initial rise of the institutional approach in labour economics is discussed, focusing on the contributions of writers such as Richard T. Ely and John R. Commons. This is followed by a critical discussion of the approach of Thorstein Veblen. Veblen assumed that humans were instinctively driven to work well and he refuted the idea that work was all painful toil. He argued, instead, that work resistance was linked to the evolution of a 'pecuniary culture' in society that valued leisure over work. Veblen's views on work, while insightful and useful, are argued to contain several problems. His notion of the 'instinct of workmanship' is found to be flawed. Calling the human propensity to work creatively an 'instinct' is to confuse the distinctive nature of human work. In arguing that the machine process would have a largely positive impact on worker well-being, Veblen is also seen to have underestimated the human costs of work under industrial capitalism. The latter part of the chapter considers the demise of institutional labour economics after the mid-1950s, addressing some of the reasons for and consequences of its replacement by neoclassical labour economics.

Chapter 7 assesses the efforts made by modern mainstream economists to uncover the hidden abode of production. It deals first with the theory of compensating wage differentials and then examines the contribution of recent theories such as transaction costs economics and personnel economics that deal with issues surrounding the internal organisation of work. These latter theories are found to be defective in several respects. Particular problems are associated with the analysis of the employment relationship. A key aspect of such analysis is the assumption that all workers have identical (negative) preferences for work; hence the commonly held view in modern mainstream economics is that workers are prone to 'shirk' the activity of work itself. Although the interests of workers and employers can be seen as opposed under capitalism, the chapter argues that such an opposition must be linked to the objective conditions of production, rather than to the alleged shirking proclivities of individual workers. There are also reasons to believe that consent by workers will be an important element of the actual operation of the employment contract, regardless of the existence of incentives that seek to ensure compliance from workers. The organisation of conflict and consent under conditions of unequal power can be seen to define the employment relation under capitalism.

Chapter 7 also considers the contribution of the new 'economics of happiness' that confronts the relationship between the quality of work and worker well-being in a direct way. This literature is shown to create confusion by suggesting that well-being is a purely subjective construct, whereas, in fact, it ought to be understood in terms of the concept of human need. Researchers connected with the economics of happiness suggest that the well-being or 'happiness' of workers can be interpreted directly from survey data on preferences and hence tend to ignore the significant qualitative variation in well-being across jobs. It is argued that the equation of well-being with utility impedes rather than enhances the understanding of the quality of work life.

Chapter 8 concludes the book. It considers the main insights to be drawn from the examination of the history of ideas on work in the economics literature and focuses upon the key challenges that remain in the development of the study of work within modern economics and social scientific research more generally. In contrast to established approaches in mainstream economics, the concluding chapter argues for a political economy of work that is directly focused on the improvement of worker welfare through the transformation of work.

2 In the sweat of thy brow

Concepts of work in pre-classical and classical economics

Everyone but an idiot knows that the lower classes must be kept poor, or they will not be industrious.

(Arthur Young 1771)

Introduction

It has become an accepted opinion in the history of economic thought that the mid-eighteenth century witnessed a change in the prevailing attitude to labour within political economy (Coats 1958; Baird 1997; Hatcher 1998; Firth 2002; Dew 2007). Before this point, in the 'mercantilist' literature, the view was widely held that workers needed to be coerced to work by the threat of poverty and the achievement and maintenance of low wages was seen as a necessary foundation of a prosperous economy and a stable social order (see Furniss 1920). In the third quarter of the eighteenth century, however, economic writers began to recognise the role and power of economic incentives as a positive inducement to the supply of labour and to see the economic and social advantages of high wages. This move to embrace a more 'liberal' attitude to labour is regarded as most clearly evident in the work of Adam Smith, who argued against the necessity of subjecting workers to poverty and supported an increase in the living standards of the working population on economic as well as moral grounds (see Marshall 1998; Firth 2002). Later classical economists, it has been further argued, were not wholly hostile to the interests of workers and indeed were broadly in favour of the improvement in the material condition of the working class (see Coats 1967).

The debate on labour in political economy did, indeed, change over the course of the eighteenth century. But how deep rooted and fundamental was this change? Historians of economic thought, most notably A.W. Coats (1958), have argued that political economists after 1750 took a profoundly different approach to labour than that suggested by the earlier mercantilist writers. Several factors such as the 'Enlightenment' and the increased use of mechanised forms of production are seen to have helped promote greater sympathy for the plight of the labourer (see McNulty 1980: 32–5).

Historians, on the other hand, have looked to emphasise the influence of changing economic conditions on the direction of economic debates on labour in the eighteenth century. John Hatcher (1998), thus, has argued that a harsher economic environment in the post-1750 period prompted political economists to acknowledge the economic and social costs of low wages. In the view of Hatcher, the change in attitudes to labour in the mid-eighteenth century took place within the context of a 'portfolio of enduring beliefs' (Hatcher 1998: 104) and thus was far less profound than most historians of economic thought have tended to imply (see Dew 2007).

This chapter takes a different focus in considering the approach of the mercantilists and the classical economists to the concept of work. It is argued that an instrumental view of work survived the transition from mercantilism to classical economics. Even though economic writers in the second half of the eighteenth century believed in the effectiveness of incentives as a positive enticement to work, most still started from the same basic premise that work was irksome. Like the mercantilists, the classical economists were broadly in agreement that work had to be extracted from unwilling workers. The continuity in the conceptual analysis of work had two important consequences. First, it meant that human needs were defined in a narrow way: there was no clear recognition that workers along with the rest of humanity might have a need for work, not just as a means to secure their basic needs, but also as a source of creative activity. Work was seen as a means to an end, rather than an end in itself. Second, the view of work as an inherent bad deflected attention away from the possibility of making work into a more rewarding activity, via the reform of the institutions and organisation of work. Hence it appeared that each worker was born to labour in a joyless fashion since work was by its very nature painful. There was a general failure to see the endogenous roots of workers' resistance to work and the consequent scope for progress in the quality of work. At worse, the ideology of work as 'toil and trouble' (Smith 1976b vol. 1: 47) served to condone and legitimate the drudgery and deprivation of work in the real world.

A partial exception to the above was J.S. Mill. While he recognised the inherent hardships of work under all economic systems, he acknowledged the fact that the aversion to work was linked in a direct way to the system of work under capitalism. Indeed, he argued for reforms in work organisation to overcome the specific costs of capitalist work organisation. However, he vacillated about whether in fact capitalism should be replaced by an alternative economic system.

The chapter is divided into five main sections. The next section sets out the key aspects of the labour doctrine of the mercantilists. This is followed by a section that looks at the debate on labour in the economics literature during the period 1750–76. The third section examines Adam Smith's conception of work. The fourth section discusses the development of ideas on the nature and role of work within classical economics. The fifth section focuses on the specific contribution of J.S. Mill. The sixth section concludes.

Mercantilist labour doctrine

'Mercantilism' is the term commonly used to describe the body of opinion that held sway in economic thought from the sixteenth through to the mid-eighteenth centuries. The mercantilists believed that the affluence of a nation depended on its ability to achieve and maintain a positive trade surplus. Based on this, it was seen as of vital importance that a nation kept down the price of its exports (see Heckscher 1935; Magnusson 1994). At the time when the mercantilists wrote, labour was the chief input into production and hence also the major cost of production. Consequently, there was a keen focus on the level of wages. It was argued that wages should be kept as low as possible not just to minimise direct labour costs and hence also export prices, but also to maximise the supply of labour (Furniss 1920; Coats 1958; Hatcher 1998; Firth 2002). The mercantilists believed that low wages were necessary to ensure that workers worked on a regular and continuous basis. The above ideas formed the basis of the so-called 'utility of poverty' thesis: the argument that the wealth of the nation was greatest where those who laboured were poor (Furniss 1920: 8). The paradox in mercantilist labour doctrine was that, while the labourer was seen to provide the source of the nation's wealth, he or she was argued to have no right to any greater share of economic wealth than was necessary to meet his or her most basic material needs.

A number of ideas and opinions informed the case put forward by the mercantilists in support of low wages. First, the view was taken that the English labourer was innately opposed to work. Daniel Defoe thus wrote scathingly in 1704 about the 'taint of slothfulness' (Defoe 1704: 27) that was possessed by the working population in England. In the absence of poverty, workers would be certain to remain idle and higher wages were to be avoided as a means of enforcing a regular pattern of work that was required to increase national wealth. Thomas Mun's view that 'penury and want do make a people wise and industrious' (Mun 1664: 182), was typical of the mercantilist period as a whole (see Furniss 1920: 117–18). Alongside low wages, the workhouse was to act as a 'school of industry' (Furniss 1920: 109) to instil in the poor the habit of regular and diligent work. Second, it was claimed that workers had very low material horizons, and would be unresponsive to wage incentives. High wages were seen to result in increased idleness with a negligible or zero effect on consumption levels (Hatcher 1998: 69–70), and low wages and high prices were recommended as a means to coerce the workforce into working long hours. Third, workers in England were condemned for drinking excessive amounts of alcohol and for leading debauched lives. Defoe lamented that 'there's nothing more certain than for an Englishman to work until he has got his pocket full of money, and then to go and be idle, *or perhaps drunk*, till 'tis all gone' (Defoe 1704: 27; emphasis in original). It was argued that if wages were allowed to rise then workers were sure to indulge their passion for 'vice' (see Furniss 1920: 99–101).[1] Low wages, in this case, were to be encouraged to ensure that the labouring population adopted more godly habits of abstinence and prudence (Firth 2002: 46). Fourth, there was a fear that a rise in the living standards of the labourer would lead to disorder and sedition in society (Hatcher 1998: 70–1). A low level of wages, therefore, was needed to thwart the political ambitions of the lower classes and to preserve the existing social order.

The mercantilists were in favour of state regulation of the labour market to maintain wages at the subsistence level (see McNulty 1980: 24). Acceptance of an unregulated or 'free' labour market in political economy was to come later on. Among those who felt that the actual wage had come to exceed the subsistence level, a not uncommon view in the period before 1750, the conclusion was reached that wages should be reduced, either by lowering money wages or by raising the price of basic foodstuffs (Furniss 1920: 177). Other routes to lower wages involved measures such as increased immigration that helped to increase competition in the labour market (McNulty 1980: 28; Firth 2002: 47). The majority of authors, however, believed that English workers should be paid slightly higher wages than their foreign counterparts on account of their superior subsistence needs (see Furniss 1920: 183–7). These writers, which included Sir Walter Harris, Josiah Tucker, and Jacob Vanderlint, advocated measures to lower the subsistence wage, principally through the reduction in food prices. In this case, the state was to play a leading role in ensuring that the price of food was minimised.

Not every contributor to the mercantilist literature was opposed to the principle of high wages (see Wiles 1968). Several writers, including Defoe, pointed to the positive impact of high wages on consumption, and hence on accumulation and wealth creation (Wiles 1968: 117–21). Others, like John Cary and Josiah Tucker, believed that high wages could lead to a rise in productivity as well as the quality of labour (Wiles 1968: 122–6). Yet, these views were qualified (see Hatcher 1998: 104–5). Defoe, who was 'perhaps the most outstanding exponent of the relation between wages and consumption' (Wiles 1968: 119), continued to condemn the 'crimes of indolence and sloth' (quoted in Furniss 1920: 138) of overpaid English labourers. Josiah Tucker, 'one of the most able writers of the era upon economic subjects' (Wiles 1968: 124), declared that if 'the price of labour is continually beat down, combinations of journeymen against their masters are prevented, industry is encouraged, and an emulation is excited: All which are greatly for the public good' (Tucker 1750: 42). High wages could not be tolerated, in effect, while evidence showed that they acted to lower the available supply of labour (see Hatcher 1998: 105–6).

The mercantilists sought to portray the dedication to work as a national as well as moral duty. In the first place, it was argued that work was 'good', not in itself necessarily, but rather as a means of creating and advancing national wealth. Hard work was needed to maintain the wealth of the nation, and was to be performed with an attitude of service to one's fellow citizens. Those who worked ceaselessly for the nation were to be treated with respect, while those who avoided work were to be treated with the contempt they deserved. The nationalistic understanding of the 'duty of labour', hence, was important to mercantilist writers in condoning and legitimating the economic as well as social degradation of the labourer (see Furniss 1920: 200–1). In the second place, work was regarded as praiseworthy because of the evil of idleness (see McNulty 1980: 32). The imposition of endless toil via the maintenance of low wages was seen to keep the labourer away from an assortment of evils and to enable him or her to live a more virtuous and ultimately 'happier' life (see Furniss 1920: 121–2; Firth 2002: 47). Thus, Josiah Child concluded in 1693 that workers 'lived better' (18) where they were industrious, a view that served to justify the utility of hard times.

An underlying belief was that workers had a rightful position at the bottom of the social hierarchy and that they were born to carry out 'the menial tasks of society' (Furniss 1920: 147). Poverty thus was to be used to prevent social mobility and to preserve the extant class divisions in society (see Firth 2002). The notion that workers could be encouraged to acquire higher consumption wants and aspirations and to gain personal reward from work would have struck most mercantilist writers as absurd and nonsensical. Rather, they saw it as the duty of workers to toil in an unremitting fashion for low wages.

Henry Fielding, writing in 1751, used religious doctrine to justify the position of workers as the burden-bearers of society. Thus, he wrote that:

> To be born for no other purpose than to consume the fruits of the earth is the privilege (if it may be really called a privilege) of very few. The greater part of mankind must sweat hard to produce them, or society will no longer answer the purposes for which it was ordained. Six days shalt thou labour was the positive command of God in his own republic.
> (Fielding 1751: 5)

Fielding's view was shared by other mercantilist writers, who argued that the labourer was to accept his or her lowly status in society as a necessary requirement for national prosperity (Furniss 1920: 147–56).

The views of the mercantilists were, of course, influenced by the prejudices and biases of the ruling classes. Many of these writers were themselves property owners and stood to gain from the policies they recommended. It was a convenient ideology to paint the working population as idle and dissolute, since it helped to justify the payment of low wages (Hatcher 1998: 72). The mercantilists had a point when they asserted that the labour supply of workers varied negatively with the level of wages (see Furniss 1920: 118). Historians, thus, have shown that in the period before 1750 rises in wages were associated with a reduction in total hours worked (see Harrison 1984: 145). But the negative relationship between work hours and wages at this time had little to do with the natural indolence of workers. Rather it was largely explained by cultural and historical factors.

It is important to recall that in the period before the industrial revolution there was no established pattern of regular working. Workers who were in control of their work lives, instead, were used to performing work on an irregular basis: their time alternated between bouts of intense labour and periods of relative inactivity and the work they performed was extended and curtailed in line with the tasks that needed to be completed (Thompson 1967: 73). The proliferation of the wage-labour system challenged these traditions, although it initially failed to fully displace them (see Hatcher 1998: 82). Hence, throughout the eighteenth century, many workers in paid occupations continued to honour 'Saint Monday': an additional day off from work that offered an opportunity to recuperate from the excesses of the weekend (Thompson 1967: 73–5). The point to stress here is that when the mercantilists accused the working population of increased idleness they did so from a position that reflected the new expectations and requirements of industrial capitalism. Their own expectations concerning the amount of work to be performed were much greater than those of workers, and they failed to observe that the traditional pattern of working that had been established over several centuries included frequent and prolonged leisure taking (see Dew 2007: 1217).

Other factors militated against the adoption of a regular work pattern. These included the real adversities of work under the system of wage-labour. Workers, hence, cherished their rights and privileges as 'free born Englishmen' and looked to oppose the lack of freedom of paid work (see Hill 1967). There was resistance, too, to the harshness and severity of the actual conditions of work. Waged work, thus, frequently took the form of hard manual labour and generally lacked opportunities for creative activity (Hatcher 1998: 82). Given these circumstances, it is hardly surprising that many workers before 1750 forfeited the opportunity to earn greater income from work as wages rose. It can be argued that, for these workers, leisure time became a relative safe haven from the drudgery and hardship of hours of paid work.

The mercantilists, in short, were largely ignorant of the endogenous reasons for the resistance to work that was evident at the time they wrote. They saw the problem of labour as rooted in the alleged character faults of individual workers when, in fact, it was fostered and encouraged by the wage-labour system that acted to convert work into a painful and despised activity. Their writings ultimately sought to reconcile workers to the toil of work by arguing that it was their duty to labour without pleasure and they thus contributed to the myth that work was intrinsically and irredeemably unrewarding. The next section explores the debate on labour within political economy in the period after 1750.

Continuity and change: attitudes to labour in the years 1750–76

A growing number of political economists in the third quarter of the eighteenth century began to dispute the view that poverty was the most appropriate mechanism for inducing workers to work hard. It was increasingly recognised that the persistence of low wages could undermine the motivation and morale of the working population, placing artificial limits on the level of output and productivity. Instead, there was an increased focus on the role and importance of economic incentives in creating a workforce that was willing and dedicated to increasing national wealth.[2] By far the most important factor explaining this change in attitude, according to Coats (1958: 46–7), was the realisation at the level of economic theory that high money wages and high unit labour costs were not inextricably linked. In contrast to earlier mercantilist accounts, there was growing recognition that wages could have a positive impact upon labour productivity. There was also greater appreciation of the efficiency advantages of mechanical devices and labour-saving technologies, and this helped to moderate support for low wages as the principal method of lowering costs of production (Coats 1958: 47–8).

Changes in the economic environment after 1750 also played a significant part in the shift in viewpoint towards labour in the economics literature at this time (Hatcher 1998: 98). The period before 1750 saw a rise in the living standards of the working population: a trend that many contemporary economic writers associated with a fall in the available supply of labour, leading them to advocate the utility of low wages (see above). In the late 1750s and 1760s, by contrast, the economy in Britain experienced periods of rising food prices together with contractions in economic activity. The rising destitution of the working population during this period, far from being welcomed, was increasingly believed to undermine the prosperity as well as security of the nation (Coats 1958: 43; Hatcher 1998: 98). In this context, increased interest was shown in the potential economic as well as social benefits of improved living standards for the lower classes.

One of those to express sympathy with the plight of the working poor was Malachy Postlethwayt (see Coats 1958: 38–9). He questioned in 1759 the motives for reducing wages as a mechanism for increasing the supply of labour: 'is it not apparent, that the working people not only can, but would do a great deal more work than they do, if they were encouraged in a proper and effectual manner, by prevailing motives to industry and sobriety?' (Postlethwayt 1759: 44). Writing a few years later, he suggested that the working population of Britain deserved much credit for their efforts in improving national wealth. Britain, thus, had grown rich on:

> the ingenuity and dexterity of her working artists and manufacturers, which have heretofore given credit and reputation to British wares in general. ... Were they obliged to toil the year round, the whole six days in the week, in a repetition of the same work, might it not blunt their ingenuity and render them stupid instead of alert and dexterous?
>
> (Postlethwayt 1774: xiv)

Postlethwayt challenged the view that workers were lazy by dint of some inherited character flaw and instead drew attention to the loss of freedom and liberty associated with the wage-labour system in creating an unnatural limit to increased labour supply and hence increased economic wealth (see Hill 1967: 347–8).

Pro-labour sentiments were expressed by other writers of the period. Nathaniel Forster, in 1767, questioned whether the pursuit of low wages was of benefit to the nation. He wrote that:

> If a man sees that the harder he labours, the higher he shall be taxed, or if he finds in private life that his wages are lowered in proportion to his industry, is it in nature that either of these circumstances should tend to increase his industry? They must always have a contrary effect, and will necessarily crush and extinguish it.
>
> (Forster 1767: 58)

Forster criticised those who argued that the poor 'lived better' in bad than in good times and sought to promote the case for a higher standard of living for the labourer (see Coats 1958: 40–1). He concluded that 'I cannot but think it as good a general maxim as ever was advanced, that the sure way of engaging a man to go through a work with vigour and spirit is, to ensure him a taste of the sweets of it' (Forster 1767: 61).

A similar stance was taken by Thomas Mortimer. Writing in 1772, he argued that 'the combined plagues of dearness of provisions, incessant labour and low wages' (Mortimer 1772: 90) had prevented the harnessing of the skills and creativity of workers. The worker, who faced on the one side 'a hard-hearted, mercenary employer', and on the other side 'a numerous, distressed family', derived satisfaction from neither work nor leisure. Mortimer believed that it was only where work was generously remunerated that the workforce would dedicate themselves to the task of working in a diligent and assiduous manner (see Coats 1958: 42–3).

The above writers are representative of a large body of opinion in the years 1750 to 1776 that objected to the suffering of the working population induced by falling real wages. Underlying this opposition was a belief that the fall in living standards would reduce the working poor to a state of despair and hopelessness, rendering them unwilling and perhaps also unable, due to the high cost of basic provisions, to perform work as effectively as they could. In addition to being a barrier to greater productivity, it was felt that low real wages were likely to cause large-scale emigration, or worse still, political protest (Coats 1958: 44); in both cases, the prospects for the nation were extremely grave. Many of those who expressed these sentiments were influenced by the events of their day, and it is arguable whether they would have come to support a rise in living standards, if economic conditions had not changed so sharply against the working population. The debate in the lean years of the third quarter of the eighteenth century did see some adjustments in the policy responses of political economists to the labour problem; however, as Hatcher (1998: 66–7, 104) argues, such adjustments took place within the broad parameters of a commonly agreed set of ideas and beliefs which had been built up over previous centuries and which were capable of being adapted to a wide variety of very different labour market conditions.

Much of the support for high wages during the period under review was derived from the belief that very low wages would have adverse economic as well as social consequences. A high level of wages was advocated not out of a sense of altruism towards the labourer but rather as a pragmatic means to prevent the destruction of work incentives and to head-off disorder in society (Hatcher 1998: 102). Many writers, as Coats (1958: 44) admits, failed to progress beyond the definition of an 'optimal wage' which aimed to balance the needs of workers with those of employers. Within such discussion, it was still generally recognised that workers' motivation to work would tend to diminish at high wage levels, and that some degree of necessity was required to ensure productivity and discipline in the workplace (Baird 1997: 505; Hatcher 1998: 107).

David Hume illustrates the contrasts and similarities in the debate on labour after 1750. He was of the opinion that economic hardship had an important part to play in enhancing the industry as well as morality of the working poor (see Hatcher 1998: 106–7). Hume wrote in 1752 that 'in years of scarcity, if it be not extreme, ... the poor labour more, and really live better than in years of great plenty, when they indulge themselves in idleness and riot' (Hume 1752: 118). He believed that moderate taxes should be levied on basic consumption goods, in order to increase the supply of labour (Hume 1752: 115–16; see Furniss 1920: 136). He also (1752: 13), on the other hand, argued that the expansion of the labourer's wants and the improvement of his or her standard of living would help to enhance work motivation (see Furniss 1920: 180; Coats 1958: 38–9; Marshall 1998: 313). Moreover, Hume saw a case for higher wages on equity grounds (Hume 1752: 18). Yet, he at no point asserted that he wished to see an increase in the present level of wages, and his views on the importance of necessity as a labour disciplinary device point towards a rejection of high wages per se. As Hatcher (1998: 107) argues, 'Hume sought refuge in the airy postulation that wages should not be so high as to encourage idleness, nor so low as to cause severe distress, and in this respect at least he was captive of the circumstances of his age' (see also Dew 2007: 1221).

What of Hume's apparent acknowledgement of the utility of work activity? It has been argued that he imparted to all human beings a basic desire for 'action', inclusive of work activity (see Marshall 1998: 312). Indolence, he thought, would be desired principally as a respite from prolonged activity, and would not normally be pursued as an end in itself (Hume 1752: 25–6). Indeed, it was quite possible that people would endure unpleasant activities rather than tolerate the 'insipid languor, which arises from perfect tranquillity and repose' (Hume 1739–40 vol. 2: 263–4; see Rotwein 1955: xlviii). Hume also felt that humans possessed a desire for interesting action (or what was termed 'liveliness') and he maintained that the thwarting of this desire could result in increased indolence (Rotwein 1955: xlix). He disputed the view of earlier mercantilist writers that workers' resistance to work could be overcome by its constant repetition. Hence such a method could only ever lead the workforce to develop a 'passive habit' of work (Hume 1739–40 vol. 2: 263); for workers to become truly dedicated to labour and hence to acquire an 'active habit' of work, they had to be offered some opportunity for variety and difficulty in it (Rotwein 1955: xliii).

Such sentiments have been drawn upon by historians of economic thought as further evidence of Hume's repudiation of mercantilist labour doctrine. Coats (1958: 40), drawing upon Rotwein (1955: xlix), writes that 'Hume rejected the widely-held view that the best way to create a disposition towards industry was to enforce an endless repetition of toil, since he believed that human beings responded more effectively to variety and the challenge of difficulty' (see also Marshall 1998: 312–15). However, it is not at all clear that Hume felt that the poor would embrace work, even under favourable circumstances. If it is to be believed that Hume thought all humans (including the lower classes) were eager to work, then it requires explanation as to why he considered that the working poor would look to indulge in 'idleness and riot' when times were good. Further, Hume was nowhere explicit that inferior working conditions were the direct cause of work resistance among the poor. Nor did he state explicitly that 'variety' and 'the challenge of difficulty' should be introduced into the everyday work of the labourer. Although Hume espoused more 'liberal' attitudes to labour than many of his predecessors, his views on wages, work motivation, and the plight of the labourer, were still conditioned by older preoccupations and concerns.

Adam Smith's conception of work

Adam Smith was a critic of the doctrine of the 'utility of poverty' and he sought through his writings to promote the case for high wages (see Baird 1997: 510; Marshall 1998: 318; Firth 2002: 51–3). By imposing on workers a low standard of living, employers ran the risk of destroying not only the physical health of workers but also the basic incentive to work. Workers could not be expected to work effectively if they faced little prospect of thereby improving their material condition. Smith, in a departure from mercantilist labour doctrine, emphasised the innate ambition of human nature. The rich were not the only ones to respond positively to economic incentives: the poor also possessed a desire to better their condition and could be motivated to work hard by the allure of financial gain. Viewed from this perspective, there was a strong economic rationale for paying workers higher wages. In particular, the increase of wages promised to raise the effort and productivity of workers. 'Where wages are high', Smith (1976b vol. 1: 99) wrote confidently, 'we shall always find the workmen more active, diligent, and expeditious, than where they are low'.

Smith (1976b vol. 1: 100) argued that the frequently observed leisure taking of workers was largely the outcome of their previous exertions in the time when they were at work. Workers thus worked sufficiently hard in three days to justify spending the other four days of the week as leisure. Without sufficient rest from work, indeed, workers were liable to suffer a decline in their health and efficiency. Smith, thus, warned employers against over-working their employees. The best results in terms of output and productivity were achieved where workers were allowed to perform work 'moderately' (see Marshall 1998: 318; Firth 2002: 52).

It was apparent to Smith that employers had greater bargaining power in the labour market than workers and he acknowledged that employers would seek to use this advantage to reduce wages as far as possible (Smith 1976b vol. 1: 83–5). He felt that it was only in circumstances where the demand for labour was rising that wages would increase and this outcome depended on the economy growing (Smith 1976b vol. 1: 87). From this vantage point, workers could be seen to share with the rest of society an interest in the accumulation of capital and the expansion of national wealth.

Smith did not just support high wages on economic grounds; he also felt that a high level of wages was consistent with the creation of a 'happy' as well as equitable society. According to him:

> No society can surely be flourishing and happy, of which the far greater part of the members are poor and miserable. It is but equity, besides, that they who feed, clothe and lodge the whole body of the people, should have such a share of the produce of their own labour as to be themselves tolerably well fed, clothed and lodged.
>
> (Smith 1976b vol. 1: 96)

It should be said that Smith saw potential problems with a high wage policy: hence, in the case of piecework, there was a real danger that workers would burn themselves out in the pursuit of available wage incentives (Smith 1976b vol. 1: 100) and this implied the case for wage moderation as a means to reproduce a healthy and efficient workforce.

Nonetheless, as has been well established in the secondary literature, Smith was in favour of an increase in wages as a means of motivating the labourer to work hard. One commentator, indeed, has described Smith as the 'ultimate high wage theorist' (Baird 1997: 510). Smith's positive views on wages have been used to exemplify the 'liberal' character of his general attitude to labour (see, for example, Marshall 1998). However, other (less frequently cited) parts of his work point in a quite different direction. Smith, in a direct echo of earlier mercantilist accounts, accused the poor of being naturally lazy and averse to work. Thus, he wrote that:

> in the poor the hatred of labour and the love of present ease and enjoyment, are the passions which prompt [them] to invade property, passions

much more steady in their operation, and much more universal in their influence.

(Smith 1976b vol. 2: 709)

Smith, to be sure, believed that the mass of humanity was prone to idleness (see Rotenberg 1960: 557). 'It is the interest of every man to live as much at his ease as he can', according to Smith (1976b vol. 2: 760). Yet, he seemed to think that the desire to avoid work was greatest among the poor. Accordingly, while members of the lower classes could be encouraged to work by the allure of bettering their condition, there was still an important role for the state in regulating the behaviour of the poor: 'Civil government, so far as it is instituted for the security of property, is in reality instituted for the defence of the rich against the poor, or of those who have some property against those who have none at all' (Smith 1976b vol. 1: 715). Based on these quotations at least, Smith does not come across as an ally of the labouring classes.[3]

Smith (1976b vol. 1: 47) defined work as a source of 'toil and trouble'. He indicated how workers would suffer discomfort from work, *regardless* of how and where it was performed, and so would have to be induced to give up their leisure time by some outside stimulus. In this respect, as argued by early critics of his analysis, such as Marx (1973: 611), there was no recognition in Smith's analysis of the potential merits of work as a creative activity (see Chapter 4). Hume (1752: 25–6), it seems, offered a more developed conception of work than Smith, in that he acknowledged the role that work might play in providing a source of variety and challenge to workers.

Smith's negative portrayal of work might not have been such a problem if it had been rooted in an understanding of the type and quality of work that existed under the wage-labour system. Thus, for many wage labourers, work did represent 'toil and trouble'. However, in terms of his broad definition of work, Smith made no direct connection with the actual system of work as such: rather, as he saw it, *all* work was irksome and painful. This lent legitimacy to the idea that workers were supposed to feel work as pain and thus gave an air of necessity and inevitability to the real world costs of work.

What of Smith's recognition of the degradation of work due to the division of labour? Smith, as is well known, pointed to the negative impact of repetitive work on the intelligence of workers. The effect of the division of labour was to render the labourer 'as stupid and ignorant as it is possible for a human creature to become' (Smith 1976b vol. 2: 782). But Smith viewed this cost as a necessary evil: it was required to prevent the labourer from indulging his or her preference for leisure. Without the division of labour, according to Smith, the mass of labourers would be apt to acquire a 'habit of sauntering and of indolent careless application' (Smith 1976b vol. 1: 19), lowering the level of labour productivity. The division of labour, thus, fulfilled an important function in imparting to the labourer a habit of regular and constant work, thereby creating a necessary condition for greater economic growth which promised to benefit all classes in society.

Smith claimed that, in the 'progressive state', where an economy was growing at a rapid rate, the labourer would be able to earn wages in excess of the subsistence level. In such a situation, it was argued that the condition of 'all the labouring poor, of the great body of people, seems to be the happiest' (Smith 1976b vol. 1: 99). Here the 'happiness' of the working poor was seen to be safeguarded, in spite (and indeed because) of the fact that they had to endure a dehumanising work environment (see West 1975: 549). Smith implied that the economic benefits of high wages would more than offset the human misery of repetitive and uninteresting work and he argued that the net impact of the division of labour on human welfare was positive.[4]

From a different vantage point, Smith (1976b vol. 1: 116–17) argued that wages would adjust to equalise the net advantages in different jobs. In what has become known as the theory of compensating wage differentials, he claimed that wages would tend to be lower in 'good jobs' and higher in 'bad jobs' (see Chapter 7). This theory raised several issues. On the one hand, it seemed to imply that work, at least under certain conditions, might be agreeable to workers. As a result, it appeared to contradict Smith's view of work as an inherent disutility. On the other hand, there was the implication that workers would be fully compensated for the negative experience of work by the level of wages. The labour market, if left unimpeded, was assumed to effectively resolve the problem of differences in work quality. Hence, it appeared that if workers were in unfavourable jobs they were there out of choice: they had chosen such jobs because of their preference for increased income. In this sense, Smith seemed to rule out the necessity for external intervention (e.g. by the state) to improve working conditions.

Smith did recommend state education to counteract the negative impact of the division of labour on the intelligence of the working class. This was a palliative rather than a cure, since the productivity benefits of the division of labour were seen as too significant to dispense with. It was still expected that workers would perform work in the same dehumanising way, only now with the opportunity of some years of schooling it would be possible for them to improve their minds when they were not at work. Significantly, Smith did not seek to promote the case for the reform of the existing institutions of work, in order to alleviate and overcome the human costs of work. Rather his analysis presupposed the fact that workers would endure work as a painful activity.[5]

Smith's theory of labour, in short, bore some similarities to that of earlier political economists. To be sure, he disagreed with his predecessors on the indispensability of poverty as a deterrent to work avoidance and his writings gave some support to the raising of wages for the working class. Yet, he was also inclined to see the working population as naturally slothful. He remained of the opinion that some element of state regulation would be needed to police the actions of the poor. Further, his view of work as an inherent pain was a barrier to a full understanding of the true costs of work associated with the wage-labour system. Even when he recognised the links between the costs of work and the division of labour, he believed that these costs were justified to increase economic wealth. Ultimately, Smith offered the working class no hope of a future without the monotonous routine of toil. In the next section, we consider the ideas on work and labour of later classical economists.

Classical economics and labour theory

In the closing decades of the eighteenth century and the earlier decades of the nineteenth century, changes occurred in production and in society more generally that helped to foster a more positive attitude to labour within classical economics. Rapid progress in technology coupled with the growth of consumer wants during this period, on the one hand, added significantly to the support for higher wages as a potentially effective mechanism for motivating the working class to work hard. Advances in the scale of industrial production units and in the division and supervision of labour, together with adverse shifts in real wages, on the other hand, made it more difficult for workers to avoid work and promoted more regular patterns of working (Hatcher 1998: 113). Among the classical economists, there was growing optimism about the possibilities of reforming the habits of workers to fit the new disciplines and demands of capitalism, and it was increasingly argued that higher living standards were a necessary and indeed desirable component of a prosperous and stable economy. Yet, as this section will show, there were also continuities in the debates regarding work and labour within classical economics. As in earlier times, hence, there remained an acceptance that work was a painful undertaking and it was denied that much of significance could be done to overcome the direct costs of work.

The classical economists, following Smith, believed that work was essentially a disutility. It was argued that workers would refuse to work, in the absence of some external inducement. There was an admission that the labourer had a desire to better his or her condition and thus would be responsive to wage incentives. However, it was also maintained that the carrot of higher wages alone would not be enough to induce the labourer to perform work: there was also a need to subject him or her to some degree of necessity. As in previous economic debates, there remained a concern with establishing a wage level that was not so low that workers faced difficulties in meeting their basic needs and not so high that workers could remain idle (see Coats 1967: 111).

Robert Malthus argued that human beings were naturally inclined to avoid work. He saw virtue in necessity as a means to overcome the natural laziness of mankind. He argued that the economic hardship in society created by the tendency for food supplies to grow more slowly than the size of population was not altogether a bad thing; on the contrary it had a beneficial effect in creating the necessary stimulus for people to undertake work and hence to develop their intellect. 'Necessity has been with great truth called the mother of invention', Malthus (1926: 358) asserted in a manner that was reminiscent of earlier mercantilist discourse. As a religious man, Malthus wished to reconcile the law of population with the benevolence of God and he was able to do this by insisting that this law, as a cause of necessity and want in society, was required for intellectual progress. According to him:

> It seems ... every way probable, that even the acknowledged difficulties occasioned by the law of population, tend rather to promote, than impede the general purpose of Providence. They excite universal exertion, and contribute to that infinite variety of situations, and consequently of impressions, which seems, upon the whole, favourable to the growth of mind. It is probable, that too great, or too little excitement, extreme poverty, or too great riches, may be alike unfavourable in this respect. The middle regions of society seem to be best suited to intellectual improvement; but it is contrary to the analogy of all nature, to expect that the whole of society can be a middle region.
>
> (Malthus 1926: 366–7)

Malthus saw an unequal distribution of income as a necessary and indeed desirable feature of society. Without the poverty of the lower classes, on the one hand, there would be no deterrent to idleness among the middle class. Without the wealth of the upper class, on the other hand, there would be no incentive for the middle class to better their condition. Dismissing the utopian schemes of William Godwin and others, Malthus argued in 1798 that there was no scope for progress in the material as well as intellectual condition of the labourer.[6] Hence he wrote that:

> the principal argument of this essay tends to place in a strong point of view the improbability that the lower classes of people in any country should ever be sufficiently free from want and labour to attain any high degree of intellectual improvement.
>
> (Malthus 1926: 217–18)

Other classical economists portrayed work as a loathsome activity, believing that workers would avoid it whenever and wherever possible. Jeremy Bentham, writing in 1817, claimed that:

> *Aversion* – not *desire* – is the emotion – the only emotion which *labour*, taken by itself is qualified to produce. ... In so far as *labour* is taken in its proper sense, *love of labour*, is a contradiction in terms.
>
> (Bentham 1983: 104; emphasis in original)

Workers worked simply to meet their basic needs and had no desire to work for its own sake.

J.R. McCulloch invoked the language and rhetoric of the Bible in arguing that work was by necessity a pain:

> The consumption of wealth is indispensable to existence; but the external law of Providence has decreed, that wealth can only be procured by industry; that man must earn his bread in the sweat of his brow.
>
> (McCulloch 1849: 7)

McCulloch, like Malthus, was a believer in the role of necessity as a goad to human labour:

> It is idle to suppose that men will be industrious without a motive; and though the desire of bettering our condition be a very powerful one, it is less so than the pressure of want, or the fear of falling to an inferior rank.
>
> (McCulloch 1849: 239)

Although McCulloch argued that higher wages could act as a positive inducement to labour (see Coats 1967: 115–16; Marshall 1998: 321–4), as the above quotation makes clear, he remained of the opinion that want and necessity were required to deter idleness and to enforce a regular habit of work.[7]

Yet, while the classical economists argued that work was intrinsically irksome, they were mostly reluctant to implicate the actual system of work as a source of its human cost. Malthus's opinion on the impact of the industrial revolution changed over time. Writing in 1798, he argued that workers had been unable to consume most of the goods created by modern industry and had been forced to endure unstable and unhealthy employment inside factories (Malthus 1926: 309–10). Malthus took issue with Adam Smith's optimistic vision of untrammelled economic growth as being consistent with a 'happy' society. Based on the experience of Britain, it was evident that 'the increase of wealth of later years has had no tendency to increase the happiness of the labouring poor' (Malthus 1926: 321). In later editions of his *Essay on Population*, however, Malthus came to adopt a less critical position regarding the effects of industrialisation on the welfare of workers (see Gilbert 1980). While there were still examples of industrial abuses, these were seen to be offset by evidence of improved conditions. Indeed, by the fifth edition (1817), Malthus was confident enough to write that the expansion of industry, 'whether it consists principally in additions to the means of subsistence or to the stock of conveniences and comforts, will always, *ceteris paribus*, have a favourable effect on the poor' (quoted in Gilbert 1980: 95). In reaching this conclusion, Malthus was insensitive to the economic setbacks (falling wages together with rising unemployment) suffered by the working class during the years of depression that followed the battle of Waterloo in 1815, and to the existence and persistence of very long work hours and poor working conditions that acted to undermine the health of workers.

Nassau Senior questioned whether factory work was detrimental to the well-being of workers. Indeed, from his perspective, the conditions of work in many workplaces had a broadly positive impact on the lives of the labouring population. Hence he wrote in 1837 that:

> The factory work-people in the country districts are the plumpest, best clothed, and healthiest-looking persons of the labouring class that I ever seen. The girls, especially, are far more good-looking (and good looks are fair evidence of health and spirits) than the daughters of agricultural labourers.
>
> (Senior 1837: 23)

Such sentiments were shared by other classical economists. McCulloch, thus, wrote boldly in 1827 that 'the health, morals and intelligence of the population have all gained by the establishment of the present manufacturing system' (quoted in O'Brien 1970: 283n). Further, in a decisive step, McCulloch claimed that Adam Smith's criticisms of the dehumanising effects of the division of labour were 'marvellously incorrect' (McCulloch 1849: 186). The division of labour had actually increased the intelligence of the working class. Thus:

> by working together, those employed in manufacturing establishments have constant opportunities of discussing all topics of interest and importance. They are thus gradually trained to habits of thinking and reflection; their intellects are sharpened by the collision of conflicting opinions; and a small contribution from each individual enables them to establish lectureships and libraries, and to obtain ample supplies of newspapers and periodical publications.
>
> (McCulloch 1849: 187)

McCulloch adhered consistently to the view that the division of labour and machinery were advantageous to workers. It is true that, in response to the Chartist protests of the 1840s, McCulloch (1849: 189–94) began to worry about the negative effects of falling wages and income inequality on the stability of society. But, as much as McCulloch came to regret the distributional consequences of the factory system, he never doubted that the latter was beneficial to the population as a whole. Mark Blaug's (1958a: 241–2) suggestion that McCulloch became a critic of the factory system in his later work, as Denis O'Brien (1970: 284) has argued, overlooks the unchanging optimism of McCulloch's underlying vision of the process of industrialisation. McCulloch conceded that the size of the manufacturing sector in the economy might have grown too large, and even suggested that employers ought to take an interest in the condition of their workforce (O'Brien 1970: 285); however, while there was a case for alleviating the plight of the working poor, the solution to the problem would have to await the attention of a future generation of economists (McCulloch 1849: 195).

The classical economists were reluctant to embrace the argument for the regulation of work hours that formed part of the nineteenth-century Factory Acts (see Blaug 1958b; Nyland 1986). While they agreed with factory legislation aimed at child workers, they remained opposed to interference between employers and adult workers. On the one hand, a legal limit to the working day was thought to be unnecessary in the case of adult workers since they were seen to be able to decide for themselves. Those above the age of consent were deemed to be 'free agents' and work time legislation was viewed as an unwarranted violation of the adult worker's right to negotiate his or her own work hours. Although the classical economists came to accept the Factory Acts once they were implemented, they strongly opposed further legislation out of fear that it would lead to the regulation of adult workers (Nyland 1986: 519). On the other hand, from the 1840s onwards, it was argued that legal restrictions on work time would undermine the profitability of production and hence the wealth of the nation. Senior's (1837) infamous 'last-hour' thesis, although itself a target of criticism, was largely successful in promoting the idea that a reduction in work hours would lead to a proportionate fall in output (Blaug 1958b: 217). Thus, it was argued that workers would suffer increased unemployment if work time legislation was extended.

These arguments were clearly open to question (Nyland 1986: 520). First, the idea that adult workers had control over when and how they worked contradicted with the realities of the labour market in which the vast majority of the workforce were forced to sell their labour power for wages. Work hours remained the prerogative of employers and workers of all ages were obliged to work long hours, regardless of their preferences. Malthus (1926: 292) referred glibly to workers as being in 'an amicable exchange' with employers, seemingly unaware of the power imbalances in the workplace which enabled employers to impose a crippling burden of work on workers. Ironically, it was principally the inability of workers to decide their own hours which had provided the initial impetus for state regulation of work time. Second, it did not strike the critics of factory legislation that a shorter working day might, if a significant increase in productivity occurred, lead to a rise in output. William Thornton (1846) realised this possibility, but his ideas failed to make any impact on the content of debate within classical economics (see Blaug 1958b: 219).

Overall, the classical economists, like their predecessors, argued that the worker had to be coerced to work and while they insisted that economic incentives could be effective they continued to believe in the power of necessity as a means of securing a productive and compliant workforce. They also gave the strong impression that work was necessarily painful and they remained sceptical about the possibilities for converting work into a rewarding activity. To say that the classical economists wished 'to enlist the workers as accessories of reform' (Coats 1967: 130) by a process of 'embourgeoisement' is not to deny that they opposed the extension of factory legislation even though existing laws had been shown not to undermine output, and that they defended the factory system in spite of its manifold economic and social ills. Such beliefs, in practice, drew them into conflict with the working class.[8] Advocates of work reform did, though, find a potential ally in the form of J.S. Mill. His contribution is discussed in the next section.

The labour theory of J.S. Mill

J.S. Mill offered an original account of work and labour that was noteworthy for the emphasis it gave to the human costs of industrialisation, as well as to the case for a radical transformation of the existing system of work. Mill adopted a common starting point with most of his contemporaries by stressing the innate costs of work. However, as will be shown below, he also argued that the system of private property was a key contributory factor in the creation and reproduction of the problem of work avoidance in modern society.

A good insight into Mill's ideas on work can be found in his critical response to Thomas Carlyle's (1849) vitriolic attack on classical political economy for supporting the abolition of the slave trade (Mill 1984a).[9] In his article, written in 1850, Mill rejected Carlyle's argument that there was virtue in performing work for its own ends. Carlyle held that selfless devotion to work was the key to spiritual development, and that idleness was a threat to individuality:

> To do competent work, to labour honestly according to the ability given them; for that, and for no other purpose was each one of us sent into this world; and woe is to every man who, by friend or by foe, is prevented from fulfilling this the end of his being.
>
> (Carlyle 1849: 355)

In upholding the sanctity of productive activity, Carlyle argued that the free slaves of the Caribbean were no better off, and in many ways were worse off, since they now faced no guarantee of work; instead, in their new role as wage labourers, they were forced into a nomadic existence, vainly searching for jobs in different locations and only caring for the money they could earn from selling their labour services. As such, they were denied the opportunity to experience the 'joy of work'. Odiously, Carlyle's rhetoric contained a strong racist element, and his views amounted to an apology for the oppression of the black population (see Chapter 3). Mill responded that work was by its very nature a pain and that it was absurd to think people could ever come to enjoy work for its own sake: 'Work, I imagine, is not a good in itself. There is nothing laudable in work for work's sake' (Mill

1984a: 90). He maintained, in utilitarian terms, that work was, instead, undertaken for the sake of its extrinsic rewards. In opposition to Carlyle's 'gospel of work', Mill proposed his own 'gospel of leisure', on the basis 'that human beings *cannot* rise to the finer attributes of their nature compatibly with a life filled with labour' (Mill 1984a: 91; emphasis in original). Mill looked forward with confidence to a time when work would occupy a less dominant role in human life:

> To reduce very greatly the quantity of work required to carry on exis-
> tence is as needful as to distribute it more equally; and the progress of
> science, and the increasing ascendency [*sic*] of justice and good sense,
> tend to this result.

(Mill 1984a: 91)

Mill agreed with Carlyle that modern industrial capitalism had come to blight the lives of the working population; however, he argued against his proposals for social reform. Carlyle wished to return society to the feudal age in which each individual was assigned to a fixed role in the social hier-archy and was governed by strong leadership. He blamed the policy of lais-sez-faire for creating an idle and dissolute workforce, and invoked the 'gospel of work' to justify the reestablishment of the compulsion to work. Mill objected that Carlyle promised only tyranny for the masses. Carlyle had committed 'the vulgar error of imputing every difference which he finds among human beings to an original difference of nature' (Mill 1984a: 93). He had not supposed that those who started out life as strong were able to inhibit the development of the weak, and that the protection of the strong was likely to compound the existing inequalities in society. Contra Carlyle, Mill (1984a: 95) wished to see an end to despotism and was committed to human freedom and development.

In the *Principles*, first published in 1848, Mill argued that the expansion of economic wealth had come at the expense of a decline in the quality of life among the labouring class. All the great technological improvements that had occurred in society had simply 'enabled a greater population to live the same life of drudgery and imprisonment' (Mill 1965: 756). Mill considered that the 'stationary state' of growth, so much maligned by previous classical economists, was actually to be welcomed as a means to promote the 'art of living' instead of the 'art of getting on' (ibid.). He looked forward to a time when fewer people would be employed in endless and uninteresting toil, and when leisure would be sufficient for all in society 'to cultivate freely the graces of life' (Mill 1965: 755).

Mill's views on social reform underwent a fundamental revision between the first and third editions of the *Principles*. Having come down in favour of private property in the first edition, Mill adopted a more critical position towards it in the third, published in 1852 (see Robbins 1953: 147–55). This shift has been variously attributed to the influence of his wife Harriet Taylor (they married in April 1851) and to his positive impression of the socialist experiments in post-revolutionary France (Claeys 1987: 130–1). Thus, by the third edition, Mill was convinced that communism had certain merits over private property.

Of particular interest here are Mill's views about the respective impacts of private property and communism on work incentives, wages and workers. First, he came to hold the view that the 'cash-nexus' under private property was a poor inducement to labour, in comparison with the form of incentives available under communism:

> A factory operative has less personal interest in his work than a member of a Communist association, since he is not, like him, working for a partnership of which he is himself a member.
>
> (Mill 1965: 204)

While the direct link between reward and effort would be removed with the movement to communism, it was possible that this disadvantage would be more than offset by the growth of public spiritedness, allowing for a net improvement in labour productivity (Mill 1965: 205).

Second, in an effective riposte to Adam Smith's theory of compensating wage differentials, Mill (1965: 207) argued that private property had a tendency to reward workers in inverse relation to the actual hardships of work: those employed in the least favourable jobs, thus, received in most cases the lowest wages. Although there were problems to resolve in relation to the apportionment of labour under communism, 'the worst and most unjust arrangement ... under a system of equality, would be so far short of the inequality and injustice with which labour (not to speak of remuneration) is now apportioned, as to be scarcely worth counting in the comparison' (Mill 1965: 207).

Third, Mill objected to the essentially undemocratic nature of the capitalist employment relation:

> The generality of labourers in this and most other countries, have as little choice of occupation or freedom of locomotion, are practically as dependent on fixed rules and on the will of others, as they could be on any system short of actual slavery.
>
> (Mill 1965: 209)

Work under private property thus deprived workers of both the individual independence and the collective self-government that were required to realise the benefits of economic freedom (Baum 1999: 495–6; Medearis 2005: 140). Communism, to be sure, posed a threat to human liberty and spontaneity. Yet, Mill wrote that: 'The restraints of communism would be freedom in comparison with the present condition of the majority of the human race' (1965: 209). He outlined the advantages, economic as well as social and cultural, of moving to a system of production in which workers could own productive assets and also exercise an effective input into the governance of the firm. The formation of democratic and cooperative forms of work organisation thus promised, not only a vast improvement in 'the productiveness of labour', but also:

> the healing of the standing feud between capital and labour; the transformation of human life, from a conflict of classes struggling for opposite interests, to a friendly rivalry in the pursuit of a good common to all; the elevation of the dignity of labour; a new sense of security and independence in the labouring class; and the conversion of each human being's daily occupation into a school of social sympathies and the practical intelligence.
>
> (Mill 1965: 792)

Here Mill emphasised that work could be converted into a 'dignified' and positive activity. Such an outcome required that workers were given the freedom to work. Thus, with work a free activity, workers could realise and express in production their innate human powers.

Mill (1965: 790–2) drew particular inspiration from the success of the cooperative movement in Northern England, which sought to remove the distinction between capitalist and labourer, not by a bloody revolution, but by a process of incremental change. However, he thought it would be desirable, 'for a considerable time to come', that capitalist firms should 'coexist' with cooperative associations (Mill 1965: 792), and he was content to look for progress within capitalism in the first instance, advising:

> that the object to be principally aimed at in the present stage of human improvement, is not the subversion of the system of individual property, but the improvement of it, and the full participation of every member of the community in its benefits.
>
> (Mill 1965: 214)

Capitalism had not been given a 'fair trail in any country' and it could yet turn out to be the best possible system (Mill 1965: 207). Worrying about the possible negative impact of communism on the freedom of the individual, Mill wanted to see further experimentation into alternative work organisation within capitalist society.

Underlying Mill's advocacy of worker cooperatives was a 'positive' view of liberty (see Claeys 1987: 123–4; Baum 1999: 523–6; Medearis 2005: 140–1). By becoming owners of productive assets, workers would not only be set free from the restrictions on self-determination and democracy imposed by private property, but they would also in the process be able to 'enjoy' freedom. The ability to exercise control over one's own labour and person and to participate in democratic institutions was seen by Mill as vital in promoting individuality and freedom, and thereby human welfare. Mill's embrace of 'cooperative socialism', it has been claimed, was consistent with his philosophy of liberty. It reflected upon his belief that the actual enjoyment of freedom was dependent on people of all classes being able to choose between work and leisure and to gain a voice in setting the rules that govern their work lives.

Mill's approach was not without problems, however. He appeared to affirm two separate views of work, without fully taking into account the incompatibility between them. On the one hand, he took the view, in common with the classical school as a whole, that work was a bad. This view, tied as it was to the doctrine of utilitarianism, represented work simply as a means to an end, and ignored its effects on the preferences and personalities of people in their role as producers. On the other hand, Mill claimed that if people were able to work freely and to self-govern production they would come to find a new purpose and even 'dignity' in work, elevating their life-experience. In response to the Fourierists, who had claimed that all work could be rendered as pleasurable under a socialist system, Mill argued that it was the ability to act freely which determined whether work was a good or a bad: 'The liberty of quitting a position often makes the whole difference between its being painful or pleasurable' (Mill 1965: 213).[10] Mill was required to adopt a non-hedonistic view of work motivation to uphold his own arguments against the system of private property and in support of a form of cooperative socialism. The problem is that he failed to do this consistently, and on occasion, as in his critical reply to Carlyle, he gave the impression that all work was bad in itself, irrespective of where or how it was performed. To this extent, if unwittingly, he stymied his own case for radical change by suggesting that nothing could be done to alter the preferences of workers for work: it appeared that workers would avoid work and hence minimise pain, whether or not they had the freedom to work, and this necessarily weakened the argument for preferring socialism over private property.

Conclusion

This chapter has focused on the views of the mercantilists and the classical economists towards work and labour. It has been argued that, whereas the mercantilists placed emphasis on the role of negative sanctions such as poverty in inducing workers to work hard, the classical economists, in general, gave relatively more attention to the use of economic incentives as a positive spur to increased labour supply. This argument is relatively uncontroversial and fits with established thinking. What is different about the discussion in this chapter is the argument regarding the continuity in the underlying conception of work in mercantilism and classical economics. Hence a key argument of the chapter has been that the classical economists, in common with the mercantilists, regarded work as a painful necessity that was only performed for monetary gain. The transition from mercantilism to classical economics, in short, consolidated and reinforced the view that work was a disutility.

The mercantilists, having assumed that workers were naturally lazy and unable to overcome the pain of work, believed that it was necessary for workers to be subject to a low standard of living to ensure the prosperity of the nation. After 1750, despite a growing sympathy for improvement in the material condition of workers, most economists continued to accept that workers would be averse to work. It was also still customary to view work resistance as a natural state-of-affairs, rather than as a product of the actual system of work evident under capitalism. Adam Smith did admit that the division of labour would brutalise the worker by taking away his or her capacity to function as an intelligent human being. Yet, he saw the human costs of the division of labour as more than offset by the economic benefits of higher labour productivity and consequently higher wages. Smith suggested that the costliness of work was an inevitable aspect of the real world and he was doubtful that humans could find any intrinsic benefit in work. Classical economists in the nineteenth century took a similar view in suggesting that work was only ever a means. They made little systematic attempt to explain the structural reasons for work resistance and generally were sceptical towards the case for work reform, believing in the essential advantages of laissez-faire capitalism.

J.S. Mill's contribution stands out on a number of levels. He argued that capitalism gave the worker little incentive to work and he also criticised the lack of democracy in the capitalist firm. Mill supported the democratisation of work not only to raise the motivation to work but also to make work itself into a free and dignified undertaking. But Mill's claims about the possibilities for altering the character of work were overshadowed by his insistence that work was a pain which was undertaken for the sake of its product.

Neither mercantilism nor classical economics, in summary, offered any precise recognition of the potential benefits of work activity as an end in itself. In making this point, it is not to say that one ideology – that work is necessarily bad – should be replaced by another – that work is necessarily good. The 'work as good' ideology, like the 'work as bad' ideology, would be deficient in respect of concealing the impact of the social conditions of work. What remains important in understanding the form taken by work is the way in which it is organised. This makes the crucial difference in terms of whether people are able to find work rewarding or not. As we shall see in the following chapter, this point was recognised by some notable critics of classical economics.

3 Work contra the classical economists
Pro-work sentiments in the late eighteenth and nineteenth centuries

As long as the work is repulsive it will still be a burden which must be taken up daily, and even so would mar our life, even though the hours of labour were short. What we want to do is to add to our wealth without diminishing our pleasure. Nature will not be finally conquered till our work becomes a part of the pleasure of our lives.

(William Morris 1915b)

Introduction

The classical economists were severely criticised by a group of writers in the late eighteenth and nineteenth centuries. A general criticism was that classical economics failed to identify and explain the negative impact of industrial capitalism on the lives of workers. To their critics, the classical economists were apologists for the capitalist system and their doctrines stood in the way of the social reforms that were necessary to improve the standard of human life.

Among the authors to advance such a criticism were William Godwin, Charles Fourier, Thomas Carlyle, John Ruskin, and William Morris. These authors, while writing at different points in time and, in the case of Fourier, in a different country, pointed to similar flaws in classical economics and were led to endorse certain common themes, including some on the nature of work. These authors, in particular, paid close attention to the hardships faced by workers in production. The form of work evident in industrial capitalism, when available to workers, was invariably corrupting of individual character and accordingly had to be enforced by employers. This was not how work should be, they suggested. Hence it was argued that work retained, in essence, a positive character, and would be embraced by workers in different circumstances. One purpose then was to show how work could be converted from its current status as a chore into a rewarding activity that added to human happiness.

This chapter considers the pro-work doctrines of William Godwin, Charles Fourier, Thomas Carlyle, John Ruskin, and William Morris. It illustrates the way in which all five authors linked the costs of work with the organisation of work under capitalism. Rather than seek to condone work as a living hell, they sought to make the case for change in the nature of work, in order to realise the full benefits of work activity. Contra the classical economists, they believed that there was hope for 'good work' in the future, provided society was willing to accept certain fundamental reforms.

The five writers considered in this chapter did not, of course, agree on all issues. Indeed, on the matter of social reform their ideas diverged, sometimes in quite profound ways. Further, while they all accepted that work could be fulfilling, they failed to reach a common view about why this was the case. Morris, for example, distanced himself from the view promoted by Carlyle that there was an underlying dignity in all kinds of work: in Morris's view, only work that was under the direct mastery of the worker could be a source of pleasure and delight.[1] Nonetheless, all five writers embraced the idea that capitalism was an impediment to the achievement of intrinsically rewarding work and they were committed to the task of building a new society in which work could be enjoyed for its own sake rather than simply for its product. Their joint recognition of the personal and social advantages of work, it is shown below, drew them into conflict with the classical economists. Carlyle, for instance, clashed with J.S. Mill over whether work could be virtuous or not.

The chapter is organised as follows. The following section looks at the concept of work in the writings of William Godwin. The second section considers the views of Charles Fourier on the possibility of 'attractive labour'. The third examines Thomas Carlyle's and John Ruskin's so-called 'gospel of work'. The fourth discusses William Morris's conception of work under capitalism and socialism. The fifth section concludes.

Dissent in the making: William Godwin's *Political Justice*

William Godwin, early English anarchist philosopher and famous adversary of Malthus, criticised those who sought to portray work as a universal bad. Writing in his *Political Justice* (1793), he argued that the system of private property was the principal cause of the idleness of the working population. Workers were not idle from choice; rather their poor life conditions had driven them to avoid work and to seek leisure:

> Let us survey the poor; oppressed, hungry, naked, denied all the gratifications of life, and all that nourishes the mind. They are either tormented with the injustice, or chilled into lethargy.
>
> (Godwin 1946 vol. 1: 456)

In Godwin's view, private property brought all classes down to the same level and acted to frustrate and inhibit the progress of the human mind. While the lives of the lower classes were blighted by poverty and an oppressive working environment, the lives of the rich were harmed by the constant pursuit of material wealth that robbed them of opportunities to develop their intellect. As an early critic of materialism, Godwin claimed that human happiness could not be realised by the accumulation of consumption goods, but rather required the exercise and development of human intelligence. He believed that under private property no class could hope to lead a full and happy life. Thus, he wrote that:

> the established administration of property, is the true levelling system with respect to the human species, by as much as the cultivation of intellect is more valuable, and more characteristic of man, than the gratifications of vanity or appetite. Accumulated property treads the powers of thought in the dust, extinguishes the sparks of genius, and reduces the great mass of mankind to be immersed in sordid cares.
>
> (Godwin 1946 vol. 2: 460)

Society's ills, according to Godwin, could not be overcome without the abolition of private property and the move to a 'system of equality'. One important feature of such a system was its capacity to reduce and overcome the burden of work. Under private property, workers toiled very long hours and were subject to unintelligent work. In the ideal society of the future, by contrast, workers could look forward to working only a few hours each day and to extended periods of leisure time during which they could realise their latent capacities in activities of their own choosing. Godwin described his vision of utopia as follows:

> Every man would have a frugal, yet wholesome diet; every man would go forth to that moderate exercise of his corporal functions, that would give hilarity to the spirits; none would be made torpid with fatigue, but all would have leisure to cultivate the kindly and philanthropic affections of the soul, and to let loose his faculties in the search of intellectual improvement.
>
> (Godwin 1946 vol. 2: 460–1)

In parallel with later writers such as Marx, Godwin believed that it was important to extend free time, so as to allow people the space to discover and develop their faculties. He was clear that mankind, far from being naturally idle, could be led to embrace all kinds of activities, including in the work domain, via the transition to an equal system of property.

Godwin argued that in the ideal society the incentive to work would be enhanced and as a result there would be much greater scope for productivity improvements than under the present system of private property. This was, in part, because people would have a common interest in production and would be able to see the direct worth in their labour. However, it was also explained by the high intrinsic rewards from work. Hence, in a system of equal ownership, the volume of work, being the collective responsibility of all in society, would be 'so light, as rather to assume the guise of agreeable relaxation and gentle exercise, than of labour' (Godwin 1946 vol. 2: 482). Even those who had previously been exempted from all manual labour would gain from its performance on a moderate basis: 'The mathematician, the poet and the philosopher, will derive a new stock of cheerfulness and energy, from the recurring labour that makes them feel they are men' (ibid.). Godwin envisaged that in the utopian society of the future there would be little problem in motivating people to work hard.

In short, while Godwin accepted that work was characterised by pain and discomfort in the society of his day, he believed that this was not true of all possible societies. Rather, he argued that it was necessary to create a different kind of work system, in which work was valued for its own ends. Unlike the classical economists, Godwin recognised that the aversion to work was endogenous to the social system and that it could be transcended by appropriate institutional reform. As he wrote:

> Laborious employment is a calamity now, because it is imperiously pre-scribed upon men as the condition of their existence, and because it shuts them out from a fair participation in the means of knowledge and improvement. When it shall be rendered in the strictest sense voluntary, when it shall cease to interfere with our improvement, and rather become a part of it, or at worst be converted into a source of amusement and variety, it may then be no longer a calamity, but a benefit.
>
> (Godwin 1946 vol. 2: 494)

In order to achieve the perfect society, Godwin was happy to rely on the forces of persuasion and reason: 'I have no concern ... with factions or intrigue; but simply to promulgate the truth, and to wait the tranquil progress of conviction' (Godwin 1946 vol. 2: 539–40). Godwin, then, did not share with Marx the vision of a bloody revolution in the transformation of society.

Godwin was a harsh critic of classical economics. In his view, classical economists such as Malthus were blind to the exploitation and unequal power evident under the system of private property. Their writings, indeed, were ultimately an attempt to justify the status quo (Godwin 1820). Godwin's criticisms, however, largely fell on deaf ears. Certainly, there was no move by the classical economists to reconsider their attitudes towards private property, especially in relation to its influence on the character of work. In the next section, we consider the contribution of Charles Fourier, who like Godwin was an opponent of classical political economy.

Charles Fourier: the possibility of attractive work

The French utopian writer, Charles Fourier, provided a forceful defence of the intrinsic merit of work activity.[2] He argued that while work was loathed by workers in modern capitalist society this was not because work per se was painful. Rather resistance to work had been caused by the prevailing capitalist system that prevented people from experiencing pleasurable work. Fourier argued that by creating a new system of work it was possible to transform it into a satisfying and pleasurable activity.

Based on his own experiences as a paid salesman and commercial clerk, Fourier acquired a firsthand knowledge of the many hardships faced by workers in what he termed ironically 'civilisation' (Fourier 1983: 5–13). The working class, when not unemployed, faced a bleak existence in production. Workers were forced to undertake very long hours in dull and repetitive tasks. Matters were made worse by the unwholesomeness and filthiness of the workplace which served to ruin their health (Fourier 1983: 28–30). Given the high costs of work, it came as little surprise to Fourier that workers resisted it.

Fourier observed a double standard in the rhetoric of the rich: while the rich were happy to preach the benefits of hard work to the poor, they themselves had no desire to undertake the work they carried out:

> 'We must love work', say our sages. Well! How can we? What is loveable about work in civilisation? For nine-tenths of all men work procures nothing but profitless boredom. Rich men, consequently, find work loathsome and do only the easiest and most lucrative kinds of work such as managing companies. How can you make a poor man love work when you are not even able to make work agreeable for the rich?
>
> (Fourier 1983: 148)

The fundamental problem of work in civilisation was that it was not freely undertaken. Wage labourers had no control over their work, but instead had to take orders from employers. There also existed in civilised society a strong 'work ethic' that inhibited the ability of all classes to work freely (Fourier 1983: 31–2). Fourier believed that human beings could not realise their innermost 'passions' and hence achieve happiness in their lives where they were denied the opportunity of free work. An overriding goal of Fourier, then, was to restore work as a free activity and thus as a means for passional fulfilment.

Fourier identified twelve 'passions' in total, consisting of the five senses (sight, hearing, smell, touch, and taste), four affective passions (friendship, love, ambition, and parenthood), and three distributive or 'mechanising' passions (the Cabalist or intriguing passion; the Butterfly or love of variety and contrast; and the Composite or passion of blind enthusiasm) (see Fourier 1983: 37–43). These last three were important for the realisation and satisfaction of the other nine. All of the passions had been bequeathed to mankind by God and were present in each person to a varying degree.[3] Fourier argued that civilisation acted to suppress the three distributive passions. Hence, for example, in the modern industrial setting, workers were forced to perform work on a repetitive basis and were unable to meet their passion for contrast and variety (or Butterfly). Unlike Adam Smith, Fourier was opposed to a strict division of labour, arguing that the psychological damage it inflicted on workers was of far greater importance than any economic benefit it might offer. In fact, as we shall see below, Fourier believed that there were productive advantages in allowing workers to undertake different tasks.

In Fourier's ideal society, work was to become a servant of the passions and thus a route to self-expression and self-realisation (Fourier 1983: 43). In such a society, production and consumption were to be organised and conducted on a communal basis. Work, thus, was to be performed in small self-sustaining production units (or 'phalanxes'), and was to be allocated according to the preferences of those who were employed within them. The transformation of work into an attraction and pleasure required an assortment of reforms, including the improvement of working conditions, the reduction of work time, and the guarantee of a basic annual income (Fourier 1983: 44, 274–5). The purpose of the latter was to ensure that people had the freedom to pursue work as an end in itself, rather than as a means to income.

Fourier was confident that, in his utopia, work would be carried out by people without the need for external pressure (Fourier 1983: 46).[4] This was, in part, because work would satisfy the three distributive passions. In the first place, the Butterfly or passion for variety would be met by the curtailment of work time in any one work task to a maximum of two hours per day, a practice that eliminated the human misery of task specialisation. Although there might be some losses in output from the movement of workers between separate work tasks, these losses would be more than offset by higher productivity from 'impassioned workers' (Fourier 1983: 48, 278).[5] In the second place, the Cabalist or the desire for intrigue and rivalry would be satisfied by the creation of emulation between groups of workers who performed the same or similar work tasks. Hence Fourier thought that production should be organised in the form of a 'passionate series', with work divided among small groups of workers who would compete against one another to produce the best output (Fourier 1983: 46–7). In the third place, the Composite or impulse of blind enthusiasm would be realised by the formation of kinship among fellow workers, and by the aesthetic appreciation of the items that arose from the passionate endeavour of the competing work groups (Fourier 1983: 50).[6]

Fourier, like Godwin, opposed the doctrines of the classical economists. He accused the proponents of classical economics of promoting an acceptance of society's existing institutions and of blocking social reform. He wrote scathingly that those:

> who are called the *Economists*, do not have the welfare of the people in mind. They think only of enriching empires without worrying themselves

about the fate of the individual. Thus the theories of the Economists
have greatly enriched England without enriching the English.

(Fourier 1983: 88; emphasis in original)

The classical economists, Fourier complained:

advocate theories that run counter to human destiny. They encourage us
to submit passively to civilisation, with its system of incoherent and
loathsome work, when we should be trying to attain our true destiny
which is societary work.

(Fourier 1983: 157)

In its depiction of work as an inherent bad, specifically, classical economics
perpetuated the falsehood that people were to labour without pleasure on a
constant basis and thus prevented the promotion of measures that could
bring about an improvement in the quality of work.

But the views of Fourier made little impact on the development of ideas
within classical economics. Only J.S. Mill seemed to take his ideas seriously.
'The most skilfully combined, and with the greatest foresight of objections,
of all the forms of Socialism', Mill wrote in the *Principles*, 'is that commonly
known as Fourierism' (Mill 1965: 211–12). The Fourierist system of socialism appealed to Mill because it did not entail the abolition of private property. He apparently approved of the Fourierist proposals for a basic annual
income and for a new system of incentives to labour. Mill also mentioned the
Fourierist proposition that work could become attractive under socialism.
However, he claimed that 'the argument founded on it could be stretched too
far' (Mill 1965: 213). Whether work was or was not agreeable depended on the
freedom enjoyed by the person performing it: 'If occupations full of discomfort and fatigue are freely pursued as amusements, who does not see that
they are amusements exactly because they are pursued freely, and may be dis-
continued at pleasure?' (Mill 1965: 213). Yet, evidently part of Fourier's
argument was that members of the phalanx could choose the work tasks
they perform and that this was an essential ingredient in their enjoyment of
work. Hence Mill's remark about the importance of individual liberty as a
necessary condition for pleasurable work, far from exposing any weakness in
Fourier's argument, was actually supportive of it. Further, as argued in Chapter 2,
Mill's apparent awareness that work activity could be agreeable, at least
under conditions where workers were 'free' to pursue labour, contradicted his
and the classical economists' conception of work as a disutility.

Fourier, on the other hand, received praise from Marx and Engels for his
biting satire and for his criticisms of capitalism. Marx and Engels (1976:
572) referred in *The Germany Ideology* to 'Fourier's brilliant satires on the
conditions of life of the bourgeoisie'; while Engels (1993: 67) wrote in his
Socialism: Utopian and Scientific that 'Fourier is not only a critic; his eternal
sprightliness makes him a satirist, and assuredly one of the greatest satirists

of all time'. Yet, Marx and Engels remained unsympathetic to Fourier's socialist schemes. Like the so-called 'Ricardian socialists', Fourier had failed to understand that capitalism would beget socialism as a necessary part of its own development and that socialism must be comprehended in scientific terms rather than simply proposed as some kind of ethical ideal (see Fourier 1983: 69–70). Marx also questioned the basis of Fourier's argument that labour could become attractive under socialism. Fourier had indeed been correct to stress the importance of labour as a means of self-realisation; however, he had shown '*grisette*-like naïveté' in claiming that labour could become 'mere fun, mere amusement' (Marx 1973: 611; emphasis in original). The problem was that Fourier had not understood that there was a need to increase free time by utilising the technology of capitalism and that the reduction of necessary work time was required to convert labour or work into a free activity (see Sayers 2003).[7] Fourier conceived of freedom only in terms of the ability of humans to choose the work they perform. Marx subscribed to a different vision of freedom that incorporated the ability of humans to undertake free creative activity within and outside necessary work time (see Chapter 4).

Fourier's system of thought contained elements that were outlandish and plain nonsensical (Fourier 1983: 64). For example, some critics have ridiculed Fourier's claim that in the transcendence of civilisation the sea would be turned into lemonade and wild animals would be transformed into servants of mankind (see Engels 1975: 614–15). Notwithstanding these elements, Fourier did make an important case against the prevailing institutions of capitalist society and his proposals for reform communicated a significant and abiding message about the need to restore the pleasure of work.[8]

Thomas Carlyle and John Ruskin: the gospel of work

Two important nineteenth-century critics of classical economics were Thomas Carlyle and John Ruskin. Both writers criticised the free market doctrine and 'do-nothing' ideology of the classical economists. For Carlyle and Ruskin, the encouragement of free competition in the labour market promised only increased destitution and discontentment for the working poor in society. These two writers believed that work was an essentially virtuous activity; however, they claimed that its positive features could not be fully realised without radical social reform.

Carlyle regarded work as a moral and religious obligation. In his view, there was goodness in all kinds of work. Thus, he wrote in 1843 that, 'even in the meanest sorts of Labour, the whole soul of a man is composed into a kind of real harmony, the instant he sets himself to work' (Carlyle 1843: 196). In Carlyle's words:

> Labour is Life: from the inmost heart of the Worker rises his god-given Force, the sacred celestial Life-essence breathed into him by Almighty

God; from his inmost heart awakens him to all nobleness, – to all knowledge, 'self-knowledge' and much else, so soon as Work fitly begins.

(Carlyle 1843: 197–8)

In addition to being an ennobling activity, work was also a basis for affirming masculine identity. 'Manliness' was exhibited by the person who devoted himself to work:

a man perfects himself by working. Foul jungles are cleared away, fair seed-fields rise instead, and stately cities; and withal the man himself first ceases to be a jungle, and foul unwholesome desert thereby. ... The man is now a man.

(Carlyle 1843: 196)

One of Carlyle's main criticisms of capitalism was that it had reduced work to a purely money-driven activity. Work was governed by the 'cash-nexus' and workers had no interest in their work beyond the receipt of wages (see Persky 1990: 170). As we saw in Chapter 2, Carlyle believed that the freedom given to slaves had not improved their lives, since they faced no security of regular work and hence were unable to obtain the advantages of hard work (see Carlyle 1849). Here, as argued by J.S. Mill, Carlyle failed to observe the direct hardships of the work performed by slaves and he maintained the false view that the imposition of work on people improved human happiness. His support for slavery as an antidote to the problems of industrial capitalism was despicable. Yet, in his criticisms of the dominance of pecuniary rewards and the neglect of the quality of work in modern society, Carlyle did help to reveal important shortcomings in the prevailing capitalist system of work.

He expressed mixed views towards the factory system and its impact on the welfare of workers. On the one hand, he acknowledged that manual workers had been made worse off by factory work:

Industrial work, still under the bondage of Mammon, the rational soul of it not as yet awakened, is a tragic spectacle. Men in the rapidest motion and self-motion; restless, with convulsive energy, as if driven by Galvanism, as if possessed by a Devil.

(Carlyle 1843: 207)

Yet, on the other hand, Carlyle saw a latent saintly quality in the work performed inside the factories of industrial Britain. Thus, he wrote that: 'Labour is not a devil, even while encased in Mammonism; Labour is ever an imprisoned god, writhing unconsciously or consciously to escape out of Mammonism!' (Carlyle 1843: 207). Those afflicted by factory work would be rewarded in heaven for their industriousness (see Knowles 2001: 133):

Who art thou that complainest of thy life of toil? Complain not. Look up, my wearied brother; see thy fellow Workmen there, in God's Eternity; surviving there, they alone surviving: sacred Band of the Immortals, celestial Bodyguard of the Empire of Mankind.

(Carlyle 1843: 202)

Ironically, by reconciling the working population to their lives under capitalism, such rhetoric served as a means to justify the status quo and to inhibit the case for radical change. As argued by Robert Breton (2005: 40–1), Carlyle's preaching of the gospel of 'good work' to the working class provided an effective apology for the hardships of work within industrial capitalist society.

In formulating his own vision of utopia, Carlyle looked back in time to the institutions of feudalism. His ideal society was to feature a strict social hierarchy and was to be governed by strong leadership (Thompson 1976: 30–1; Breton 2005: 43–5). Those with wisdom and strength who stood at the top of society were to take responsibility for compelling the rest of society to do work. In contrast to Fourier, Carlyle wished to deny people the freedom to choose their occupation. People were to be content with the fact that their lives were filled with work, since it was by their assiduous and diligent actions in the work sphere that they affirmed their identity and achieved self-realisation. The restoration of a society based on feudal obligations and relationships appeared to Carlyle to be infinitely more desirable than the present capitalist system where human life was ruled over by the anonymous forces of supply and demand and people were denied the chance to perform work on a regular basis.[9]

Carlyle's pro-slavery stance, coupled with his regressive reform agenda, make him unappealing to the modern reader. Yet, in his day, his views attracted the support of some prominent social reformers. John Ruskin, a nineteenth-century art historian and critic, became a leading advocate of Carlyle's ideas (Hobson 1904: 39). He appreciated the argument that Carlyle had made in support of the intrinsic benefits of work activity. However, in his own writings, he attempted to shift the focus away from the spiritual aspects of work and towards the connections between work and art (see Thompson 1976: 32). Work, according to Ruskin, offered people an opportunity to express their creative powers and hence was an important source of self-expression and personal achievement. His views on the creative dimensions of work were informed directly by his own experiences as a working artist.

Ruskin argued that the capitalist system had robbed work of all its expressive qualities. The great increase in the availability of consumption goods had coincided with a significant decrease in the welfare and happiness of the workforce. In *The Stones of Venice* (1853), Ruskin wrote that 'we manufacture everything ... except men' (quoted in Thompson 1976: 35). He thought that the conditions of work in the industrial age were many times worse than those in the earlier medieval period, where workers had been able to devote themselves to the creation of great works of art. The magnificent Gothic architecture of the Middle Ages was seen by Ruskin as evidence of the joy which the craftspeople who built these structures gained from their work. The contrast was to be made with the worker in modern capitalist society who was forced by necessity to labour in a manner that afforded few (if any) opportunities for the realisation and development of his or her creative energies. With the standardisation of production, and the separation of mental and manual labour, work under capitalism was endured by the worker as a degrading and alienating activity. From Ruskin's perspective, industrialisation in capitalist society had led only to bad workmanship and to the proliferation of useless things (Hobson 1904: 132, 304–5). He saw the capitalist system as devoid of art and beauty and identified this outcome with the absence of pleasurable work.

Like Carlyle, Ruskin believed that work had an essentially positive character, almost regardless of how and where it was performed (Hobson 1904: 307). The difference from Carlyle was that Ruskin emphasised the importance of *creative* labour: the free expression of 'the intellectual and moral – and not only physical and mechanical – powers of the labourer' (Thompson 1976: 35). He related the misery of the modern worker to the lack of creativity of industrial work and he was unsurprised that the working class were inclined to seek pleasure in the accumulation of goods. Ruskin conveyed the problems of modern society as follows:

> It is not that men are ill-fed, but that they have no pleasure in the work by which they make their bread, and, therefore, look to wealth as the only means of pleasure. It is not that men are pained by the scorn of the upper classes, but they cannot endure their own; for they feel that the kind of labour to which they are condemned is verily a degrading one, and makes them less than men.
>
> (Ruskin 1904b: 194)

But there was hope for a better society in the future. Ruskin believed that certain reforms needed to be implemented to build a future utopia, in which work could be enjoyed rather than loathed. 'In order that people may be happy in their work', Ruskin wrote in *Pre-Raphaelitism*, 'these three things are needed: They must be fit for it. They must not do too much of it. And they must have a sense of success in it' (Ruskin 1904a: 341). It was important that people called upon all their creative capabilities in the work they performed and that they gained intrinsic reward from the work itself. J.A. Hobson summarised the ideals of Ruskin's utopia in the following way:

> Every man must do the work which he can do best, and in the best way, for the common good and not for individual profit, receiving in return

property consisting of good things which he has honestly got and can skilfully use.

(Hobson 1904: 154)

Ruskin was prepared to see a role for modern machinery in the ideal society of the future; however, he did not wish for machines to take the place of the skill and craftsmanship of working people, and he was prepared to sacrifice some of the economic advantages of mechanisation if this helped to preserve the skill and craft content of work.[10]

A key aim of Ruskin was to create a society where power was concentrated in the hands of a superior (though benevolent) elite or aristocracy and democracy was denied to the masses (Hobson 1904: 185–9; Spear 1984: 154–5). Like Carlyle, Ruskin believed that some people were born superior to others and he saw little possibility for widespread social mobility. Thus, he wrote that:

> if there be any one point insisted on throughout my works more frequently than another, that one point is the impossibility of Equality. My continual aim has been to show the eternal superiority of some men to others, sometimes even of one man to all others; and to show also the advisability of appointing such persons or person to guide, to lead, or on occasion even to compel and subdue, their inferiors, according to their own better knowledge and wiser will.

(Ruskin 1905: 74)

In contrast to Fourier, Ruskin did not want to extend to all workers the ability to work freely, but on the contrary wished to impose on them a fixed set of duties and tasks. He believed that the unskilled, partly for reasons of natural inferiority, were preordained to live a life of hard toil. Ruskin had no qualms about the imposition of routine manual tasks on this group of workers, since he felt it was their destiny and duty to perform unintelligent and uninteresting work (see Hobson 1904: 159; Breton 2005: 88).[11]

Ruskin (1905) rejected the approach of the classical economists and instead looked to promote his own brand of 'social economics'. Such an approach was to take account of the human costs as well as benefits of work in the evaluation of wealth. Yet, Ruskin's ideas failed to change the opinion of many economists. His critique of classical economics was deemed too subversive and consequently was largely ignored.[12] Despite Ruskin's protestations that they should do the opposite, most economists continued to adopt a narrow focus on the material advantages of production and ignored the needs of producers for 'good work'.

Overall, Carlyle and Ruskin shared a common vision of the virtuousness of work. Whereas Carlyle's 'gospel of work' was based on ideas of morality and spirituality, Ruskin also brought into consideration issues of aesthetics and art. Further, both writers believed in the necessity of imposing work and were quite willing to remove the autonomy and freedom of the lower classes in order to ensure that they worked regularly. Their proposals for reforming society, although based on an earnest belief in the need to reinstate the goodness of work, were essentially backward-looking.

The revolutionary vision of William Morris

The nineteenth-century English writer and artist, William Morris, was influenced by the work of Ruskin. Indeed, Morris referred to Ruskin as his 'master' (Morris 1915e: 279). In line with Ruskin, Morris emphasised the relation between work and art. He agreed with Ruskin that great art stemmed from pleasurable work (Morris 1915a: 173). Work was not just a means to meet consumption wants; it was also a potentially creative activity that could enrich human life. Thus he wrote that:

> man at work, making something which he feels will exist because he is working at it and wills it, is exercising the energies of his mind and soul as well as of his body. Memory and imagination help him as he works. Not only his own thoughts, but the thoughts of the men of past ages guide his hands; and, as a part of the human race, he creates. If we work thus we shall be men, and our days will be happy and eventful.
>
> (Morris 1915b: 100)

But work was far from pleasurable for the working class in capitalist society. For most workers, work was a joyless affair and was undertaken out of necessity (Morris 1915b: 108). Morris was especially hostile to the use of machinery in capitalist production. While machines had the potential to liberate people from the drudgery of work, they were used presently to destroy jobs and also to deskill labour (Morris 1915b: 117; 1915d: 69). In Morris's view, industrial capitalism had created a form of work that was lacking in art and hence in happiness and there was a pressing need to build a different system of production (Thompson 1976: 645–6; Spear 1984: 228).

The critique of capitalism offered by Morris went beyond anything written by either Carlyle or Ruskin. The latter, to be sure, had resisted the institutions of capitalism, yet they failed to offer the kind of systematic understanding of the ills of capitalism contained in Morris's writings:

> Where Ruskin had jabbed an indignant finger at capitalism and had often (guided by Carlyle's wrath at the 'cash-nexus') indicated, in the worship of Mammon, the source of its degradation and horror, Morris was able in page after page of coherent and detailed historical exposition to reveal in the very processes of production, the common economic root both of capitalist exploitation and of the corruption of art.
>
> (Thompson 1976: 643)

Indeed, Morris was led to oppose some of the ideas of Carlyle. Specifically, Morris rejected Carlyle's view that work had a positive quality even under industrial capitalism (Thompson 1976: 647). The notion of the sacredness of all work was 'a convenient belief to those who live on the labour of others' (Morris 1915b: 98), but it was, in truth, a distortion of the actual realities of industrial work in modern capitalism, which inflicted great harm on the labouring population.

The critical content of Morris's later writings on capitalism owed much to his reading of Marx. He read a French translation of the first volume of *Capital* in 1883 (Thompson 1976: 270–2; Spear 1984: 226–7). He came to believe, like Marx, that the problems of modern society could only be fully resolved by the abolition of capitalist production relations. Here Morris disagreed with the proposals of Fourier, and of Carlyle and Ruskin. On the one hand, he opposed Fourier's idea that progress could be made through the reform of capitalism (Kinna 2000: 502). On the other hand, he dismissed the case put forward by Carlyle and by Ruskin for a return to a feudal society. In Morris's view, genuine and decisive progress in society necessitated the move to socialism.

Following Marx, Morris saw the potential to use the machinery of capitalism in a future socialist society (Morris 1915c: 19).[13] Compared with Fourier and Ruskin, he was much more positive about the role that machinery could play in the ideal society of the future. Machines were not bad per se: it was their use under capitalism that was the problem. As Morris (1915c: 24) wrote, 'it is the allowing of machines to be our masters and not our servants that so injures the beauty of life nowadays'. While it was important to preserve as far as possible the craftsmanship of people, it was equally important to reduce the drudgery and toil of necessary work, and this required some mechanised forms of production (Morris 1915b: 117). Morris did contemplate that technology might be curtailed under socialism and greater emphasis be paid to handicrafts (Morris 1915c: 24), and this raised issues about possible reductions in free time in a future socialist society (see Kinna 2000: 509). However, he adopted an open mind about the evolution of technology within a socialist system. He was aware thus that the exact form of socialism could not be fully anticipated ahead of its actual realisation.

Morris argued that socialism would bring about a great transformation in the experience of work. Hence, as a loathed activity under capitalism, work was to become an enjoyable activity under socialism. Indeed, a socialist society promised to lessen and ultimately remove the distinction between work and leisure and between work and art. Morris felt that with radical changes to the form of work organisation, including the encouragement of variety of work and improved working conditions, people would come to embrace work with a renewed enthusiasm and vigour.[14] He thus wrote that under socialism:

> people would rather be anxious to seek work than to avoid it; our working hours would rather be merry parties of men and maids, young men and old enjoying themselves over their work, than the grumpy weariness it mostly is now. Then would come the time for the new birth

of art, so much talked of, so long deferred; people could not help showing their mirth and pleasure in their work, and would be always wishing to express it in a tangible and more or less enduring form, and the workshop would once more be a school of art, whose influence no one could escape from.

(Morris 1915c: 21)

In short, Morris believed that work could be made into a satisfying and pleasurable activity. His key argument against capitalist production was that it deprived people of the ability to enjoy work. In turn, his support for socialism was built upon the idea that such a system offered the best hope of returning joy to productive activity. He dismissed the pessimism of those in classical economics who believed that work was intrinsically irksome. In contrast, Morris provided an optimistic vision of a future society in which work would be restored as a free creative activity. Believing that capitalism would founder under its own internal contradictions (Morris 1915d: 79–80), he came to believe, like Marx, that socialism was inevitable and that pleasurable work was realisable in the not-too-distant future.

Conclusion

The five writers considered in this chapter all believed that work could and should play a positive role in human life. The reasons that these writers gave for why work was, or could be, a 'good thing', were not uniform, and each offered his own explanation as to how work could be made into a rewarding activity. However, they were united in the view that capitalism was a cause of work resistance and that measures were urgently needed to alter the way in which work was organised. They thus rejected the notion that work was naturally and inevitably irksome. Rather they stressed how the costs of work were linked to the structures and institutions of capitalism and pointed to the necessity for a radical reorganisation of production, in order to enhance the qualitative experience of work.[15]

The ideas and proposals of all five writers contain clear weaknesses. The stress on the alleged natural differences between the classes and races contained in the writings of Carlyle and Ruskin, for example, is not just morally objectionable, but also plain wrong. There were also acute problems in terms of the reforms proposed by Carlyle and by Ruskin. Nonetheless, their work, along with that of Godwin, Fourier, and Morris, helped to move the debate on work in a fundamentally new direction. In contrast to the classical economists, they showed that pain was not an inherent and universal part of work activity and that it was necessary and possible to create a form of work that not only met the consumption requirements of society but also enhanced the lives of producers. The vision of a future society in which work could be valued in its own right, as we shall see in the next chapter, took centre stage in the writings of Marx.

4 The Marxian view of work

Milton produced *Paradise Lost* for the same reason that a silk worm produces silk. It was an activity of *his* nature.

(Marx 1969; emphasis in original)

Introduction

Few scholars can claim to have written more on the subject of work and labour than Karl Marx.[1] His ideas on work permeated most aspects of his philosophical, economic, and political thought. For Marx, work was not just an economic activity performed for extrinsic reasons. It was also an essential human activity that could be a source of creative fulfilment and self-actualisation. With his long-time friend and co-writer Fredrick Engels, Marx explained how capitalism had come to 'alienate' workers from their work, leading them to suffer great personal harm in the course of meeting their basic material needs. In Marx's view, capitalism had to be abolished, if work was to once again become a central part of human life.

Marx, importantly, was a critic of classical economics. He resisted the support given by the classical economists to capitalism. There were, indeed, important insights to be gained from the classical school, such as the recognition of the importance of labour as the source of value. Yet it was necessary to transcend classical political economy to gain a full understanding of the capitalist economy. Marx noted, in particular, how the classical economists failed to provide a proper theorisation of work and labour. They were guilty of seeing only the negative aspects of work, and were unable to relate such aspects to the capitalist system of work. Further, they had not realised the potential for work to be made into a positive and creative activity by the removal of capitalism. As was noted in Chapter 3, Marx was also critical of some 'utopian' writers of the nineteenth century. These writers had done a good thing in promoting the case against capitalism; however, they had failed to offer a 'scientific' understanding of the movement from capitalism to socialism and communism.

The purpose of this chapter is to examine some of the central aspects of the conception of work and labour found in the writings of Marx. In addition to focusing on Marx's key concept of 'alienation' and his explanation of the nature and transformation of work under capitalism, attention will be given to his views on what work could be like in a future communist society. The following discussion on Marx does not pretend to be exhaustive or comprehensive; in particular, it does not fully engage with the vast secondary literature on Marx and Marxism. Rather, the aim is to provide a summary account of Marx's analysis of work. In the final part of the chapter, some critical discussion is offered on more recent debates surrounding the Marxian view of work, especially those sparked by the seminal work of Braverman. In addition, weak or undeveloped aspects of Marx's writings on work and labour are identified.

Work and human nature

Marx (1976: 283) defined work as 'a process between man and nature, a process by which man, through his own actions, mediates, regulates and controls the metabolism between himself and nature'. Here it was emphasised that humans were required to transform nature to meet their basic needs and that work as such was performed out of necessity. The labour process, 'in its simple and abstract elements', provided:

> the universal condition for the metabolic interaction [*Stoffwechsel*] between man and nature, the everlasting nature-imposed condition of human existence, and it is therefore independent of every form of that existence, or rather it is common to all forms of society in which human beings live.
>
> (Marx 1976: 290)

Work was not a unique activity of humans. Other non-human life forms acted on nature to aid their survival: 'A spider conducts operations which resemble those of the weaver, and a bee would put many a human architect to shame by the construction of its honeycomb cells' (Marx 1976: 284). Yet, the work done by humans was unique in being governed by the power of conceptual thought: what was produced was not predetermined by instinct, but was imagined in the minds of producers prior to its actual realisation. According to Marx, 'what distinguishes the worst architect from the best of bees is that the architect builds the cell in his mind before he constructs it in wax' (Marx 1976: 284). Human labour, then, represented for Marx purposeful activity.

The activity of work in human society, however, was much more than just a means to survival. It was also the activity through which people affirmed and realised their humanity. Conscious work, in Marx's view, was the root of man's 'species being'. As he put it:

> the productive life is the life of the species. It is life-engendering life. The whole character of a species – its species-character – is contained in

the character of its life activity; and free, conscious activity is man's species-character.

(Marx 1977: 68)

According to Marx, humans could achieve self-development and self-realisation in and through productive activity. Work, far from being irredeemably painful, was an essential life-activity that could and should be fulfilling in its own right.

Marx's theory of labour was built upon a particular view of human nature. He believed that human beings were naturally inclined to undertake some productive activity not simply to enjoy the benefits of consumption but also to realise their innate creative powers. The human need for creative activity led people to actively seek out the challenge and difficulty of work. Instead of aiming for a life of ease, he thought, people gained great personal reward from engaging in productive activities that enabled them to exercise their physical and mental capacities. Marx stressed that human work had a vital role in the expression of creativity and thus was to be regarded as an essentially positive activity.

The intimate connection between humanity and work remained an important and enduring theme in the writings of Marx and Engels.[2] Both stressed the way in which people were themselves transformed by the process of work (Marx 1976: 283). In the opinion of Marx and Engels, the identities and personalities of people were shaped by their participation in work activities. Whether people could or could not achieve fulfilment in their lives was seen to depend upon the ways in which they experienced work.

Stress was also placed upon the social character of labour. In human society, Marx wrote, people must 'enter into definite connections and relations with one another and only within these social connections and relations does their actions on nature, does production take place' (Marx 1968: 80). Only by working together could people produce the things they needed to live. Marx emphasised that production created not just the means of life, but also the essence of society itself. The point was well made by Marx and Engels in *The German Ideology* when they objected to the classification of production as a process orientated towards human reproduction:

The way in which men produce their means of subsistence depends first of all on the nature of the means of subsistence they actually find in existence and have to reproduce. This mode of production must not be considered simply as being the production of the physical existence of the individuals. Rather it is a definite form of activity of these individuals, a definite form of expressing their life, a definite *mode of life* on their part. As individuals express their life, so they are. What they are, therefore, coincides with their production, both with *what* they produce and with *how* they produce. Hence what individuals are depends on the material conditions of their production.

(Marx and Engels 1976: 37; emphasis in original)

For Marx and Engels, people were to be understood as 'social beings'. Human labour forged important social ties between people that determined the form of society as a whole. In this materialist view of human behaviour, activities in the sphere of production were considered to have a major bearing on the way that people thought and behaved.

However, the labour process took different forms depending on the stage of history that was reached. Its form under capitalism thus was very different from the one it had taken under feudalism. One of Marx's chief criticisms of the classical economists from Adam Smith onwards was that they had failed to draw out the distinctive aspects of labour within capitalist society. Instead, there was a tendency in classical economics to confuse capitalist production with the labour process itself, and to ignore the historical specificity and thus transitory nature of social relations. The classical economists, in effect, had treated history as a process that ended with capitalism. Marx made this criticism most clearly in *The Poverty of Philosophy*:

> Economists express the relations of bourgeois production, the division of labour, credit, money, etc., as fixed, immutable, eternal categories. ... Economists explain how production takes place in the above-mentioned relations, but what they do not explain is how these relations themselves are produced, that is, the historical movement which gave them birth.
>
> (Marx 1975b: 97)

In contrast, Marx and Engels were concerned to uncover the *specific differentiae* of production in capitalist society. In this way, they wished to show that capitalism was neither necessary nor inevitable; rather it was only one possible form of society that would be transcended in the future, by the pressure of collective action from the working class. As we shall see below, Marx argued that one of the peculiar features of the capitalist labour process was the 'alienation' of the worker.

The concept of 'alienation'

Marx first introduced the concept of 'alienation' in the *Economic and Philosophical Manuscripts*. Alienation, in essence, represented the inability of people to exercise control over their labour. Although serfs had not been able to fully determine their labour in earlier feudal society, this paled into insignificance as compared with the alienation suffered by the working class under capitalism. The private ownership of the means of production meant that the majority of people in society were now unable to meet their needs through their own labour and instead were forced to undertake paid work in order to survive. This situation, Marx believed, had come to exert a profound negative influence on the lives of producers.

Marx identified four different dimensions of alienation under capitalism. First, wage labourers were alienated from the product of their own labour because it was owned by the capitalists who hired them for a specified period of time. They were unable to use the things that they produced to sustain life, since these things were the property of capitalists. Marx stressed that the workers' alienation would grow in proportion with the number of commodities they yielded in production. Normally, it would be expected that greater production would advance the welfare of workers, by enlarging the goods available to them. Yet, in capitalism, the reverse was the case. Hence, by adding to the volume of produced commodities workers only increased the 'hostile and alien' force that dominated over them (Marx 1977: 64). For Marx, increased production led necessarily to the impoverishment of the working class:

> It is true that labour produces wonderful things for the rich – but for the worker it produces privation. It produces palaces – but for the worker, hovels. It produces beauty – but for the worker, deformity. It replaces labour by machines, but it throws one section of the workers back to a barbarous type of labour, and it turns the other section into a machine. It produces intelligence – but for the worker, stupidity, and cretinism.
>
> (Marx 1977: 65)

Second, it was argued that workers were alienated from the activity of work itself. In working for capitalists, workers relinquished control over the direction of their own labour within production. What and how work was done were decided upon by capitalists, not workers. Marx stressed that this loss of control over the labour process would mean that work itself would no longer exist as a creative force; rather it would be viewed by workers as a purely functional activity that was performed to earn wages. Marx indicated too that the power of capitalists in production would be used to the disadvantage of workers; under the pressure to make profit, capitalists thus would find it in their own interests to lengthen work time, and to intensify work. In these ways, the alienation of workers from work itself would grow even more severe.

The third dimension of alienation was the estrangement of workers from their 'species being'. As pointed out above, Marx viewed the ability to participate in creative work as an essential part of human nature. The fact that under capitalism workers were unable to exercise any control over the product and process of labour meant that they were effectively denied the opportunity to work creatively and freely. Work, instead of being the foundation of human development, thus had become a simple means to income and was associated with endless toil and drudgery.

Finally, Marx (1977: 69) argued that workers were alienated from each other. Under capitalism workers were treated as commodities rather than as people and were unable to forge positive social connections. More concretely, workers were alienated from one another by the fragmentation of tasks which undermined cooperation, by the imposition of a hierarchical work structure which made workers compete against one another, and by the lack of any form of collective decision making over the organisation and control of work.

Marx argued that alienation ultimately was the source of great misery to the working class as a whole and was the cause of opposition to the activity of work itself. Thus, according to Marx, under capitalism:

> The worker ... only feels himself outside his work, and in his work feels outside himself. He feels at home when he is not working, and when he is working he does not feel at home. His labour is therefore not voluntary but coerced; it is *forced labour*. It is therefore not the satisfaction of a need; it is merely a *means* to satisfy needs external to it. Its alien character emerges clearly in the fact that as soon as no physical or other compulsion exists, labour is shunned like the plague.
>
> (Marx 1977: 66; emphasis in original)

Here we may note that Marx stressed the historical origins of the temporal divide between work and leisure, and argued that instrumental attitudes towards work, instead of being a ubiquitous feature of reality, were in fact the product of capitalism. Workers possessed a positive preference for leisure and a negative preference for work, not because of their natural proclivity for idleness, but instead because of their 'alienation' in capitalist production. Marx argued that the commonsense view of work as an unpleasant necessity was symptomatic of the alienated experience of work under capitalism. Indeed, such a view played a vital role in justifying the suffering of the working class by denying that anything could be done to resolve the costs of work.

Marx contended that alienation would not just affect the working class; it would also impact on the capitalist class as well. Capitalists, thus, had no way of realising their true humanity, since their own needs were subordinated to those of capital accumulation. All members of capitalist society effectively were enslaved by the structures and processes of capitalism: their lives were governed by conditions that appeared to exist independently of them, and over which they had no control. Thus, while commodities expressed definite social relations between people, as Marx (1976: 165) put it, these relations assumed 'the fantastic form of a relation between things'. Capital, value, money, and so on commanded power over the lives of people and restricted the opportunity for free activity (see Fromm 1961: 49).

In *The Holy Family*, Marx and Engels indicated that while capitalists were alienated under capitalism they had interests in not overcoming this situation:

> The propertied class and the class of the proletariat present the same human self-estrangement. But the former class feels at ease and

strengthened in this self-alienation, it recognises estrangement *as its own power* and has in it the *semblance* of a human existence. The latter feels annihilated in estrangement; it sees in it its own powerlessness and the reality of an inhuman existence.

(Marx and Engels 1975: 36; emphasis in original)

In spite of their alienation, capitalists would defend capitalism in order to ensure that their own material advantage over the working class was preserved. In contrast, Marx envisaged that the working class would come to develop an awareness of its own alienation under capitalism and would seek to negate the power of capitalists. Thus, for Marx, proletariat revolution was a necessary and inevitable consequence of the development of capitalist society. The next section considers Marx's views on exploitation under capitalism and on the nature and development of capitalist work relations.

Expolitation and the transformation of work under capitalism

Capitalist production, according to Marx, operated through the purchase and sale of commodities formally owned by the capitalist class. Capitalists were able to buy commodities such as labour power and machinery, and utilise them in the production of new commodities that realised a sum of money in exchange much greater than the initial monetary cost of the commodities used as inputs in production. Marx stressed that the positive return to capitalists in this case was not the product of any kind of imperfection in the marketplace. All commodities, including the commodity labour power that workers sold to capitalists in exchange for wages, traded at their underlying values. Here Marx applied a labour theory of value to understand the formation of prices. Thus, in the case of labour power, the wages received by workers matched exactly the socially necessary labour time employed in the production of the commodities that made up the subsistence wage bundle. Equally, all non-labour inputs were bought and sold at prices set by the socially necessary labour time required in their production. Marx deduced then that for profit to exist at least one input must be able to contribute a greater amount of value in production than its own value. This input, Marx claimed, was labour power. Unlike non-labour inputs that transferred their value to commodities in an unchanged form, labour power had the unique property of being able to create new value when set to work in production.

It was stressed that there was a difference between what capitalists paid for labour power in the labour market and what labour power could actually produce in the workplace. The socially necessary labour time required to meet the needs of the worker, according to Marx, was less than the actual time for which labour power could be employed in production. In Marx's view, the working day contained both a paid and unpaid element. Paid labour time was equal to the labour time that was needed to produce the value of the worker's level of subsistence. Unpaid labour time was equal to the labour time that was performed by the worker for the benefit of the capitalist. During unpaid labour time, the worker produced 'surplus value', that is, an amount of new value in excess of the value of labour power, and this provided the essence of the capitalist's profit.

Marx thus argued that profit was based on the exploitation of workers by capitalists. Here exploitation existed not because of any direct 'theft' or 'robbery' from workers in terms of the underpayment of wages; on the contrary, wages continued to match the value of labour power. Rather it arose from the fact that capitalists were able to force workers to work longer hours than were needed to meet their own requirements. That they were able to do so was due to their ownership of the means of production, which transformed labour power into a commodity and which denied workers control over the determination of working time.

Marx emphasised the way in which the pursuit of surplus value by capitalists led to the constant transformation of the production process in capitalist society. Capitalists would strive to generate additional surplus value through two main routes. First, they would aim to increase 'absolute surplus value' by prolonging the duration of the working day. This had a direct benefit to capitalists in increasing the length of unpaid labour time. However, it ran the risk of destroying the health of workers, and thus reducing the duration of their labour power. Although capitalists would be driven to extend the working day, they would retain interests in establishing a 'normal working day' that suited the reproduction of labour power (Marx 1976: 376–7). In this sense, work time legislation such as the nineteenth-century Factory Acts was not incompatible with the requirements of capitalists, since it mitigated the problem of overwork. Second, capitalists would seek to increase 'relative surplus value' by reducing the length of paid labour time. The latter required the progress of technology and hence productivity in production. Such progress thus would allow for a cheapening in the commodities consumed by workers, leading to a reduction in the value of labour power and an increase in unpaid labour time within a given working day. As Marx wrote:

> The objective of the development of the productivity of labour within the context of capitalist production is the shortening of that part of the working day in which the worker must work for himself, and the lengthening, thereby, of the other part of that day, in which he is free to work for nothing for the capitalist.
>
> (Marx 1976: 438)

Production under capitalism was seen by Marx as an inherently dynamic process that was driven by the profit imperative. He stressed how changes in the design and organisation of work as well as in science and technology were made to advance the wealth of capitalists rather than to benefit society as a whole. Indeed, the changes that occurred in production were in most cases to the detriment of workers. Hence the detailed division of labour that was used by capitalists to reduce the cost of labour power had resulted in the reduction of labour to a homogenous form. Many workers, instead of being able to develop their knowledge in work, were forced to perform the same dull and repetitive tasks. Although such work was suited to the needs of capitalists, it was ultimately destructive of the physical and mental health of the workforce. The industrial worker thus faced being converted 'into a crippled monstrosity' (Marx 1976: 481).

Marx (1976: 483) welcomed Adam Smith's candour on the human costs of job specialisation. But he emphasised that these costs were to be understood as the specific outcome of the capitalist drive to make profit. Capitalists had imposed a harsher work environment on workers in order to meet their own material interests. The use of machinery was also seen to blight the lives of workers. While the machine drove up the productivity of labour and hence reduced the value of labour power, it also had the effect of allowing women and children to be employed in the workplace, by reducing the dependence of production on muscular strength. This provided capitalists with additional labour power to exploit and also made possible further reductions in wages (Marx 1976: 517–18).

Work performed inside factories was seen by Marx as especially damaging to the well-being of workers:

> Factory work exhausts the nervous system to the uttermost; at the same time, it does away with the many-sided play of the muscles, and confiscates every atom of freedom, both in bodily and intellectual activity. Even the lightening of the labour becomes an instrument of torture, since the machine does not free the worker from work, but rather deprives the work itself of all content. Every kind of capitalist production, in so far as it is not only a labour process but also capital's process of valorisation, has this in common, but it is not the worker who employs the conditions of his work, but rather the reverse, the conditions of work employ the worker.
>
> (Marx 1976: 548)

What had the potential to liberate workers from common drudgery, machinery, thus had become under capitalism a mechanism to control and exploit them. In the capitalist workplace:

> all means for the development of production undergo a dialectical inversion so that they become means of domination and exploitation of the producers; they distort the worker into a fragment of man, they degrade him to the level of an appendage of a machine, they destroy the actual content of his labour by turning it into a torment.
>
> (Marx 1976: 799)

There were, though, inherent contradictions in the development of capitalist production. For example. in the movement to mechanised forms of production, there was a tendency for workers to be expelled from production. Given that capitalists relied for their wealth on the unpaid labour time of workers, this tendency posed significant challenges to the continuous creation of profit. Indeed, Marx's law of the tendency for the rate of profit to fall was premised on the idea that capitalist production was characterised by labour saving technical change, leading to an ever increasing ratio of means of production to labour power. Further, in bringing workers together in one place and by subjecting them to a common experience of alienated work, it was argued that capitalism would tend to create a united working class that was opposed to its very existence. Thus, in spite of the objectification of capitalist control in machinery and the rise in the reserve army of the unemployed caused by increased mechanisation, workers would come to acquire the collective strength and organisation to challenge the power of capital. As Marx wrote, while the constant revolution of the labour process:

> creates the real conditions for the domination of labour by capital, perfecting the process and providing it with the appropriate framework, ... by evolving conditions of production and communication and productive forces of labour antagonistic to the workers involved in them, this revolution creates the real premises of a new mode of production, one that abolishes the contradictory form of capitalism. It thereby creates the material basis of a newly shaped social process and hence of a new social formation.
>
> (Marx 1976: 1065)

In effect, the very processes which augmented capitalist domination would also tend towards its demise. Marx claimed that capitalism would ultimately founder under its own internal contradictions.

Marx's vision of the future

Marx believed in the necessity and desirability of building a future communist society. He dismissed as apologetic measures aimed at reforming capitalism. Higher wages advocated by trade unions, for example, were viewed as 'nothing but *better payment for the slave*', for they 'would not win either for the worker or for labour their human status and dignity' (Marx 1977: 72–3; emphasis in original). By showing how exploitation under capitalism was compatible with a 'free' and 'fair' labour market, Marx established the futility of manipulating wages to alleviate the plight of the working class. The end of exploitation required no less than the abolition of capitalism itself. Adam Smith's proposals for state education to combat the degrading effects of the division of labour were also derided by Marx as 'homoeopathic doses', since they failed to deliver any decisive or lasting change in the life-situation of producers (Marx 1976: 484). Revolution as opposed to reform was required to achieve genuine progress in society.

In presenting his vision of an ideal society, Marx emphasised the importance of increasing 'free time' at the expense of necessary labour time spent on meeting the needs of society. In his opinion, people could only develop their innate creative capacities to the fullest possible extent if they were granted the freedom to pursue activities of their own choosing. Were they to spend most of their time undertaking the instrumental activity of work their actions would be restricted by essential external constraints and they would be unable to lead fully creative lives. These ideas were well conveyed by Marx in the third volume of *Capital* when he drew a clear distinction between 'the realm of necessity' and 'the true realm of freedom':

> The realm of freedom actually begins only where labour which is determined by necessity and mundane considerations ceases; thus in the very nature of things it lies beyond the sphere of actual material production. Just as the savage must wrestle with nature to satisfy his wants, to maintain and reproduce his life, so must civilised man, and he must do so in all forms of society and under all possible modes of production. This realm of natural necessity expands with his development, because his needs do too; but the productive forces to satisfy these expand at the same time. Freedom, in this sphere, can only consist in this, that socialised man, the associated producers, govern the human metabolism with nature in a rational way, bringing it under their collective control instead of being dominated by it as a blind power; accomplishing it with the least expenditure of energy and in conditions most worthy and appropriate to their human nature. But this always remains a realm of necessity. The true realm of freedom, the development of human powers as an end in itself, begins beyond it, though it can only flourish with this realm of necessity as its basis. The reduction of the working day is the basic prerequisite.
>
> (Marx 1992: 959)

The point was that economically necessary work continued to be circumscribed by material needs and was not a truly free activity. This was in contrast to other kinds of activity such as the arts where people were able to carry out activities not for the sake of external needs but for their own ends. In such activities, hence, it was possible for people to be freely creative. The purpose, then, of communism was to expand the opportunities for free creative activity by economising on labour time during which people were obliged to perform activities which met their physical requirements. However, as we shall see, Marx held that in a future communist society, labour would be transformed into an end in itself.

Marx felt that 'the realm of freedom' could be expanded under communism by the development of the forces of production. He was confident that with production liberated from the contradictions endemic to capitalism there would be plentiful scope for the progress of technology which could be harnessed to reduce the length of the working day. Unlike nineteenth-century 'utopian' critics of capitalism such as Fourier (see Chapter 3), Marx believed that modern machinery constituted the highest point of human creative activity; the point was to liberate it from capitalism and to employ it as a means to enhance the lives of all in society.

Whereas under capitalism the reduction in necessary labour time was used to increase surplus value, in the ideal society of the future it would be used to increase free time. In this way, there would be much room for 'the free development of individualities' (Marx 1973: 706). Marx thought that free time would be used for the 'artistic' as well as 'scientific' development of individuals and thus would be the catalyst for the creation and appropriation of great beauty and truth. Based on this, Marx (1973: 708) foresaw that after capitalism's demise 'wealth' itself would be defined in terms of 'free time', not in terms of labour time.

Marx did not see freedom as incompatible with the realm of necessity, however (Sayers 2003). On the contrary, he set out two necessary conditions for free activity in this realm. First, it was essential that 'the associated producers govern the human metabolism with nature in a rational way, bringing it under their collective control instead of being dominated by it as a blind power' (Marx 1992: 959). This effectively meant that production was undertaken in a way that did not alienate producers, but rather was orientated to the satisfaction of the needs of society. Second, there was a need for necessary work to be performed 'with the least expenditure of energy and in conditions most worthy and appropriate to their human nature' (ibid.). Thus, with the socialisation of productive forces, it would be possible to devote fewer hours to hard, physical work, and longer hours to creative work. Marx seemed to have in mind the idea that in a future communist society machinery and technology could be used to reduce and eliminate unpleasant and irksome forms of work.

The purpose of reducing work time was not simply to expand the freedom for people to pursue activities as ends in themselves and thus to fully realise their creative powers. It was also to provide a necessary basis for the conversion of work into a free and fulfilling activity (see Sayers 2003). Hence:

> It is self-evident that if labour-time is reduced to a normal length and, furthermore, labour is no longer performed for someone else, but for myself, and, at the same time, the social contradictions between master and men, etc., being abolished, it acquires a quite different, a free character, it becomes real social labour, and finally the basis of *disposable time* – the *labour* of a man who has also disposable time, must be of a much higher quality than that of the beast of burden.
>
> (Marx 1972: 257; emphasis in original)

Here it was emphasised that necessary work in a future communist society would be much more productive than it was in capitalism where productivity was artificially constrained by the hierarchal and coercive nature of the wage-labour relation. Marx asserted that productive activities under communism would draw upon the fully developed capabilities of individuals and would be executed to the full benefit of the community, improving their attractiveness among producers. The development of individual capabilities, in turn, would allow for further improvements in the productive forces of society, adding to the potential for a shorter working day.

Commenting on the work of James Mill, Marx expressed clearly what he saw as the positive transformation that would occur in the character of labour under conditions where people 'carried out production as human beings':

> Let us suppose that we had carried out production as human beings. Each of us would have in two ways affirmed himself and the other person. 1) In my production I would have objectified my individuality, its specific character, and therefore enjoyed not only an individual manifestation of my life during the activity, but also when looking at the object I would have the individual pleasure of knowing my personality to be objective, visible to the senses and hence a power beyond all doubt. 2) In your enjoyment or use of my product I would have the direct enjoyment both of being conscious of having satisfied a human need by my work, that is, of having objectified man's essential nature, and of having thus created an object corresponding to the need of another man's essential nature. 3) I would have been for you the mediator between you and the species, and therefore would become recognised and felt by you yourself as a completion of your own essential nature and as a necessary part of yourself, and consequently would know myself to be confirmed both in your thought and your love. 4) In the individual expression of my life I would have directly created your expression of your life, and therefore in my individual activity I would have directly confirmed and realised my true nature, my human nature, my communal nature.
>
> Our products would be so many mirrors in which we saw reflected our essential nature.
>
> This relationship would moreover be reciprocal; what occurs on my side has also to occur on yours.
>
> (Marx 1975a: 227–8)

The contrast between the work carried out under communism and that carried out under capitalism could not be starker. Rather than suffer pain in work, people in a communist society would find joy in its performance. Thus, their 'work would be a *free manifestation of life*, hence an *enjoyment of life*' (Marx 1975a: 228; emphasis in original).

In order to enhance individual capabilities under communism, Marx saw it as important that individual workers were given the opportunity to vary their work tasks. In contrast to Adam Smith, Marx did not see any necessary or permanent role for the division of labour as a means to increase labour productivity. Rather, in the ideal community, each person would be able 'to do one thing today another tomorrow, to hunt in the morning, fish in the afternoon, rear cattle in the evening, criticise after dinner, ... without ever becoming hunter, fisherman, shepherd or critic' (Marx and Engels 1976: 53).[3] By giving people some say in what tasks they performed, communism would help to augment the intrinsic rewards from work.

To say that work would become attractive within communist society, however, was not to agree with Fourier that it could be converted into mere 'play' (Marx 1973: 712). According to Marx (1973: 611): 'Really free working, e.g. composing, is at the same time precisely the most damned seriousness, the most intense exertion'. Equally, it would be wrong to draw any insight from Adam Smith's negative concept of labour (see Chapter 2). Smith (1976b vol. 1: 34) had reasoned falsely that all labour was 'toil and trouble', when in fact this was a peculiar aspect of work under capitalism. Further, Smith had failed to recognise the possible intrinsic benefits of work. Contra Smith and what has since become the established view in the economics literature, there was a rejection in Marx's writings of any notion of human nature as indisposed to work. Instead, Marx felt that mankind retained interests in undertaking productive activity for its own ends. Labour, understood by Marx (1973: 611) as 'self-realisation, objectification of the subject, hence real freedom', in fact, could be a potentially life-enhancing activity, provided the transition was made from capitalism to communism. Within Marx's ideal future society, in short, labour would become 'not only a means of life but life's prime want' (Marx 1978: 531; see also Pagano 1985: 57).

Marx's discussion of the ideal society emphasised the idea that work was not a bad thing in and of itself; rather its character as a scourge on human life was peculiar to capitalism and was resolvable by the creation of a communist society. It was emphasised that for people to find intrinsic benefit in work they first had to be given the freedom to develop their creative capacities in as many activities as possible and this required of necessity a reduction in the length of the working day. Working under communal conditions and free to pursue activities for their own ends, Marx contended, people would come to develop an interest in performing work for its own sake.

Debates and criticisms

Marx's analysis of work remained largely undeveloped, up until the 1970s. That renewed interest has been shown in this analysis over the last thirty years is largely down to the efforts of Harry Braverman, whose *Labor and Monopoly Capitalism* (1974) injected a critical content into debates on work in the social sciences. Braverman's (1974: ix) own role was that of creative adaptor of Marx's theories and ideas. He wished to show the contemporary relevance of the Marxian analysis of work, by illustrating the way in which work relations in the twentieth century had been transformed by the forces of capital accumulation. He focused in particular on the degradation of work caused by the development of science and technology.

The 'labour process debate' that followed the publication of Braverman's book, however, has been distinctive for the failure to take forward the Marxian approach of Braverman. The story of the brief history of labour process analysis has been one of the progressive exclusion of Braverman and Marxian concepts from debate (Spencer 2000a). A favourite criticism has been that Braverman, and by implication Marx, offered a one-sided (objectivist) conception of the labour process which ignored the subjective dimensions of work. Braverman supposedly painted a unilinear picture of the process of management that saw workers as overwhelmed by a strategy of 'deskilling' implemented by all-powerful capitalists. In this case, he is claimed to have missed the complexities and contradictions entailed in managing the labour process. Empirical-based studies too have challenged Braverman's view that skills have declined. Indeed, some have claimed that the transformation of work in the late twentieth century actually resulted in an increase in skill levels (see Hodgson 1999: 186).

These criticisms can be misleading, however. To begin with, Braverman's purpose was not simply to describe the trends in management practices and outcomes. Rather his main aim was to connect developments in the workplace with the imperative of capital accumulation. He was critical of previous sociological research for failing to grasp the importance of such a connection. Hence industrial sociologists had tended to see things out of context, by focusing on the effects of capital accumulation rather than on its underlying causes. Braverman (1974: 27) stressed that his neglect of subjectivity was a 'self-imposed limitation'. Thus, it was designed to bring out the objective basis of capitalist production that was located in capitalist class conflict. He wished in this case to avoid the problems encountered in established industrial sociology where social relations in the workplace were treated as free-floating and undetermined.

Braverman drew particular attention to the view of 'alienation' in the work of modern sociologists. Most studies in sociology had tended to see alienation as a state of mind, rather than as the specific product of the organisation of society:

> Class, 'status', 'stratification', and even that favourite hobby horse of recent years which has been taken from Marx without the least understanding of its significance, 'alienation' – all of these are for bourgeois social science artefacts of consciousness and can be studied only as they manifest themselves in the minds of the subject population.
>
> (Braverman 1974: 27–8)

The very fact that workers responded positively to questionnaires which asked them to rate their level of job satisfaction was enough to convince researchers that 'alienation' was not a problem.[4] There was a failure to go beyond the psychology of individuals, to investigate the social underpinnings of capitalist production. In focusing on individual consciousness, the industrial sociologist was seen to share with management the belief that the capitalist labour process was 'natural' and 'inevitable'. Thus:

> for industrial sociology the problem does not appear with the degradation of work, but only with overt signs of dissatisfaction on the part of the worker. From this point of view, the only important matter, the only thing worth studying, is not work itself but the reaction of the worker to it, and in that respect sociology makes sense.
>
> (Braverman 1974: 29)

It was precisely the attempt to form a more critical analysis of the organisation of work – one that could act to promote rather than inhibit the Marxian critique of capitalist production – that prompted Braverman to focus so heavily upon the objective foundations of production under capitalism.

Braverman (1974: 19) looked to defend Marx against the charge of 'simpleminded "determinism"'. Not only did Marx show how the same technologies could persist in very different societies, but he also indicated the way in which technology could produce social relations, as much as be produced by them. According to Braverman:

> If Marx was not in the least embarrassed by this interchange of roles between social forms on the one side and material production processes on the other, but on the contrary moved comfortably among them, it was because – apart from his genius at dialectic – he never took a formulistic view of history, never played with bare and hapless correlations, 'one-to-one relationships', and other foolish attempts to master history by means of violent simplifications.
>
> (Braverman 1974: 21)

Braverman for his own part was happy to emphasise the complex and uneven development of capitalism. 'Social determinacy', he argued:

> does not have the fixity of a chemical reaction, but is a *historic process*. The concrete and determinate forms of society are indeed 'determined' rather than accidental, but this is the determinacy of the thread-by-thread weaving of the fabric of history, not the imposition of external formulas.
>
> (Braverman 1974: 21; emphasis in original)

Such sentiments jar with the commonly espoused view that Braverman was at heart a determinist.

Braverman was clearly aware of the importance of historical mediation in the complex determination of capitalist alienation and domination. He argued that through the effects of capital accumulation: 'The subjective factor of the labour process is removed to a place among its inanimate objective factors' (Braverman 1974: 171). However, he stressed that this was only 'the ideal towards which management tends', one which could be 'realised by capital only within definite limits, and unevenly among industries' (Braverman 1974: 171–2, 172). The separation of conception from execution:

> is itself restrained in its application by the nature of the various specific and determinate processes of production. Moreover, its very application brings into being new crafts and skills and technical specialities which are at first the province of labour rather than management.
>
> (Braverman 1974: 172)

Thus, not only were contingencies in the workplace seen to produce counter-pressures against deskilling forces, but also scientific management itself was suggested to require, if only for a temporary period, the creation of new skills and competencies (Armstrong 1988: 146). In Braverman's analysis, workers were not relinquished of skills in a straightforward and inexorable fashion. The process was presented as altogether more complex, involving frequent shifts, setbacks, and transformations.

Braverman's so-called 'deskilling thesis', so maligned by his critics for its perceived determinism, represented no more than a tendency inherent within capitalism that could not ever be realised in some complete and all-conquering form. The contradictions and counter-pressures created by the separation of mental and manual labour did not refute the 'law of deskilling' as such, but rather indicated its actual causal movement and dynamic. Critics of Braverman would do well to remember his important comment that:

> the shape of our society, the shape of any given society, is not an instantaneous creation of 'laws' which generate that society on the spot and before our eyes. Every society is a moment in the historical process, and can be grasped only as part of that process.
>
> (Braverman 1974: 21)

Although Braverman identified deskilling as an important long-run tendency under capitalism, he neither posited nor sought an invariant law of deskilling. He emphasised that deskilling would only be actualised where conditions allowed it to develop. At a minimum, this demonstrated the opportunity for collective opposition to the degradation of work.

Marx was aware too that skills would survive and even increase as a result of capital accumulation. Thus, in the expansion of mechanised forms of production, he realised that new demands would be placed on workers to adapt to the constantly evolving technical conditions of work. The contradiction was that the established division of labour tended to tie workers to particular tasks and thus produced inflexibilities in the use of labour in production, inhibiting the extraction of surplus value. As Marx (1976: 617) wrote, while 'large-scale industry, by its very nature, necessitates variations of labour, fluidity of functions, and mobility of the work in all directions ... in its capitalist form it reproduces the old division of labour with its ossified particularities'. The tension would force upon capital a relaxation of the division of labour to facilitate the valorisation process. As Marx explained:

> large scale industry, through its very catastrophes, makes the recognition of variation of labour and hence of the fitness of the worker for the maximum number of different kinds of labour into a question of life and death. This possibility of varying labour must become a general law of social production, and the existing relations must be adapted to permit its realisation in practice. That monstrosity, the disposable working population held in reserve, in misery, for the changing requirements of capitalist, must be replaced by the individual man who is absolutely available for the different kinds of labour required of him; the partially developed individual, who is merely the bearer of one specialised social function, must be replaced by the totally developed individual, for whom the different social functions are different modes of activity he takes up in turn.
>
> (Marx 1976: 618)

The fact that Marx thought capitalist production could throw up tendencies to raise skill levels among workers undermines the view that he saw a uniform movement to deskilling under capitalism. Based on the above quotation, G. Hodgson's (1999: 185) claim that Marx 'paid inadequate attention to the growing complexity of socio-economic systems and the increasing need for knowledge-based skills' can be questioned.

Moreover, in contrast to some interpretations, Marx was not blind to the different influences on human motivation. He was aware, for example, that the preferences and interests of workers would be moulded by the social and institutional environment. Hence a central implication of his idea of the 'fetishism of commodities' was that workers would be led to see capitalism as a natural and inevitable system. Here ideology played a major role in aligning the interests of capital and labour. Hodgson (1999: 130–1) has repeated the claim made by Thorstein Veblen and other 'old' institutional economists that Marx missed the part played by culture and habit in determining how people think and behave in society. Yet, consider the following quotation taken from volume one of *Capital*, where the influence of 'tradition' and also 'habit' on workers' attitudes and behaviour is mentioned explicitly: 'The advance of capitalist production develops a working class which by education, tradition, and habit looks upon that mode of production as self-evident laws' (Marx 1976: 899). In terms of his basic conception of work, as shown above, Marx was clear that changes in the organisation of production would impact upon the preferences of workers for work and for leisure.

There do remain places, though, where Marx's analysis can be improved upon. Marx's apparent certainty about the development of a revolutionary working class can be seen as particularly problematic (see Hyman 2006: 48). At times, Marx seemed to imply that workers only had to experience capitalist production on a sustained basis to develop a class consciousness, prompting them to overthrow capitalism. Notwithstanding his recognition of possible mediating factors, Marx tended to underplay the role of ideology and culture in channelling the behaviour of the working class into non-revolutionary ends not just for temporary periods but on a potentially enduring basis. Here the work of contemporary writers such as Michael Burawoy (1979) can be seen as useful in showing the way that cultures and ideologies developed by workers themselves in the course of their working lives can help to elicit and reproduce their consent to the rules and institutions of capitalist production (see Hodgson 1999: 131; Spencer 2000b; 2002).

In terms of the way in which surplus value was extracted from workers, Marx and also Braverman tended to place a strong emphasis upon the disciplinary role of technology in the workplace. In Braverman's work, there was an underlying view that capitalist employers would seek to gain control over the labour process by reducing the discretion of workers. In practical terms, this entailed capitalist employers harnessing the forces of production to subordinate workers. However, there remains the question of whether in fact the ability of workers to resist can be fully vanquished. Even with heavily mechanised forms of production, workers may be expected to retain some discretion to inhibit production. This suggests that capitalist employers will have interests in eliciting the consent of workers, in addition to directly controlling them. Without such consent, indeed, there would be little opportunity for capitalist employers to utilise the creativity and ingenuity of their workforce. This view of the labour problem can be seen as more subtle than the one that Braverman took from Marx. Hence, as Richard Hyman argues:

> Management strategy necessarily involves a *dialectic* between capital and labour: an attempt by employers to impose control while still evoking consent, with both elements of this contradictory set of objectives conditioned by the actual and potential recalcitrance of their employers.
> (Hyman 2006: 41; emphasis in original)

An important contribution of recent labour process analysis has been to demonstrate the codetermination of control and consent in the management of labour, extending the standard Marxian account of the way in which capitalist employers seek to manage the labour process.

There is also the issue of Marx's seeming vagueness on the transition to communism (Hodgson 1999: 21–2). Marx envisaged that the division of labour and machinery could be turned in favour of humanity, once capitalism had been transcended. Thus, in an initial transitional stage of socialism, production would be carried out with the objective of increasing productive forces, so as to free up time for the activities that were undertaken in the true realm of freedom, the full realisation of which would be achieved in the final stage of communism. But this can be seen to raise several questions. How were workers to deal with the machine production and task specialisation that were required to bring forth the benefits of a shorter working day? If these production methods caused distress to workers under capitalism how could they be transformed into a basis for fulfilment under socialism?

Marx's argument, of course, turned on the view that science and technology would be deployed for the benefit of all in a socialist society (Sayers 2003: 126). However, there remained the issue of how production was to be organised. To the extent that production was to be aimed at maximising material wealth under socialism, there was a danger that workers could be enslaved once again by the very methods of production that so harmed their lives under capitalism. Pagano (1985: 58–9) suggests that at the stage of socialism workers could be made worse off than their counterparts under capitalism, because they would be forced to endure the negative consequences of mechanised production and the division of labour, without a labour market that would otherwise operate, however imperfectly, to ensure movement between jobs. According to Pagano (1985: 59), Marx failed to realise the possibility for the accumulation of wealth to become the end goal of socialism, resulting in a potentially diminished welfare for workers. Marx can be seen to have neglected the precise conception of socialism because he regarded this as a matter for debate in an actual socialist society, and not something to be pre-empted by theorists beforehand. Nonetheless, this neglect can be seen to have left a number of ambiguities in Marx's case for socialism and the details about how society would evolve from socialism to communism can be regarded as one element of his work that requires some further development.

Conclusion

Marx emphasised the central importance of work in human life. Humans were seen to realise their essential being in work. Unlike the majority of economists (both past and present), Marx did not consider that work was universally and inevitably irksome. Quite to the contrary, he maintained that humans were productive and creative beings. Far from being a means to an end, work could be a potentially fulfilling activity. However, Marx pointed out that work could only be regarded as a source of self-realisation and self-development, if people were able to exert mastery over their own labour. As he stressed, in a capitalist society the reverse was the case: work under capitalist production conditions thus had come to 'alienate' the worker from his or her work. Workers did not find meaning in work, but instead were impoverished by it. Marx's theory of alienation, however, was not simply aimed at the critique of work under capitalism. It also had a vital role to play in demonstrating what could be achieved, if capitalism were to be abolished. Hence stress was placed upon the opportunities for rewarding work in a future communist society where people laboured under relations of mutual recognition and were afforded the free time to develop their own capacities in activities that they themselves chose to undertake. Such conditions, in turn, provided the basis for work in the 'realm of necessity' to become a source of freedom and satisfaction.

Marx's ideas on work were not taken on board by economists. Neoclassical economists, as we shall see in the following chapter, attacked the basis of Marx's labour theory of value. Their own utility theory of value was developed specifically to counter the view put forth by Marx that work was alienating and exploitative under capitalism. While there was greater engagement with Marx's work outside economics, the development of a Marxian analysis of the work process was relatively slow in coming. It was only in the 1970s with the publication of Braverman's *Labor and Monopoly Capitalism* that such analysis became a prominent aspect in sociology.

However, the Marxian contribution in the 'labour process debate' has been steadily undermined over the last thirty years. Labour process analysis has been characterised by a drift away from Marxian political economy and towards post-modernism. This shift has created specific problems around the definition of the specificities of capitalist production, and has also served to emasculate the critical intention of the original labour process debate as initiated by Braverman himself (see Spencer 2000a). The route taken by labour process analysis resembles research trends in other areas of radical scholarship on work issues. Thus, in the 1970s, American radical economics offered a clear and consistent critique of capitalist work relations and stood opposed to neoclassical labour theory (e.g. Gintis 1976). Yet, over the last two decades, it has moved in the direction of mainstream economics. While it has continued to offer criticisms of the mainstream, it has lost much of its original radical voice (see Fine 1998; Spencer 2000b). It can be argued that labour process analysis has similarly relinquished the opportunity to emulate Braverman's critique of capitalist production by succumbing to the dubious allure of post-modernism (Spencer 2000a).

The view taken here is that Marx's theory of labour provides essential insights into the nature of work under capitalism. It too helps to promote thinking about the possibility for a different kind of work beyond capitalism. Marx showed how a society as dynamic as capitalism could produce great progress in technology while at the same time increasing the misery of the working class. Marx argued for the abolition of capitalism in order to restore work as a fulfilling and free activity. Of course, there remain aspects of Marx's original analysis that can be developed. For example, further work is required to understand the actual organisation and development of labour within contemporary capitalism. Issues of power and conflict, in particular, need to be better understood. Analysis of alternative systems of production and of planning is also warranted. Yet, with all such developments, the writings of Marx remain an important basis for research on the place of work in human life.

5 From pain cost to opportunity cost

The eclipse of the quality of work as a factor in economic theory

> Man ought to work in order to live: his life, physical, moral, and mental, should be strengthened and made full by his work.
>
> (Alfred Marshall 1966a)

Introduction

The last decades of the nineteenth century have been conventionally viewed as a major turning point in the history of economic thought. It is the period that witnessed the occurrence of the so-called 'marginalist revolution'. The trio of W.S. Jevons, Carl Menger, and Léon Walras published significant works in the early 1870s that challenged some of the core ideas of the classical school and their own theories have been credited with providing the foundation for 'neoclassical economics' that subsequently came to dominate economic thought. This transitional episode, importantly, heralded a shift in the focus and content of value theory. Hence Jevons, Menger, and Walras sought to promote a subjective theory of value based on the concept of 'marginal utility'. These writers rejected the classical theory of value that laid emphasis on costs of production. Instead, they argued that value was an essentially subjective category linked to the act of consumption.

The transformation of value theory had important ramifications for the study of work and labour in economics. Most obviously, it served to challenge the idea that the cost of labour was the principal source of value in exchange. Politically, this was an important step given the use by Marx of the labour theory of value to critique capitalism (see Chapter 4). But it would be wrong to see the marginalist revolution as putting aside all issues of labour cost in the theory of value. On the contrary, such issues remained a focus for intense discussion in economics during the late nineteenth and early twentieth centuries. In the 'cost controversies', as they became known, there was specific disagreement over the nature of the cost of labour and its relationship to the value of output.

There were two sides in these controversies (see Pagano 1985: 76–94). On the one side, Jevons argued in support of the psychic measurement of the 'pain' or 'disutility' of actual work done. Jevons believed that the supply of labour was affected by the dissatisfaction as well as satisfaction that workers experienced from work, and he argued that the direct costs and benefits of work were an important influence on the supply of output and hence relative prices. This approach to cost was not just accepted by Jevons; it was also supported by other English economists, most notably Alfred Marshall. On the other side, Austrian economists (e.g. Wieser 1892) emphasised the importance of the alternative uses or 'opportunity cost' of work time. They argued that workers resisted work not because of the displeasure of work but rather because of the putative benefits of leisure time, and they identified the advantage of work with the utility of its product. By effectively dispensing with the disutility concept, the Austrians were able to articulate and promote a 'pure' subjective theory of value that focused upon the marginal utility of final consumption.

The divide between Jevons and Marshall, and the Austrian economists over the status of the cost of labour was substantial. Jevons and Marshall were willing to admit a role for the subjective experience of work in economic analysis. The Austrians, by contrast, saw work as a means only and sought to deny that it had any wider significance in the understanding of individual welfare.

This chapter seeks to re-evaluate the debate regarding the cost of labour in early neoclassical economics. It considers, in particular, the significance of this debate for the conception of work in the neoclassical paradigm. The 'cost controversies' have been the subject of relatively little discussion in modern economic debates. Yet, the resolution of these controversies had an important bearing upon the nature and scope of subsequent neoclassical research. In the theory of labour supply, as is argued below, the critique and ultimate rejection of Jevons's notion of the marginal disutility of labour in favour of the Austrian concept of opportunity cost culminated in the eclipse of the quality of work as a factor in neoclassical economics. With the move to embrace the Austrian approach, neoclassical economists came to view the supply of labour as a simple trade-off between income and leisure and as a result ignored the role and impact of work itself.

The chapter is organised as follows. The following section reconsiders Jevons's original definition of the marginal disutility of labour. Jevons portrayed work as a direct source of pain and pleasure and he looked to include the qualitative aspects of work in the analysis of the supply of labour. The second section considers the Austrian counterchallenge to Jevons's approach. Austrian economists redefined the cost of labour in terms of the loss of leisure time rather than the painfulness of work activities and this led to the conflation of the marginal disutility of labour with the marginal utility of leisure time. The third section deals with the contribution of Alfred Marshall. Marshall's theory of labour was distinctive in several respects. Not only did he consider directly the impact of work on the process of character formation but he also argued for improvement in the conditions of work, in order to enhance the physical as well as moral health of the working class. The fourth section discusses the reasons for and implications of the triumph of the Austrian notion of opportunity cost in terms of the theoretical understanding of labour supply within neoclassical economics. The fifth section concludes.

Work as pain and pleasure

Jevons, in his book the *Theory of Political Economy* (1871), maintained that the value of a commodity was determined by the marginal utility of consumption. Where the supply of commodities was fixed, he argued that commodities would exchange according to the ratio of their marginal utilities. On the other hand, in circumstances where supply was flexible, he thought that cost of production would enter as an additional variable in the theory of value. Jevons was particularly concerned with the cost of work and its impact on the value of output. To be sure, he rejected the idea that labour was a direct source of exchange value. Yet, he felt that it could play an indirect role in the determination of relative prices by affecting the supply of consumption goods. 'Labour is found often to determine value, but only in an indirect manner, by varying the degree of utility of the commodity through an increase or limitation of the supply', Jevons (1970: 77) explained. In Jevons's view, the painfulness of work was an important influence on the supply of labour and hence on the opportunities for consumption.

On the surface, Jevons appeared to agree with Adam Smith that labour was 'toil and trouble', defining labour as *'any painful exertion of mind or body undergone partly or wholly with a view to future good'* (Jevons 1970: 189; emphasis in original). In portraying labour as a source of marginal disutility, however, Jevons did not wish to suggest that all labour was intrinsically dissatisfying. On the contrary, he was quite prepared to admit that labour could be pleasurable of itself and he indicated that labour would be performed in many cases independently of the level of wages. Jevons emphasised the pain cost of work to show the limits to the supply of labour, especially due to the physical demands of work, and he drew direct attention to the non-pecuniary advantages of work.

In his theory of labour, Jevons set out a simple model in which a 'free labourer' was assumed to equate the marginal disutility of labour with the marginal utility from the reward of that labour (see Blaug 1985: 313–14; White 1994a; Spencer 2003a, 2004b).[1] Within this model, he argued that work was painful to begin with. Workers, it was suggested, faced some difficulty in turning their mind and body to productive activity. Yet, once this initial pain was overcome, work became a source of marginal utility and was performed independently of any extrinsic benefit from the produce of labour. Jevons referred to work as giving the worker 'an excess of pleasure ... due to the exertion itself' (Jevons 1970: 191), a clear statement of his view that work could be a 'good thing'. After some point, however, the worker was likely to experience work as a disutility at the margin, in consequence of long work hours or intensive labour. Jevons argued that the point of stopping work would be reached where the marginal utility of the product was equal to the marginal disutility of creating it.[2]

Jevons highlighted through this simple model the fact that work could be a source of both pain and pleasure. Work was not merely a means for workers to obtain consumption goods; it also had a direct negative as well as positive impact on their welfare. Resistance to work, from Jevons's perspective, was caused by the irksomeness of work itself. He denied that leisure was rewarding of itself; rather he argued that the actual costs of work were the main reason why workers looked to spend time away from it. It was not the allure of leisure which determined the marginal disutility of labour but rather the marginal disutility of labour which determined the allure of leisure. As Michael White (1994a) has argued, Jevons thought that leisure was not a valid area of study for economics, since it raised issues of 'higher ethics' that were to be confronted by non-economists. In contrast to later analysis, Jevons's conception of the supply of labour did not accommodate an independent role for the marginal utility of leisure. Instead, it focused direct attention on the intrinsic costs and benefits of work itself.

A key assumption in Jevons's simple model of labour supply was that the worker was 'free' to determine his or her hours of work. He thus implied that the worker was able to maximise his or her utility through allocating his or her time to work. This view can be questioned. In the real world, most workers do not have the option of deciding when and how long they work. On the one hand, workers must work in order to earn wages, and they may be forced to accept jobs that cause them an excess of dissatisfaction, due to the lack of suitable alternative options. On the other hand, workers cannot exercise direct control over the length of the working day. As argued by Blaug (1985: 313), work hours are largely determined by employers on a take-it-or-leave-it basis, and in many instances workers must work longer and harder than they would if they had a genuine say over how their labour was allocated in production. The displeasure of work can affect attendance at work as well as effort levels, but it is unrealistic to assume that all workers can find a balance between the pain of work and the pleasure of the commodities obtained from that work. Whether work is agreeable or not also depends on the environment and quality of work, and these are factors over which workers have virtually no control (Blaug 1985: 314). Jevons's representation of the work decision as a marginal choice, in short, can be seen to have contradicted the actual facts of the labour market in modern capitalism. As we shall see below, this criticism was used by the Austrian school to challenge the 'real cost' doctrine of Jevons and his allies.

When he turned to the actual work patterns of different groups of workers, Jevons took into account a number of factors, including the type and quality of work and class and racial characteristics. For example, he recognised that the work motivation of professional workers (solicitors, architects or engineers) would be strengthened significantly by their positive experience of work. Thus, he wrote that:

> the case of an eminent solicitor, architect or engineer is one where the work is to a great extent done by employees, and done without reference to social or political rewards, and where yet the most successful man endures the most labour, or rather is most constantly at work. This indicates that the irksomeness of the labour does not increase so as to overbalance the utility of the increment of reward. In some characters and in some occupations, in short, the success of labour only excites to new exertions, the work itself being of an interesting and stimulating nature.
>
> (Jevons 1970: 197–8)

Those in professional occupations, it was argued, remained at work for long hours because their work was 'interesting and stimulating'. Even though they faced the option of working fewer hours as their earnings rose, these workers were disinclined to accept additional hours of leisure, due to the high levels of intrinsic satisfaction they obtained from their jobs.

But, if it was possible for professional workers to continue working because of the high quality of their jobs, was it not also feasible that manual workers might be led to avoid work and thus to seek leisure by the low quality of their jobs? Jevons neglected to address this second possibility. Although qualitative factors were mentioned by Jevons in his explanation of actual behaviour, he restricted their impact to professional workers. This oversight appears somewhat arbitrary given that part of Jevons's basic argument was that the direct costs as well as benefits of work were an important independent influence upon the individual's supply of labour. Jevons only considered the motivating effects of 'interesting and stimulating' work: he failed to examine the de-motivating effects of uninteresting and non-stimulating work. The privation and alienation of factory work escaped his attention.[3]

Jevons's explanation of the labour supply of manual workers was premised on a stereotypical and ultimately biased view of the attitudes and character of the working class in England. English workers were collectively accused of being lazy and dissolute and in a throwback to mercantilist preoccupations, it was claimed that higher wages tended to erode the incentive to work. According to Jevons:

> The English labourer enjoying little more than the necessaries of life, will work harder the less the produce; or, which comes to the same thing, will work less hard as the produce increases.
>
> (Jevons 1970: 197)

Unlike the professional classes, who were intelligent, farsighted, and industrious, manual workers in England were irrational, myopic and work-shy.

Like some earlier classical writers such as Senior, Jevons feared that higher wages would lead the working population in England to spend more of their income on 'vices' such as alcohol and he was sceptical about the merits of a high wage economy (see White 1994a).

In a further regressive step, Jevons argued that the response of labour supply to wage changes differed between the races. It was claimed, in contrast to earlier writers such as J.S. Mill, that people of different races were fundamentally dissimilar. 'Persons of an energetic disposition', Jevons (1970: 198) asserted, 'feel labour less painfully than their fellow-men, and, if they happen to be endowed with various and acute sensibilities, their desire of further acquisition never ceases'. These favourable characteristics, while common to those with wealth in modern society, were lacking in people of a 'lower race':

> A man of lower race, a Negro, for instance, enjoys possession less, and loathes work more; his exertions, therefore, soon stop. A poor savage would be content to gather the almost gratuitous fruits of nature, if they were sufficient to give sustenance; it is only physical want that drives him to exertion.
>
> (Jevons 1970: 198)

From Jevons's perspective, the 'negro' was born with a desire for indolence and he or she had no interest in work beyond the meeting of his or her most basic material needs.

Jevons's treatment of class and race was as fundamentally flawed as it was morally repugnant. Again, had he realised the full extent of his own argument about the intrinsic rewards of work being an important independent influence upon the supply of labour he would not have been required to concentrate on the putative impact of class and racial characteristics. An obvious explanation for the negative response of the English working class to higher wages was the poor conditions of factory work, which made leisure relatively more attractive than work: it had nothing to do with the supposed inferior traits of individual workers. On Jevons's discussion of what he terms 'race', the overt prejudice hardly deserves further comment. Quite obviously, where black workers did resist work this could be attributed to the harshness of their work environment.[4] Ironically Jevons's own argument based on the importance of qualitative factors could have been used to argue for improvement in working conditions as a means to raise the supply of labour. Indeed, Jevons himself pointed to the gains in productivity that could be achieved via the prevention of 'overwork'.[5] His analysis of the qualitative aspects of work, however, remained partial and unrealised.

Several features of Jevons's account of labour warrant attention. First, he argued that the resistance of workers to work was linked in a direct way to the actual pain of work itself. He recognised that the marginal disutility of labour was an important variable in its own right and he refused to privilege the pleasures of leisure in the explanation of the cost of work. A worker's desire for leisure time, in effect, was seen as a barometer of the level of his or her job satisfaction. From this perspective, the benefit of leisure time was to be considered the *consequence* rather than the cause of the marginal disutility of labour. It is only in later approaches, as argued below, that the marginal disutility of labour has come to be identified with the loss of leisure time. Second, while Jevons argued that the qualitative content of work was an important consideration in the analysis of labour supply, he also looked to give a prominent role to issues of class and race. Jevons's recognition of the intrinsic qualities of work was ultimately overshadowed by his prejudicial portrayal of the alleged differences between the classes and the alleged existence of 'higher' and 'lower' races. As we shall see in the next section, Jevons's approach to labour supply met with a hostile response from early Austrian economists.

Work as lost opportunity

Several Austrian writers challenged Jevons's notion of the marginal disutility of labour (see Böhm-Bawerk 1891; Wieser 1892). These writers looked to deemphasise the role of labour as a direct source of discomfort. Rather, in line with their mentor, Carl Menger, they sought to highlight the importance of labour in satisfying the wants of consumers. Labour was the means to utility, the ends were provided by final consumption. Austrian economists had fought hard to repel the labour theory of value and they were not about to reintroduce labour as a causal factor in the explanation of subjective value. Value, they insisted, was determined by the pleasures of direct consumption: commodities were more or less valuable depending on their fulfilment of human wants and desires. On this basis, it was superfluous to speak of workers 'enjoying' their work unless this related to their consuming the product of their labour. Whether or not workers actually enjoyed the work they performed was of trivial concern relative to the satisfaction they gained from the consumption of produced commodities.

Instead of the 'real cost' doctrine of Jevons, the Austrians gave their support to the theory of 'alternative cost' (Wieser 1892; Green 1894). According to this theory, costs were linked to losses of opportunity that arose under conditions of scarcity. Cost of production was not to be measured by the direct painfulness of work, but instead was to be defined in terms of the subjective value of output that could have been produced if factor inputs had been put to alternative uses. As argued by Friedrich von Wieser:

> Cost consists in the means of production having manifold applications, like iron, coal, and common labour, which, even when they are employed in the production of a single commodity, are still estimated according to the value they have in all their applications.
>
> (Wieser 1892: 41–2)

The Austrian theory of value showed how costs of production were in fact subjectively determined by the marginal utility of consumption and it attempted to erase any direct link between cost and the value of commodities.

From an Austrian perspective, Jevons's disutility concept took economic theory down the wrong track. It was not the cost of production which determined the subjective value of commodities, but the subjective value of commodities which determined the cost of production. As Eugen von Böhm-Bawerk argued:

> costs are not the final but the intermediate cause of value. In the last resort they do not *give* it to their products, but receive it from them. ... The principle of value is never in them, but outside them, in the marginal utility of the products.
>
> (Böhm-Bawerk 1891: 189; emphasis in original)

In this view, value was determined independently of the pain and pleasure of work activities, and the cost of factor inputs was measured by the marginal utility of the commodities that *might have been produced* if these inputs had been used differently in production (see Buchanan 1969: 11). Costs thus were ultimately subjective in nature. Yet, they were also measurable because utility was reflected in exchange value, that is, the prices commanded by commodities denoted their subjective worth and there was consequent scope for the objective measurement of the cost of forgone opportunities. The cost of production could be estimated from the prices of tradable commodities that could have been produced by the same inputs in alternative uses.

For the Austrian definition of cost to remain valid, it was necessary to assume that resources were finite. The limitation of resources thus made clear the fact that there were sacrifices of opportunity to confront in meeting the wants of individuals. Austrian economists then were led to place great emphasis on 'scarcity' as the key economic problem. The ultimate limited resource was time. There was only so much time that could be allocated to the production of output and costs could be seen to arise from the choices that individuals made between alternative uses of their time. Such choices were especially important in the case of the supply of labour. With only twenty-four hours in the day, workers had to 'choose' how to allocate their time between work and leisure. From this vantage point, the lost opportunity for leisure was seen to represent the cost of work and was regarded as the key reason why workers were paid wages for the time they devoted to work.

The work decision received specific attention in an article by David Green (1894). Green's key contribution was to formulate the notion of 'opportunity cost'.[6] In his article, he attempted to set out from an Austrian perspective the nature of the cost of work and its relation to the supply of labour. He claimed that work (time) was a source of cost because of the pleasure that could be gained from leisure time. Thus, according to Green (1894: 222): 'The labourer stops work at a certain hour, not simply because he is tired, but because he wants some opportunity for pleasure and recreation.' Work was not disliked because it was experienced as a direct source of pain; rather it was resisted on account of it taking time away from other activities that conferred utility on workers. As Green explained:

> The wages given for the first hour of a day's work are not paid on account of any discomfort endured; but the labourer secures just as much pay for the first hour as for the last, because it could be utilised for other purposes to just as good advantage. His power for doing work is an opportunity to him which he cannot afford to transfer to his employer without some return, whether the work be burdensome or not.
>
> (Green 1894: 223)

Two points can be made here. First, Green believed that the benefits of leisure were determined independently of the character of work: workers were assumed to have a high preference for leisure, almost regardless of the qualitative experience of work. Second, he argued that work was pursued for merely instrumental reasons. It was the desire to obtain income to spend on consumption goods that motivated workers to work as opposed to any intrinsic desire for work itself. Work thus was to be understood as a mere means to consumption.

Böhm-Bawerk (1894a) attacked Jevons's argument that the marginal disutility of labour would influence the supply of labour (see Blaug 1985: 314; Pagano 1985: 85–8). In arguing that workers could equate the marginal disutility of labour and the marginal utility of consumption, Jevons had effectively assumed that the supply of labour was discretionary. In reality, however, workers had little or no control over their labour supply; rather the length of work time was fixed by institutional factors (Pagano 1985: 86). Böhm-Bawerk (1894a) argued that while the marginal disutility of labour could be seen to enter as a variable in the setting of the value of output in an economy of independent producers it had no role to play in the determination of value under modern capitalism where the supply of labour was fixed. Under capitalism, he stated, utility and not disutility was the 'ultimate standard of value'.

F.Y. Edgeworth (1894a), who sided with Jevons's 'real cost' doctrine, responded to Böhm-Bawerk's criticism. While he agreed with Böhm-Bawerk that wage labourers were unable to choose the hours they work, he argued that it was possible for other aspects of labour supply to vary (Pagano 1985: 87). For example, workers could change occupations if they were dissatisfied with their work. Edgeworth suggested that the marginal disutility of labour would affect relative wages and hence also relative prices (Blaug 1985: 314). Further, he argued that, in the case of piecework, workers could adjust their effort in line with the marginal disutility of labour and thus the latter variable could still impinge on the supply of labour. Edgeworth (1894a: 521) claimed that the Austrian argument that value was determined by marginal utility was only applicable to a special case in which labour supply was inflexible; it was untrue of cases where the supply of labour was variable.

Böhm-Bawerk (1894b) replied that the constraints on labour supply were much greater than Edgeworth allowed. In Böhm-Bawerk's view, wages did not correspond closely to the discomfort or pain of work, and instances of piecework did not guarantee to workers the ability to vary their effort levels (Böhm-Bawerk 1894b: 721–4). Again he concluded that the marginal disutility of labour was not to be given any significant weight in the explanation of the determination of value. In a rejoinder, Edgeworth (1894b) reiterated his support for the theory of 'real cost'. He reasserted the point that a correct account of value must consider both utility and disutility.

As argued by Pagano (1985: 87), Böhm-Bawerk and Edgeworth ultimately agreed that the freedom of workers to determine their labour supply influenced the impact of the marginal disutility of labour on the value of output. Jevons, it was suggested, had been wrong to suppose that workers employed in modern capitalism could set their own work hours. But equally the Austrians were not able to rule out the relevance of the disutility concept where freedom was available to workers. The point, though, from an Austrian viewpoint was that such instances of free choice were an insignificant part of the real world and that it was not appropriate for analytical reasons to regard work as an independent source of marginal disutility and hence as a separate determinant of value. The Austrians went a stage further. They implied that even if workers could adjust their labour supply the cost of work was to be measured in terms of opportunity cost and not pain cost. Workers, thus, were seen to resist increases in their labour supply not because they endured added pain from working but because they suffered a greater loss of leisure hours. Austrian economists such as Wieser, Böhm-Bawerk, and Green, in essence, were concerned to diminish the significance of Jevons's conception of cost and to elevate the importance of the theory of opportunity cost (see Pagano 1985: 89–90).

Philip Wicksteed (1910) put a formal gloss on the Austrian approach to labour supply.[7] Ironically Wicksteed has often been cast in the role of the defender and ally of Jevons. Yet, on the question of labour supply, Wicksteed departed from Jevons's original theory of labour. In line with the Austrian school, Wicksteed maintained that costs of production were to be identified with losses of consumption stemming from the possible alternative uses of factor inputs, and he argued that the marginal utility of consumption was the key determinant of value. He wrote that:

> The only sense ... in which cost of production can affect the value of one thing is the sense in which it is itself the value of another thing. Thus what has been variously termed utility, ophelimity, or desiredness, is the sole and ultimate determinant of all exchange value.
>
> (Wicksteed 1910: 391)

In terms of the work decision, Wicksteed focused upon the constraints imposed by the alternative uses of work time on the supply of work hours. He criticised Jevons for identifying the cost of labour with the painfulness of work itself. In fact, the marginal disutility of labour 'is only a negative expression of one element in the desirability of rest or leisure. This latter is a positive conception, and it includes all output of effort upon the direct securing of things not in the circle of exchange, as well as rest' (Wicksteed 1910: 624). Work was a cost to society because it entailed the sacrifice of leisure time. Wicksteed rejected the argument of Jevons and his supporters that the direct pain and pleasure of work exerted an influence upon the supply of labour.

The Austrians, to summarise, viewed work as a mere conduit to income and they ignored its intrinsic costs as well as benefits. Unlike Jevons, they were prepared to focus on the uses of leisure time in the definition of the cost of work and they failed to consider directly the preferences of workers for work. Indeed, within Austrian theory, it was assumed that workers were essentially uninterested in the actual content of work itself; they were implied to be concerned only with the duration of work time and the level of wages. As we shall see in the next section, a quite different stance on the role and importance of work was taken by Alfred Marshall.

The Marshallian view of work

Alfred Marshall saw work as important in its own right. He thought that people were affected in quite profound ways by the experience of work and he argued for improvement in the quality of work. Writing in 1873, Marshall stated that: 'Work, in its best sense, the healthy energetic exercise of faculties, is the aim of life, is life itself' (Marshall 1966a: 115). This line would not have looked out of place in the writings of other nineteenth-century pro-work writers such as Carlyle and Ruskin (see Chapter 3).

Later, in the *Principles*, published in 1890, Marshall reiterated the significance of work in human life. According to him: 'man's character has been moulded by his every-day work, and the material resources he thereby procures, more than by any other influence unless it be that of his religious ideals' (Marshall 1910: 1). Marshall emphasised further the intrinsic worth of work. Hence work offered a way for people to develop and realise their 'high faculties':

> The truth seems to be that as human nature is constituted, man rapidly degenerates unless he has some hard work to do, some difficulties to overcome; and that some strenuous exertion is necessary for physical and moral health. The fullness of life lies in the development and activity of as many and as high faculties as possible.
>
> (Marshall 1910: 136)

Plainly, work was much more than just a means for people to earn a living: it also played a vital role in the development and improvement of human character.

Like Jevons, Marshall believed that people were motivated to work by the enjoyment of the work itself. Although Marshall defined work as a disutility, he emphasised that in many cases work was experienced as a source of pleasure (Marshall 1910: 141–2). Indeed, he criticised Jevons for overstating the painfulness of work:

> he [Jevons] himself points out how painful idleness often is. Most people work more than they would if they considered only the direct pleasure resulting from the work; but in a healthy state, pleasure predominates over pain in a great part even of the work that is done for hire.
>
> (Marshall 1910: 65n)

To the extent that work was experienced as a disutility at the margin, this was explained by the duration and intensity of work, or the conditions of work:

> The discommodity of labour may arise from bodily or mental fatigue, or from its being carried on in unhealthy surroundings, or with unwelcome associates, or from its occupying time that is wanted for recreation, or for social or intellectual pursuits. But whatever be the cause of the discommodity, its intensity nearly always increases with the severity and the duration of labour.
>
> (Marshall 1910: 140)

Work resistance, in Marshall's view, was not an inevitable outcome. Instead, it was seen to depend on the quantity as well as quality of work that was actually performed by workers.

In contrast to Jevons, Marshall included the marginal utility of leisure as a separate variable in his treatment of the labour supply decision (see O'Connor 1961). Thus, people were seen to consider the benefits as well as costs of leisure time in deciding how much labour to supply. But, unlike the Austrians, Marshall did not regard leisure as intrinsically rewarding. Instead, he argued that leisure could be endured as a source of pain, if it was extended over a prolonged period of time, and involved extended bouts of inactivity. Long hours of leisure thus might heighten the desire to work. Marshall thought that there were non-pecuniary as well as pecuniary costs associated with unemployment and he felt that workers who experienced long spells of unemployment might opt to work for nothing rather than remain jobless (Marshall 1910: 141).

In terms of his value theory, Marshall understood that commodities took their value from two sources: the marginal utility of consumption and cost of production, including the marginal disutility of labour. He thus refused to go along with the Austrians that value was demand determined; on the contrary he sought to promote an understanding of the dual role of utility and cost of production in the determination of market prices (see Marshall 1910: 527–8n). Marshall thought that, in terms of the establishment of the value of output, utility and disutility worked together in the same way as the two blades of a pair of scissors.[8]

He believed that humans had progressed materially as well as morally through the pursuit of 'activities', not for ulterior motives, but as ends in themselves (Marshall 1910: 86–9). In the early stages of human evolution, people had been driven to undertake activities in order to meet their basic biological needs, such as food, shelter, and clothing. In later stages, once such needs had been met, people had developed interests in carrying out activities for their own sake and in consequence had acquired new wants. An important outcome of the development of activities was the dissemination throughout all strata of society of a 'desire for excellence for its own sake' (Marshall 1910: 89). Marshall thought that human beings had acquired a propensity to work well. Those like Newton and Stradivarius were not the only ones to have shown great dedication and expertise in their work: similar characteristics were shared by workers in more routine jobs. For instance, 'the fisherman who, even when no one is looking and he is not in a hurry, delights in handling his craft well, and in the fact that she is well built and responds promptly to his guidance' (Marshall 1910: 89).

Material gain remained important in explaining the work that was performed by people, but it was by no means the only factor, and in many instances it was eclipsed by the impact of the intrinsic rewards of the work itself. Marshall argued that work was so important to people that they might even suffer some discomfort to undertake it. Hence, he wrote that:

> it is also conceivable, and almost equally probable, that people may be so anxious to work that they will undergo some penalty as a condition of obtaining leave to work. For, as deferring the consumption of some of his means is a thing which a prudent person would desire on its own account, so doing some work is a desirable object on its own account to a healthy person.
>
> (Marshall 1910: 232)

Marshall declared that 'it is to changes in the forms of efforts and sacrifices in production that we must turn when in search for the keynotes of the history of mankind' (Marshall 1910: 85). This was a profound statement in terms of the character and scope of economic science. Specifically, Marshall rejected the idea articulated by Thomas Banfield and supported by Jevons that '"the Theory of Consumption is the scientific basis of economics"' (Marshall 1910: 90). Instead, he insisted that the job of economists was to develop a theory of activities. Marshall was aware that the character and wants of humans were changed by the conditions under which they lived and worked, and he was critical of utility theory for treating activities as a mere means to the satisfaction of the (given) wants of individuals (Parsons 1931: 107–10). In parallel with Carlyle and Ruskin, Marshall distanced himself from the narrow definition of economics as the study of the accumulation of material wealth. Instead, he wanted economists to discover and explain the conditions required to enhance the character of people.[9]

The devotion of people to 'higher activities' was seen by Marshall to provide the basis for an increase in the 'standard of life'. A rising standard of life implied:

> an increase of intelligence and energy and self-respect; leading to more care and judgment in expenditure, and to an avoidance of food and drink that gratify the appetite but afford no strength, and of ways of living that are unwholesome physically and morally.
>
> (Marshall 1910: 689)

The increase in the physical, mental as well as moral health of the labouring population associated with a rising standard of life was seen to pave the way for an increase in labour efficiency and real wages. A contrast was to be made with an increase in the 'standard of comfort' which 'may suggest a mere increase of artificial wants, among which perhaps the grosser wants may predominate' (Marshall 1910: 690). Marshall clearly thought it best that people devote their energies to pursuing so-called 'higher activities' and avoid the pursuit of arbitrary or 'artificial' wants. Thus, it was through such activities that people could use and develop their human faculties and thereby enhance their character.[10]

Marshall believed that the institutions of capitalism were conducive to character development and social progress. The system of 'free industry and enterprise', hence, was seen to promote the kind of activities that help to foster and express the 'noblest qualities of human character' (Parsons 1931: 107). Yet, Marshall was also aware that there was still further to go in modern society to improve the lot of some groups and individuals. A particular concern of Marshall was the negative impact of manual work on the character of the working class. In an article, 'The Future of the Working Classes', written in 1873, Marshall lamented the fact that many workers in industrial Britain were employed in degrading and stultifying jobs:

> Let us look at those vast masses of men who, after long hours of hard and unintellectual toil, are wont to return to their narrow homes with bodies exhausted and with minds dull and sluggish. That men do habitually sustain hard corporeal work for eight, ten, or twelve hours a day, is a fact so familiar to us that we scarcely realise the extent to which it governs the moral and mental history of the world; we scarcely realise how subtle, all-pervading and powerful may be the effect of the work on man's body in dwarfing the growth of the man.
>
> (Marshall 1966a: 105–6)

It was not surprising that many workers showed little appetite to use their leisure time for self-improvement, since their work provided no scope for the development of their mental powers, but instead offered only constant drudgery and toil. Marshall, far from condemning the working class in Britain for misspending their wages on alcohol, believed that they had been driven to seek 'the coarse pleasures of the public-house', due to the harshness of the conditions they faced in the work they performed for wages (Marshall 1966a: 107).[11]

But Marshall remained hopeful that a better society could be created in the future. He looked forward to a society in which 'no one in it should have any occupation which tends to make him anything else than a gentleman' (Marshall 1966a: 109–10). To achieve such a society, certain reforms were needed. In addition to a more equal distribution of income and a proper education for the population as a whole, Marshall also saw a pressing need to curtail the hours of manual work. 'No one is to do in the day so much manual work as will leave him little time or little aptitude for intellectual and artistic enjoyment in the evening', he declared (Marshall 1966a: 110). Marshall felt that some manual work was good for the personal health of individuals and he saw advantages in all members of society performing such work.[12] In the ideal society, manual work was to be highly paid and was to be shared out among the population as a whole. Marshall (1966a: 110) thought that under conditions where everyone had the opportunity for education and refinement in their lives there would be no social stigma attached to the pursuit of manual work and the disincentive to perform such work would be lessened. A shorter working day was to be achieved by the use of science and technology and by the introduction a new pattern of shift working. Marshall thus proposed that the working day be divided into two six-hour shifts, and for really strenuous work, three four-hour shifts (Marshall 1966a: 113). In a similar way to Marx (see Chapter 4), Marshall wished to utilise the benefits of productivity to reduce the length of the working day and to increase free time during which people could strengthen and develop their character in higher activities (see Marshall 1910: 720). But Marshall, unlike Marx, was content to see progress towards a shorter working day under capitalism and was opposed to any kind of radical upheaval of society's existing institutions.

As Marshall saw it, much of the resistance to work in modern society was caused by the lack of intelligent work. He thought that with the help of science and technology much unintelligent work could be avoided and stronger incentives could be provided for people to work hard. Overall, Marshall was confident that productivity would rise rather than fall in the ideal society of the future. Thus, he wrote that:

> the only labour removed from our new society is that which is so conducted as to stunt the mental growth, preventing people from rising out of old narrow grooves of thought and feeling, from obtaining increased knowledge, higher tastes, and more comprehensive interests. Now it is to such stunting almost alone that indolence is due. Remove it, and work

rightly applied, the vigorous exercise of faculties would be the aim of every man. The total work done per head of population would be greater than now.

(Marshall 1966a: 111–12)

The same point was reaffirmed in the *Principles*, where Marshall referred to the economic as well as moral advantages of a shorter working day. Thus, the elimination of 'excessive work' was seen to lay the basis for an improvement of the standard of life and hence also the efficiency of labour (Marshall 1910: 694).

Like J.S. Mill, Marshall saw benefits in the cooperative movement (see Marshall 1910: 305–7). Cooperation provided the basis for a more demo-cratic and also more efficient mode of production than currently existed. Marshall claimed that the promise of cooperative forms of business had not yet been fully realised. This was due, in part, to the lack of experience of workers in the task of business management. Marshall (1910: 307) was con-fident, however, that cooperation would enjoy high success in the future. This success was to be built on the improved education of the working classes (Marshall 1966a: 113–14; Marshall 1966b).

While Marshall considered that much work was undignified and toilsome in modern society, he believed that it was possible and necessary to create a new society in which work was an ennobling and uplifting activity. The ultimate aim of Marshall, thus, was to reach a:

condition in which every man's energies and activities will be fully developed – a condition in which men will work not less than they do now but more; only, to use a good old phrase, most of their work will be a work of love; it will be a work, which, whether conducted for payment or not, will exercise and nurture their faculties.

(Marshall 1966a: 118)

To attain this end, however, Marshall looked for gradual and slow progress *within* capitalism (Marshall, 1910: 248). He was optimistic that, in the future, the present ills of capitalism would recede and disappear. Significant progress had already been made under capitalism and further progress was likely in the future:

All ranks of society are rising; on the whole they are better and more cultivated than their forefathers were; they are no less eager to do, and they are much more powerful greatly to bear, and greatly to forbear.

(Marshall 1966a: 115)

In the *Principles*, Marshall (1910: 716) claimed that changes in technology had led to a rise in the demand for intelligent labour and to a decline in manual labour. He estimated that around half of the population was employed in unskilled and low-skilled work, with the other half employed in high-skilled work. Circumstances were much better than in the early nine-teenth century, according to Marshall, when more than half of the popula-tion had been unsuited to anything other than unskilled work, and less than one-sixth had been able to perform highly skilled work (Marshall 1910: 716). Marshall did not share Adam Smith's pessimism that the growth of industry would lead to the loss of intelligence of the workforce; instead he believed that forces were at work in industrial society that increased the skill levels of workers (Marshall 1910: 263; see Matthews 1990: 23; Bowman 2004: 507).[13]

Marshall was a critic of socialism. In a letter to *The Times*, written on 24 March 1891, he stated that:

> the chief dangers of socialism lie not in its tendency towards a more equal distribution of income for I can see no harm in that, but in the sterilising influence on those mental activities which have gradually raised the world from barbarism.
>
> (cited in Parsons 1931: 128n)

Later, in a 1907 article on 'The Social Possibilities of Economic Chivalry', Marshall wrote that:

> I am convinced that, so soon as collectivist control had spread so far as to narrow considerably the field left for free enterprise, the pressure of bureaucratic methods would impair not only the springs of material wealth, but also many of those higher qualities of human nature, the strengthening of which should be the chief aim of social endeavour.
>
> (Marshall 1966c: 334)

Although Marshall thought that the state had a role to play in society, he was keen that the freedom and initiative of individuals was preserved as far as possible and this influenced his rejection of socialism (see Parsons 1931: 124).

A key precondition for progress in society was that capitalists act in a decorous and chivalrous way towards the rest of the population (see Marshall 1966c). Marshall believed that free enterprise provided the best conditions for realising the 'social possibilities of economic chivalry' and he was confident that capitalists could be moulded into economic heroes for society (see Marshall 1910: 719). As argued by Henderson:

> what emerges [in Marshall's writings] is a sense of the possibility of reforming capitalism by merely reforming the character of those who inherit wealth. Marshall uses 'chivalry', which must be based upon per-sonal, rather than enforced, acceptance of a code of ethical conduct, as a reactionary device to avoid the horrors of any more radical programme of action.
>
> (Henderson 2000: 173)

Marshall, in short, retained an abiding faith in the ability of capitalism to improve the conditions of life and work and he rejected the calls of utopian and socialist writers for radical social reform. While capitalism was less than perfect, it was still to be viewed as the best of all possible systems.

But Marshall did admit that political solutions might be needed to achieve social progress. Thus, he pointed to a 'residuum' of people in modern society who were 'physically, mentally, or morally incapable of doing a good day's work with which to earn a good day's wage' (Marshall 1910: 714). These people were to be subject to 'paternal discipline' to ensure that they brought up their children in an appropriate manner. Marshall wrote that 'as a last resort the homes might be closed or regulated with some limitation on the freedom of parents' (Marshall 1910: 714–15n). Moreover, he proposed an even more drastic intervention, arguing that 'progress may be hastened … by the application of the principles of Eugenics to the replenishment of the race from its higher rather than its lower strains' (Marshall 1910: 248). Racial improvement, in Marshall's view, was 'the ultimate solution' to the problem of the residuum (Levitt 1976: 429). Marshall's advocacy of the science of eugenics can be seen to tarnish his image as someone who was sympathetic to the interests of the working class.

The economic writings of Marshall contained two different strands of thought (see Parsons 1931; Levitt 1976). He developed, on the one hand, a 'pure' theory of economics based on mathematics that has since come to form the bedrock of mainstream neoclassical economics.[14] Yet, on the other hand, he emphasised the importance of moral and ethical considerations, which were not easily reconcilable within and indeed in some respects were in conflict with the utility framework that he and others such as Jevons helped to devise and promulgate.[15] These two different and potentially contradictory elements were evident in his analysis of work. Hence while Marshall argued that improvement in the quality of work was a pre-condition for progress in the quality of life, he simultaneously contributed to the development of a formal model of the work decision, in which workers were assumed to maximise their utility from working (see Marshall 1910: 843–4). Utility theory, with its assumption of unchanging preferences, was ill equipped to supply an understanding of the way that people could be changed by the qualitative experience of work. What people may or may not become in consequence of working, in short, was not something that could be readily understood in terms of the individualistic concept of disutility that implied work was undertaken for instrumental reasons (see Parsons 1931: 121). Marshall's retention of this concept can be seen to have ultimately hindered his efforts to uncover and explain the quality of work and its relation to human well-being. The next section examines the reasons for the rejection of the labour theories of Jevons and of Marshall in neo-classical economics, and its implications for the theoretical analysis of labour supply.

The disappearance of work in neoclassical economics

The 'cost controversies' of the closing decade of the nineteenth century and the early years of the twentieth century were ultimately resolved in favour of the Austrian school. The 'real cost' doctrine espoused by Jevons and supported by Marshall was eclipsed by the opportunity cost framework found in the writings of Austrian economists. The 'celebrated disputes' over the origins of cost, as Lionel Robbins (1930a) later remarked, simply paved the way:

> for the now universal recognition that even when disutilities are taken into account they are ultimately to be regarded as being the pull of foregone leisure or foregone present income – opportunity costs rather than disutilities in the sense of the old hedonistic calculus.
>
> (Robbins 1930a: 207–8)

Jevons's original definition of the marginal disutility of labour, then, underwent a remarkable transformation. While occasional reference could still be found to the marginal disutility of labour, it became common practice in the twentieth century to identify the marginal disutility of labour with the opportunity cost of work time. Any notion that the marginal disutility of labour might be defined in terms of the quality of work was thereby obscured in neoclassical economics. So successful were the Austrians in vanquishing the 'real cost' doctrine that successive generations of neoclassical economists grew accustomed to using the marginal utility of leisure time to denote the cost of labour. Neoclassical economists suffered under the misapprehension that this was the true or original definition of the marginal disutility of labour, even though it was the opposite of what Jevons intended when he used this term in his own analysis of the work decision.

A consensus was reached in the neoclassical analysis of labour supply that income and leisure were the two main influences on the welfare of individuals. According to Pagano (1985: 111–12), this way of theorising was inherited from Walras and represented a compromise between the 'English' and Austrian sides in the famous disputes over cost in early neoclassical economics. The Walrasian framework suggested that work was divided into two parts: a part that was 'consumed' as leisure and a part that was sold and used in production to create consumption goods for others in society (Pagano 1985: 111). While labour that was experienced as leisure was assumed to affect welfare, the expenditure of labour in the production process was implied to have no direct impact on welfare. Two advantages were allegedly associated with the Walrasian formulation. First, in line with Austrian theory, it allowed labour to be treated like any other consumption good and thus provided the basis for the incorporation of the work decision into consumer theory. Second, it showed that work and welfare were connected, offering a link to the approach of Jevons and Marshall. Hence it was apparent that as workers increased their work hours they would suffer a loss of leisure time and hence a reduction in welfare (Pagano 1985: 112).

Two comments can be made here. The first is that Walras offered only a very cursory treatment of the supply of labour in his most famous text, the *Elements of Pure Economics*. In the passages that Pagano (1985: 100–1) draws upon, Walras failed to make any direct reference to the impact of 'leisure' on human welfare (Walras 1977: 238). This can be contrasted with the Austrian formulation, which was clear that the sacrifice of leisure time was the key source of the cost of work. In fact, when Walras did refer to labour, he seemed to imply that it might be a direct source of utility to workers. In Walras's words: 'The pleasure enjoyed by the idler, the job done by the worker and the plea made by the lawyer constitute the incomes of these people' (Walras 1977: 215). Thus, in the case of the lawyer, it was implied that the personal rewards from work extended beyond the receipt of wages and included the intrinsic pleasures of the work itself. Such a view was clearly at odds with the Austrian view of labour supply.

The second comment to make is that the actual development of the neo-classical analysis of labour supply in the twentieth century was characterised by the acceptance of the Austrian notion of opportunity cost and was not in any way directly connected with Walras.[16] The view that leisure and not work affected welfare followed directly from the Austrian framework. Thus, if there was any compromise in neoclassical economics regarding the cost of labour and its impact on labour supply, it was a compromise that was heavily biased towards the Austrian side.

But why did the opportunity cost view of labour supply win out in debate? Several reasons can be given for this. One possible reason was the desire to address the trade-off between income and leisure: hence a short-coming of Jevons's approach was its neglect of the alternative uses of work time as an independent influence on the supply of labour. As we have seen above, however, Marshall's analysis of labour supply included the marginal utility of leisure time as a separate argument alongside the marginal dis-utility of labour. This first explanation, then, faces difficulties in account-ing for the eclipse of Marshall's contribution to the economics of labour supply.

A second possible reason for the embrace of the Austrian notion of opportunity cost was that it provided a definite break with previous theories of value found in the classical tradition. It did not require or seek an expla-nation of value in terms of cost of production, but instead sought to focus on the subjective origins of value. The problem with the approach of Jevons and Marshall was that it considered disutility as a source of cost and hence of value. The need to build a value theory that eschewed the cost of work then can be seen to have facilitated the acceptance of the Austrian doctrine of opportunity cost within neoclassical economics. There may have also been a desire to avoid the analysis of work itself out of concern that this would lead into discussion around the issues of exploitation and alienation which had proved a preoccupation of some earlier radical writers, most notably Marx. The consideration of the opportunity cost of work time, thus, provided a way of sidestepping such discussion by putting out of focus the qualitative aspects of work.

A third possible reason for the triumph of the opportunity cost concept in neoclassical economic theory was that it offered a convenient way to measure, and thus quantify, the cost as well as benefit of work. Jevons's and Marshall's focus on the marginal disutility of labour, it was argued, risked a protracted and ultimately futile discussion about the intrinsic worth of work. In contrast, the notion of opportunity cost identified the cost of work with the duration of work time and the benefit of work with the hourly wage rate. These two variables – work time and wages – could be easily inserted into a formal model and could be used to make predictions about the behaviour of individuals in the labour market.

The concern to bring greater precision to the theory of labour supply was to the fore in the minds of some early Austrian writers. Green (1894), for example, objected to the vagueness of the concept of the marginal disutility of labour. From his perspective, the 'opportunity cost' of work time was more clearly defined and easier to measure. According to Green: 'The subjective feelings of different individuals are not easily compared, but the economic opportunities which a man sacrifices by pursuing a certain course of action are more capable of objective measurement' (Green 1894: 223). Frank Knight (1921) made a similar point some years later. He rejected the attempt to identify the direct pain and pleasure of economic activities. In Knight's view: 'The pleasure-pain question belongs exclusively in the field of inner consciousness, and has no bearing on problems such as those of economics' (Knight 1921: 63). The intrinsic costs and benefits of work activities were dismissed as being 'very shadowy and elusive things, if not altogether unreal' (Knight 1921: 70). It was argued that the cost of work should be defined in terms of the opportunity cost of work time and not the actual pain cost of work itself.

This view was endorsed by Robbins in his famous book, *An Essay on the Nature and Scope of Economic Science*, first published in 1932. Robbins (1930b) had earlier set out a model of labour supply. This model demonstrated the positive and negative impact of a wage change on labour supply and offered a foundation for subsequent indifference curve-based analysis of the work decision.[17] In his *Essay*, he confronted the definition of economic science, suggesting that economic science was to be defined in terms of the allocation of scarce resources among competing ends. Here it was argued that work played a merely functional role in providing the resources needed to meet diverse ends. Work effectively was a means to the end of final consumption. Only given acceptance of the Austrian side in the 'cost controversies' could Robbins (following the Austrians) adopt the means–end definition of economics and, in so doing, decisively narrow the scope of economics to a focus on consumption and exchange equilibrium.

The Austrian approach to labour supply appeared, on the surface, to avoid value statements. Instead, it seemed to be based on 'objective' data relating to the number of work hours and the level of wages. On closer inspection, however, it could be seen to incorporate certain value judgements about work and leisure. On the one hand, it was assumed that all workers held neutral preferences for the type and quality of work. This assumption followed from the idea that workers valued only the monetary rewards from work (time). On the other hand, there was a view that leisure was a 'good'. This latter assumption was required to justify the argument that the duration of work time was a useful proxy for the cost of work. It was not that the length of work time captured the sacrifices involved in working, but that it facilitated the measurement of cost in terms of the supply of labour. As Knight wrote:

> Time does not in any sense measure the alternative or sacrifice, and ... its employment in any use is a sacrifice in the first place only because there are other uses for it, which are the real sacrifice; but it is *measurable*, and our intelligence, forced to have something quantitative to feed upon, like the proverbial drowning man catches at any straw.
>
> (Knight 1921: 73; emphasis in original)

The desire to come up with an objective measure of the cost of work and hence to formalise the theory of labour supply – a trend which gathered increased momentum in neoclassical economic theory during the second half of the twentieth century (see Chapter 7) – can be regarded as one important motivating factor behind the embrace of the opportunity cost framework in neoclassical economics.

The Austrian defence of opportunity cost over pain cost, however, can be seen to confront certain problems. If, as the Austrians argued, the notion of the marginal disutility of labour was vague analytically, then could not the same argument be applied to the assumption of the marginal utility of leisure time which underscored the Austrian explanation of the opportunity cost of work time? The opportunity cost concept did not remove from the explanation of labour supply the subjective measurement of the cost of work; rather it simply replaced one subjective measure, the marginal disutility of labour, with another, the marginal utility of leisure time. The problem, though, was that no precise explanation was given for why all workers were able to 'enjoy' their leisure time. Having rejected the idea that work was a bad, the Austrians were unable to argue that the delights of leisure time were linked to the actual pain of work itself. Instead, they were forced to make the blanket assumption that all non-work or leisure time was intrinsically rewarding. This led to obvious anomalies, such as the false view that unemployment was a 'leisure activity'. Hence it appeared that the unemployed were 'happy' to spend their time as leisure. Such a view not only obscured the costs (social as well as economic) of unemployment, but also blocked the implementation of policies designed to reduce joblessness. The idea posited by Austrian economists that leisure was a 'good thing' omitted consideration of how leisure time was actually spent by individuals and also failed to consider the links between the leisure preferences of individuals and the qualitative experience of work itself. It neglected to show, in particular, how people might have a need to work, for both extrinsic as well as intrinsic reasons.

The Austrian formulation was based on the notion that workers were concerned only with the activities they pursued during their leisure time and not with the activities they pursued during their work time. True, it was suggested that the welfare of workers was affected by work. But, in this case, workers were only assumed to care about work when not actually working. Paradoxically, once at work, workers were argued to have no interest whatsoever in how their labour was allocated. Pagano (1985: 113–14) draws out the obvious shortcomings in such an approach. The logic of the Austrian position was to assume that changes in the nature and content of work had no affect on the welfare of workers, so long as the length of work hours and wages remained constant. Yet, such changes can be seen to influence workers' experiences of work and hence their welfare. Take the case of a fall in the discretion that workers have over their work. Workers in such a situation may be expected to suffer a decline in their welfare, even allowing for no change in work hours and in wages. The experience of lower-quality work in this case may also act to lower the motivation of workers, leading to potentially reduced labour productivity. The point is that, contra the stance taken by the Austrian school and its supporters, workers do harbour strong interests in the way that they work and their experiences of work affect in a direct way their well-being.

The Austrian-inspired opportunity cost framework that came to dominate thinking in the neoclassical analysis of labour supply abstracted from the actual content of work. A key outcome of the acceptance of the above framework was that human welfare came to be defined in terms of consumption and not work. The view thus was encouraged in neoclassical economics that work was valued solely as a route to income and that it had no direct intrinsic cost or benefit. Such a view had important implications for debate over policy. In particular, it suggested that changes in the nature and conditions of work were unnecessary. Moves to improve the quality of work, in this sense, were not aided by the Austrian model of labour supply. At worst, this model promoted the view that labour could be treated just like any other input into production.[18] It was not considered that the allocation of labour might matter to the welfare of workers, and indeed it was implied that labour could be allocated in production, without direct regard to the impact on workers. It appeared that the welfare impact of work was neutral, regardless of whether work was organised on a hierarchical or a democratic basis. Unwittingly, then, the Austrian formulation became a legitimating force for all kinds of workplace policies that in reality were highly damaging to the well-being of workers.

Conclusion

This chapter has considered the nature and origins of ideas on the cost of labour and its relation to the supply of labour within neoclassical economics. It has been argued that there were two competing positions in early neo-classical debates. One position, associated with Jevons and Marshall, gave emphasis to the direct costs and benefits of work activities. According to this view, workers took into account the subjective feelings of pain and pleasure experienced from work in their decision to supply labour. The other position, adopted by early Austrian economists, argued that work itself was a source of neither utility nor disutility. Instead, it highlighted the role of the oppor-tunity cost of work time as an impediment to the individual's labour supply and emphasised the direct link between utility and final consumption.

The Austrian side in the 'cost controversies', as stated in this chapter, ultimately prevailed. There were several reasons, analytical as well as ideo-logical, for this resolution. The concern to make the economics of labour supply more tractable can be seen to be one possible influence upon the embrace of the Austrian concept of opportunity cost. This concept avoided potentially troublesome discussion concerning the direct costs and benefits of work and instead focused attention on two factors that were readily mea-surable, namely work hours and wages. There is also the possibility that the disutility concept of Jevons and Marshall was abandoned, in part at least, because of its unpalatable political implications. By dispensing with this concept neoclassical economists were able to eschew the analysis of issues such as work degradation. They too were able to abandon once-and-for-all the labour theory of value and hence also the theory of exploitation.

The contribution of Marshall stands out from those of other neoclassical economists because of its direct concern with the plight of the labouring classes. Work, for Marshall, was important in its own right, rather than simply as a route to consumption, and he regarded progress in work quality as a necessary step in the enhancement of human life. Here there remained some overlap between his approach and that of J.S. Mill, who also expressed sympathies with the interests of labour (see Chapter 2). But, as argued above, Marshall tended to undermine and contradict his views on the transforma-tive nature of work by holding to a utility theory that took the preferences and interests of individuals as given. Ultimately, Marshall has become remembered for his contribution to the development of a utility theory of value. His views on the intrinsic worth of work and on the desirability of work reform, by contrast, have tended to be overlooked and ignored.

The turn to opportunity cost, it has been argued in this chapter, had sig-nificant consequences for the nature and scope of neoclassical economics. Critically, it removed from neoclassical theory the direct study of work and instead placed at its core the analysis of consumption. It was left to non-neoclassical economists and other social scientists to deal with issues regarding the nature and content of work. Robbins's hugely successful 'scarcity' definition of economics, set out in his 1932 book, reflected this mode of thinking. It built on the Austrian framework of opportunity cost and sought to reduce work to a means only.

The development of neoclassical economics in the twentieth century saw the acceptance and entrenchment of a peculiarly slanted and unbalanced conception of labour supply. It became commonly accepted among neo-classical economists that while leisure and income affected the welfare of workers, the actual activity of work itself had no direct influence (either positive or negative) on workers. It was a classic case of Hamlet without the prince: that is, neoclassical theorists attempted to understand the supply of labour without any regard to work itself. The void left in economics in terms of the analysis of work and labour, as will be shown in the next chapter, was initially filled by American institutional economists.

6 Institutional perspectives on work

A man who is not interested in his work, and does not recognise in it either beauty or utility, is degraded by that work, whether he knows it or not.

(J.A. Hobson 1914)

Introduction

The study of work and labour occupied a central position in American institutional economics. Beginning with writers such as Richard T. Ely in the 1880s and continuing with John R. Commons and others in the early decades of the twentieth century, the institutional approach to labour research assumed a prominent and influential position in economic debates. Early institutional writers were not marginal figures within economics. Ely, for example, was a founder of the American Economic Association. These writers published in leading economic journals and also held posts in the economics departments of high profile American universities (see McNulty 1980). Further, they exerted an influence over policy making: Commons and his followers helped to shape the New Deal in America during the 1930s.

Institutionalism was very much an American venture. However, it drew on a wide set of sources, including the German Historical School and the work of the Webbs in Britain. Although there were differences between the contributions of individual institutional economists, a common theme in their work was the critique of neoclassical economics. Thorstein Veblen and John R. Commons, as founders of American institutional economics, argued that neoclassical theory was an obstacle to a proper understanding of the economy and the relations therein. Particular dissent was shown towards the conception of work and labour contained in neoclassicism. Veblen (1898) criticised the neoclassical assumption of the marginal disutility of labour. He argued that this assumption was not explained by neoclassical economists. Commons, on the other hand, highlighted the deficiencies in the 'commodity theory of labour' (Commons 1919: 17). He accused neoclassical economists of treating labour as a homogenous input into production and of neglecting the direct impact of work on the well-being of workers.

Institutional economics effectively created 'labour economics' (McNulty 1980; Boyer and Smith 2001). This term entered the lexicon of economics in the mid-1920s (Solomon Blum's 1925 book was the first to bear it as its title). The emergence of labour economics partly reflected on the state of neoclassical economics at the time, where the study of work and labour was seen as increasingly inconsequential to economic theory as such. Early institutional labour economists positioned themselves on terrain that had been vacated by neoclassical economists. Their contribution, importantly, reached out to researchers beyond economics. For example, institutional labour economics was a strong influence on the development of ideas in the subject of industrial relations.

This chapter considers the contribution of American institutional economics to the analysis of work and labour. It begins by examining the interventions of early institutional labour economists, including Ely and Commons. It then moves on to consider the work of Veblen. Veblen is shown to have provided a novel challenge to the 'work as bad' thesis, as articulated in conventional economics. On the one hand, Veblen argued that people possessed an 'instinct of workmanship': he refuted the idea that people were born lazy. Yet, on the other hand, he suggested that people had been led to acquire an aversion to work by the prevailing 'pecuniary culture' in society. Veblen's contribution is assessed critically in the second section, drawing out weaknesses in his conception of the instinct of workmanship and in his account of the evolution of industrial capitalism. Finally the chapter considers the post-war evolution of labour economics, focusing on the demise of institutional labour economics and the rise of neoclassical labour economics.

Early institutional labour economics

A central figure in the initial development of the institutional approach to labour economics was Richard T. Ely. In 1886, he published *The Labor Movement in America*. This book, which has been described as the first text in labour economics (McNulty 1980: 132; Boyer and Smith 2001: 200), adopted a historical and descriptive approach. It aimed specifically to identify 'labour problems' evident in contemporary American society, and proposed solutions to combat these problems. Ely was trained in Germany rather than in the USA and brought to his work ideas gleaned from the German Historical School of economics. He was critical of traditional economic theory for its failure to examine the distresses and hardships faced by workers in their work lives.[1] In terms of politics, Ely was committed to social reform as a means to improve the condition of the working population and he viewed organised labour as a particularly important social agent in the achievement of this end. Indeed, he was fulsome in his praise of the ambitions and aims of trade unions, writing that:

> The labour movement ... in its broadest terms, is the effort of men to live the life of men. It is the systematic, organized struggle of the masses to attain primarily more leisure and larger economic resources; but that is not by any means all, because the end and purpose of it all is a richer existence for the toilers, and that with respect to mind, soul, and body. Half conscious though it may be, the labour movement is a force pushing on towards the attainment of the purpose of humanity; in other words, the end of the true growth of mankind; namely, the full and harmonious development in each individual of all human faculties – the faculties of working, perceiving, knowing, loving – the development, in short, of whatever capabilities of good there may be in us.
>
> (Ely 1905: 3)[2]

Here Ely stressed how it was important for workers to be elevated by their work, rather than degraded by it, and he looked to various reforms to enhance the quality of work life. Indeed, he suggested that useful lessons could be drawn from experiments in communist work organisation in America, writing that:

> Early American communism has accomplished much good and little harm. Its leaders have been actuated by noble motives, have many times been men far above their fellows in moral stature, even in intellectual stature, and have desired only to benefit their kind. Its aim has been to elevate men, and its ways have been ways of peace.
>
> (Ely 1905: 33)

Ely's own reformist zeal was not directly connected to any political ideology as such, but rather was influenced for the most part by the teachings of the Christian Church (McNulty 1980: 140–1).

John R. Commons was a student of Ely. Like his mentor, he stressed the value of real-world research and he was concerned to use economics to achieve certain social ends. He was critical of the simple supply and demand conception of market exchange found in standard economic theory and instead sought to promote an approach to the study of the economy that took into account the role and importance of institutions (see Hodgson 2003; Kaufman 2007). Commons argued that neoclassical economists took for granted exactly what must be explained, namely the non-economic environment in which people make economic decisions. He advocated a 'political economy' perspective that dealt with the connection between law and economics and highlighted the role of legal rules in affecting the behaviour of individuals and groups in society (see Kaufman 2007: 16). In this regard, Commons was concerned to reconstruct economics, although as it turned out he was unable to develop a rival economic theory to compete with neoclassical economics.

The analysis of work and labour assumed a prominent position in the writings of Commons. His research on the subject of work and labour contained a number of distinctive elements. He, for example, recognised (with Marx) the fact that the employment contract was incomplete and openended. All that an employer obtained in hiring a worker was that worker's potential to work. The employer faced the task once the worker was hired of converting this potential into actual work done. Commons indicated how the amount of work performed by workers would depend upon an array of economic, social, and institutional factors present in the workplace (see Kaufman 2007: 25). In addition, he acknowledged that in terms of the employment relationship employers had greater power than workers and so could take actions that were to their own benefit but not necessarily that of their employees (Kaufman 2000: 193–4).

Also, in a significant step, Commons challenged the view that labour could be classified as a mere commodity that was indistinguishable from other factor inputs. On the contrary, he recognised the interests and preferences of workers for the type and quality of work they perform. Work was not simply a means to consumption; it was also an important end in itself (Kaufman 2000: 192). From a human welfare perspective, hence, Commons was not merely concerned with the amount of goods and services yielded from production; he also paid close attention to the impact of production on the lives of workers and he believed, like Ely, that conditions were required in the work realm that enabled workers to achieve the higher-level objective of self-realisation (see Kaufman 2007: 35–7). Commons and other institutional economists implied that sacrifices in production may be warranted to protect and improve the quality of work.

Commons, politically, was a reformer. While he felt that the capitalist system had certain faults, he thought that it could and should be improved upon, rather than abandoned for an alternative system. Trade unions were seen as an important ingredient of a more humane capitalism. Hence trade unionists helped to counterbalance the power of employers and in turn assisted in the improvement of the conditions of work. Like other institutional labour economists, Commons believed that trade unions had an important part to play in achieving both greater democracy and superior economic performance in industry (see Kaufman 2000). Despite his prounion stance, he remained unwilling to accept the case for socialism. Commons, it has been argued, embraced an overtly anti-socialist stance in his writings after 1915, partly as a response to the drift of the trade unions towards the ideology of socialism (Nyland 1996: 1005). Instead of seeking a move to a socialist system, Commons (1934: 143) aimed ultimately 'to save capitalism by making it good'.

Critical though he was of the neoclassical analysis of the labour market, Commons was unprepared to dispense with it *in toto*. He remarked that such analysis was not wrong per se, but rather 'incomplete' (Commons 1919: 17). It was implied that neoclassical economics could be enhanced by incorporating within it the study of institutions and there was the appearance that neoclassical and institutional perspectives on work and labour might be developed alongside one another. The extent to which, in fact, the work of Commons was compatible with neoclassical economics, remains an issue of debate in the secondary literature (see Kaufman 2007: 11–12). What remains the case is that Commons failed to integrate his ideas into a coherent theoretical framework (see Hodgson 2003: 548). While Commons was in no sense opposed to theory development, he was unable to forge a fully fledged alternative to neoclassicism. He also had limited success in inspiring his students to develop the theoretical foundations for a new economics (McNulty 1980: 174–5). One consequence of this failure was that the institutional economists were unable to progress much beyond criticism of neoclassical economics: in labour research as in other areas, there remained no systematic institutional economic theory that could challenge and replace the neoclassical paradigm.

Robert Hoxie (1920), another significant writer on work and labour issues within the American institutional tradition, considered directly issues of economic theory. In particular, he saw in the study of unionism the possibility for the articulation of a general theory of the capitalist economy (see Hamilton 1916). Like Commons, however, he failed to impress upon his students the need to build an alternative economics. They adopted Hoxie's strictures against standard economic theory, but made few positive steps in developing alternatives. McNulty (1980: 175–6) argued that Hoxie's untimely death in 1916 delivered a heavy blow to the formulation of a coherent institutional approach to economics.[3]

The limited progress at the level of theory, however, failed to thwart the forward march of institutional labour economics in the first third of the twentieth century. Up until the 1930s, opinion in labour economics continued to be strongly influenced by institutional economics and rival neoclassical perspectives, such as those by J.R. Hicks (1932) and by Paul Douglas (1934), failed to make any significant inroads into debates in the field. To some extent, economic circumstances played a part in this outcome. The Great Depression brought into sharp focus the limits of the laissez-faire doctrine of neoclassical economics and won support for the pro-government intervention approach of institutional economics (Boyer and Smith 2001: 202). Yet, it is also the case that the institutional approach was seen to go where neoclassical economists were reluctant to. It dealt with issues at an empirical and conceptual level that were seen to fall outside neoclassical economics. At least in the interwar period, there was no systematic effort by neoclassical economists to contribute to labour economics, a fact that helped to secure the dominant position of institutional economics. Before looking at the development of labour economics after 1945, consideration is given in the next section to the contribution of Veblen to labour research.

Thorstein Veblen on work and work aversion

The analysis of work and labour undertaken by Veblen has not been widely commented upon by those who have examined the history of labour economics (see McNulty 1980; Boyer and Smith 2001). Indeed, Veblen's contribution has largely been overshadowed by that of Commons. Yet, Veblen offered a number of novel insights that complemented and augmented the institutional approach to labour economics. In this section, particular attention is devoted to Veblen's critique of the mainstream economists' conception of work as a bad.

In an 1898 article, Veblen drew attention to the fact that 'received economic theory' painted a picture of humans as natural idlers, who wished to avoid all work. It should be stated here that Veblen did not mention any economist by name. He thus neglected to state the fact that economists such as Marshall recognised that humans might be inclined to enjoy work for its own ends (see Chapter 5). Rather he proceeded on the basis that the dominant view in economics was that work had no intrinsic benefit. This view had certain implications for the study of human welfare, as Veblen pointed out: it implied that humans aspired to consume as much as they could, in the absence of work. As Veblen wrote:

> According to the common sense ideal, the economic beatitude lies in an unrestrained consumption of goods, without work; whereas the perfect economic affliction is unremunerated labour. Man instinctively revolts at effort that goes to supply the means of life.
>
> (Veblen 1898b: 187)

The problem, however, was that conventional economists did not explain why people wished to avoid all productive activity. Instead, they simply imputed to every person the same aversion to work on an ad hoc basis. There was certainly no explanation as to why such an aversion might have developed in society. This is where Veblen sought to make a positive contribution to the economics literature, by showing the reasons why people had come to loathe work and to desire leisure. Although Veblen agreed with the established economic theory that work was a disutility, he argued that the resistance to work was culturally determined, rather than exogenously given.

Veblen's own position was that work was, or could be, a good thing. Indeed, he was confident that people would perform work, not merely to obtain income, but also for its own sake. He believed that humans were endowed with an 'instinct of workmanship' that drove them to work well and to deplore the waste and futility of effort. He thus wrote that:

> In the intervals of sober reflection, when not harassed with the strain of overwork, men's common sense speaks unequivocally under the guidance

of the instinct of workmanship. They like to see others spend their life to some purpose, and they like to reflect that their own life is of some use. All men have this quasi-aesthetic sense of economic or industrial merit, and to this sense of economic merit futility and inefficiency are distasteful.

(Veblen 1898b: 189)

The instinct of workmanship was explained by Veblen in evolutionary terms. Hence it was argued that natural selection in the course of human phylogeny had led to the evolution of a proclivity or instinct to perform work that was useful for survival (see Hodgson 2004: 196). Such an instinct had been and remained a vital element in the reproduction of the human species.[4]

The mainstream economists' argument that people had no desire to work and wished to spend their time idly, according to Veblen, faced problems in accounting for the survival of the human race. If humans had, since the dawn of their existence, submitted no effort to the production of their own means of life they would have long since died out (Hodgson 2004: 196). The fact that the human race had managed to survive as long as it had could be attributed to the evolutionary selection of the instinct of workmanship that had given to every single human being an appreciation of effective work, and a dislike for futile effort (see also Veblen 1994: 57).

Veblen believed that the instinct of workmanship had been responsible for the great progress of industry and productivity in human history. He summarised the influence of this instinct in the following way:

Obscurely but persistently, throughout the history of human culture, the great body of the people have almost everywhere, in their everyday life, been at work to turn things to human use. The proximate aim of all industrial improvement has been the better performance of some work-manlike task. Necessarily this work has, on the one hand, proceeded on the basis of an appreciative interest in the work to be done; for there is no other ground on which to obtain anything better than the aimless performance of a task. And necessarily also, on the other hand, the discipline of work has acted to develop a workmanlike attitude.

(Veblen 1898b: 191–2)

Here Veblen suggested that the activity of work could be intrinsically rewarding. The fact that humans had devoted their time and effort to work through the ages was not solely down to the extrinsic benefits of work, but rather was partly due to their interest in and enjoyment of work itself. The point was reiterated by Veblen when he suggested that people gained personal satisfaction as well as social status from taking pride in their work. Thus, he wrote that:

As regards serviceability or efficiency, men do not only take thought at first hand of the facts of their own conduct; they are also sensitive to rebuke or approval from others. Not only is the immediate consciousness of the achievement of a purpose gratifying and stimulating, but the imputation of efficiency by one's fellows is perhaps no less gratifying or stimulating.

(Veblen 1898b: 196–7)

It was implied that people would continue to work even after they have satisfied their immediate comforts, because of the intrinsic rewards obtained from doing a job well.

But instinct was not the only influence on the behaviour of people in their role as producers. Habit and culture played a vital part too. Here Veblen emphasised the scope for the instinct of workmanship to come into conflict with and be undermined by habits of thought that were selected and reproduced at the cultural level (Hodgson 2004: 196–7). An important theme in Veblen's writings related to the crowding out of productive effort by the evolution of a so-called 'pecuniary culture'. While this culture had deep roots in the evolutionary history of mankind, it remained a very significant aspect of modern capitalist society.[5]

In the capitalist world, according to Veblen, people were preoccupied with a relentless search for status through the acquisition of monetary wealth. Status was won not simply by the ownership of wealth, but by the display of owned wealth. Specifically, it was necessary for individuals to show publicly that they possessed the financial means not to work (see Veblen 1994: 28). The ability to abstain from work, thus, had become the mark of high standing in society and people were driven to spend their time unproductively in order to gain the approval of their fellow human beings. This point is well conveyed by Veblen in *The Theory of the Leisure Class*:

> Abstention from labour is not only a honorific or meritorious act, but it presently comes to be a requisite of decency. ... Abstention from labour is the convenient evidence of wealth and is therefore the conventional mark of social standing; and this insistence on the meritoriousness [*sic*] of wealth leads to a more strenuous insistence on leisure. ... According to well established laws of human nature, prescription presently seizes upon this conventional evidence of wealth and fixes it in men's habits of thought as something that is in itself substantially meritorious and ennobling; while productive labour at the same time and by a like process becomes in a double sense intrinsically unworthy. Prescription ends by making labour not only disreputable in the eyes of the community, but morally impossible to the noble, freeborn man, and incompatible with a worthy life.
>
> (Veblen 1994: 26–7)

Two routes were available to the individual in demonstrating an ability to avoid work (Varul 2006: 105). The first was labelled by Veblen 'conspicuous leisure' and entailed the increase of leisure hours at the expense of work hours. People were limited in how many hours they themselves could spend away from work since they were required to stay there to earn income. In this case, they would aim to spend their money ensuring others who were dependent on them were exempted from work. Hence much leisure took the form of 'vicarious leisure'. Veblen (1994: 50–1) thus showed how many women were detached from paid work in order to demonstrate the high status of their husbands who could afford to let them stay at home.[6] The second way of showing abstention from work was the now familiar Veblenian concept of 'conspicuous consumption', which required that individuals spend their income on non-essential or luxury items. People achieved high status in this case by forcing others to perform work in meeting their own extravagant wants.

An important point to stress is that Veblen saw the origins of work resistance in the evolution of human culture. He did not maintain that the disutility of work was in any sense an inevitable or natural feature of human nature; quite to the contrary, he argued that humans were by instinct inclined towards productive activity. While the instinct of workmanship remained of vital importance in the development of industry in capitalism, it had become submerged by a hostile cultural environment that had converted work into a disutility. The fact that capitalism encouraged pecuniary motives at the expense of productive efficiency was seen by Veblen to present deep-seated problems in terms of its future reproduction and survival (Hodgson 2004: 197). Like Marx, though for very different reasons, Veblen thought that capitalism would develop in an uneven and contradictory fashion.

Veblen, on the one hand, was critical of the waste and destruction generated by the conspicuous leisure and conspicuous consumption evident under modern capitalist society (see Wenzler 1998; Varul 2006). Yet, on the other hand, he saw a progressive side to capitalism in the form of machine process. He believed that the machinery and technology of industrial capitalism helped to inculcate in the workforce rational and scientific habits of thought which were in direct conflict with the prevailing pecuniary values of capitalism (Veblen 1904). He argued that the transformation in values and beliefs caused by the machine process created a workforce that was sceptical towards conservative standards, including the rights and privileges of private property (see Tilman 1999: 94; Hodgson 2004: 213–14). Veblen admitted that the impact of machinery would be modified by cultural and institutional factors (see Tilman 1999: 94–5; Hodgson 2004: 209–10). Nonetheless, he felt that machinery provided the basis for heightened class conflict between a working class that was increasingly hostile to private property, and a capitalist class that was narrowly interested in advancing its own pecuniary goals. Machines, in short, threatened to undermine the institutions of capitalism (Hodgson 2004: 214). Veblen thus wrote:

> Broadly, the machine discipline acts to disintegrate the institutional heritage, of all degrees of antiquity and authenticity – whether it be the

institutions that embody the principles of natural liberty or those that comprise the residue of more archaic principles of conduct still current in civilised life. It thereby cuts away that ground of law and order on which business enterprise is founded.

(Veblen 1904: 374)

The above ideas fed into Veblen's well-known and much-criticised discussion around the endemic cultural conflict between 'industry' and 'business' (Hodgson 2004: 201–5). Hence, while the culture of business upheld the virtues of money making, the culture of industry worked to promote the ideals of efficiency and serviceability. Veblen's sympathies were clearly with the latter rather than the former. He believed that modern machinery had the potential to break the stranglehold of the pecuniary culture on modern capitalist society.

Because of their direct engagement with technology and machinery, Veblen came to view the engineering profession as an important catalyst for radical social change. By training and experience, engineers were inclined towards industrial motives and disinclined towards pecuniary motives. Their behaviour accorded with the basic instinct of workmanship that had helped to ensure the survival of the human species. Veblen thought that engineers would be at the vanguard of moves to create a new mode of social organisation that would seek to promote the real needs of society as opposed to the artificial needs advanced by business. According to E. Layton:

Veblen viewed the engineers through the spectacles of his instinct psychology. He assumed that they were being led to reject business culture by the conditioning of the machine process; because they personified the instinct of workmanship they would constitute the spearhead of the revolution.

(Layton 1962: 70)

Thus, with engineers in a position of influence, workmanship and serviceability rather than acquisition and futility would become the primary values of society. Veblen implied that people would be able to lead fuller lives where they were given the opportunity to realise their inherited instinct of workmanship and he looked to a society administered by engineers as providing the best option for achieving this ideal.

The campaign to limit the role of industry in modern society associated with the Arts and Crafts movement, not surprisingly, met with a sceptical response from Veblen. A return to handicraft or household industry was liable to lower the quality of produce and to increase labour costs, in comparison with machine-produced goods. Those like John Ruskin and William Morris who saw virtue in the industry of the past (see Chapter 3), thus, were dismissed for their 'exaltation of the defective' and 'their propaganda of crudity and wasted effort' (Veblen 1994: 98). Veblen suggested that the cult of craft production was not immune to the selected 'pecuniary canons of taste' that had come to prevail in capitalist society. As he wrote: 'The superior gratification derived from the use and contemplation of supposedly costly and beautiful product, is, commonly, in great measure a gratification of our sense of costliness masquerading under the name of beauty' (Veblen 1994: 78–9).

Veblen believed in the essential superiority of the output of mechanised forms of production. Machine-made products as compared with hand-made goods displayed 'greater perfection in workmanship and greater accuracy in the detail execution of the design' (Veblen 1994: 98). Useful and beautiful items, in short, could be created with the aid of modern machinery (see Mazur Thomson 1999: 6–7). As Veblen (1902: 110–11) put it, 'these results can be attained in fuller measure through the technological expedients of which the machine process disposes than by any means within the reach of the industry of a past age'. While Veblen's vision of the ideal society of the future was vaguely and imprecisely defined, it rested on the belief that social progress depended upon the preservation of the industry of contemporary capitalism.

Useful though Veblen's ideas were in drawing out deficiencies in the standard economic account of work and work aversion, they contained several problems of their own.[7] To begin with, one may question the basis of Veblen's classification of workmanship as an 'instinct' that is possessed by humanity in general. The work of humans cannot be judged to be instinctual, in short, without confusing its status with the work of animals. Ants and bees, for example, act on and transform nature to meet their needs. Yet, their work is fundamentally different from that of humans. In contrast to animals, humans are not led to work purely out of instinct. Rather humans have the unique capacity to work in a conscious and creative fashion. Here one can usefully draw on the analysis of Marx. As shown in Chapter 4, Marx argued that humans could conceive in their minds the fruits of their labour before commencing work: their productive activity in this sense could be seen to be influenced by the power of conceptual thought. Viewed from this perspective, it cannot be regarded as appropriate or meaningful to reduce the human capacity for useful work to the level of an instinct.

The above criticism was made by Braverman (1974). For him, Veblen had misunderstood the nature of human work and its role in human evolution. In opposition to Veblen, he claimed that human beings had progressed by non-instinctual forms of labour: 'Labour that transcends mere instinctual activity is thus the force which created humankind and the force by which humankind created the world as we know it' (Braverman 1974: 50). Veblen's instinct psychology carried the false implication that humans performed work in a reflex fashion, when in reality their work contained an inherent creative and boundless quality.

Yet, Veblen appeared to understand the distinctive aspects of the human form of work. He believed that humans had the ability to act purposefully in the satisfaction of their needs. As he put it:

Man's great advantage over other species in the struggle for survival has
been his superior facility in turning the forces of the environment to
account. It is to his proclivity for turning the material means of life to
account that he owes his position as lord of creation. It is not a proclivity
to effort, but to achievement – to the compassing of an end. His primacy
is in the last resort an industrial or economic primacy. In his economic
life man is an agent, not an absorbent; he is an agent seeking in every
act the accomplishment of some concrete, objective, impersonal end.

(Veblen 1898b: 189)

Like Marx, Veblen was aware that humans worked in an intelligent way;
however, his insistence that the human activity of work be reduced to the
operation of the instinct of workmanship tended to undermine this line of
reasoning, by asserting that humans were predisposed to work in the same
involuntary manner. In persisting with the language of 'instinct', Veblen
invited unnecessary confusion as to the true meaning of human work.

There is also the question of the impact of the system of work on workers'
aversion to work. Consider, for example, work under capitalism. Within
capitalist production, workers have no direct control over what and how they
produce. Instead, being forced to sell their labour power for wages, they must
work under the direction of employers. Seen in these terms, work in capitalist society can be regarded as an external or 'alienating' activity (see Chapter
4). The important point in relation to Veblen's analysis is that work resistance need not be seen simply as a cultural phenomenon, but rather may be
linked to the structures of capitalism that deny workers the ability to work
freely and creatively.

Of course, in arguing this point, it is important not to lose sight of differences in the way that work is actually experienced by workers. In some
instances, indeed, work may be a source of drudgery and pain. In such circumstances, the aversion to work may be seen to exist independently of any
kind of pecuniary culture that devalues and denigrates work. On the other
hand, however, circumstances may arise where work is intrinsically satisfying
or enjoyable. In creative occupations, such as in the arts, for example, people
may gain significant non-pecuniary benefits from work and may stay at their
work longer than if they are motivated simply by the desire to accumulate
consumption goods for status reasons. Veblen, to be sure, recognised that
work itself could be pleasurable. Yet, he linked this to the influence of the
instinct of workmanship. He did not explain directly the way in which the
type and quality of work itself could affect the positive motives that people
hold for work. Nor did he show the way that the direct hardships of work
could influence the hostility of workers towards work.

A further issue relates to the conception of the employment relation
under capitalism. Veblen did not account for the fact that the relationship
between workers and employers is characterised by both conflict and consent. Thus, while workers seek to resist their exploitation at the hand of

employers, they also have interests in consenting in the workplace to ensure that they remain in their jobs. Consent by workers can be further supported and reinforced by specific social and cultural forces at work (Burawoy 1979; Edwards 1990). The view of Veblen that conflict over work was linked to the dominance of pecuniary values in society and consent to work was linked to the instinct of workmanship thus failed to appreciate how conflict and consent could be endogenously created and reproduced within the workplace itself.[8]

Veblen's account of the impact of modern industry can also be seen as deficient in several respects. In his opinion, the machine process provided a means to liberate the instinct of workmanship from the pecuniary culture of capitalism, by engendering 'matter-of-fact' and causal habits of thought among those who worked in the production sphere (Hodgson 2004: 208–9). Veblen failed to recognise the adverse effect of machines on the lives of workers. He did not consider that machines might impair the qualitative experience of work: in many instances, the adoption of mechanised forms of production under industrial capitalism has coincided with a reduction in the autonomy and discretion enjoyed by workers over their work. Machines have not given to all workers a scientific understanding of production, but on the contrary have often reduced their capacity to acquire new knowledge, by imposing on them a repetitive and monotonous pattern of work (see Braverman 1974). Ironically, the machinery of industrial capitalism has often engendered an antagonism towards work among workers that has strengthened rather than weakened the preoccupation with pecuniary rewards (see Wenzler 1998: 572). Machine technology, in short, has aided in the promotion of the culture and ideology of money making.

In practice, many workers have tended to perceive mechanisation as a functional process that is external to their own needs. This is because the machine process has been designed and implemented in the interests of employers. Its primary use in capitalist society thus has been to increase profits. Indeed, the increase in profits has come before other objectives, including that of improving the knowledge and discretion of workers. Contrary to what Veblen argued, the machine process cannot be regarded as independent of the pecuniary values of capitalism. In contrast, it may be seen to be influenced by the same economic imperatives that shape the rest of capitalist society.

A comment can also be made about Veblen's advocacy of Taylorism. Veblen saw in Taylorist methods the opportunity to improve the efficiency of production and to raise wages. He was not alone in this regard: several other institutional writers of the period also gave their support to scientific management (see Nyland 1996; Hodgson 2004: 222–3). Veblen denied that Taylorism would create any tendency to deskilling and was confident that it could be implemented without any great loss in the intelligence of workers (see Veblen 1904: 313). This view, in hindsight, was a mistake: in practice, Taylorism has not proved a progressive force in all workplaces. Indeed, it has often served to undermine the skill and knowledge content of work and has been invariably associated with lower rather than higher job quality (see Braverman 1974).[9]

In order to draw out further the problems in Veblen's analysis of the machine process and the nature of work more generally, it is useful to examine the contribution of the British institutional economist J.A. Hobson. Inspired by Ruskin, Hobson sought to focus on the human costs of work incurred by workers. He argued that modern machinery, far from being a means to enhance the quality of work, had actually increased the hardship of work for many workers (Hobson 1914: 61–2). He claimed, in particular, that scientific management reduced the freedom and initiative of workers, and in turn, threatened to lower labour productivity (Hobson 1914: 219–20). Unlike Veblen, Hobson believed that the costs of Taylorism far outweighed the benefits and he was against its introduction in modern industry.

Hobson, importantly, rejected the view that work was to be accepted as a purely economic activity. Rather, he argued that work was a potentially rewarding activity in its own right. While there was a shortage of opportunities for rewarding work in modern industrial society, it was possible and necessary to expand such opportunities in the future by the implementation of several specific reforms. These included the imposition of a minimum or 'living' wage to ensure that all workers could gain enough income to meet their basic physiological needs (Hobson 1914: 196–7: see Townshend 1990: 85–6; Lutz 1999: 92). There was also a need to provide workers with secure and stable employment (Hobson 1914: 199). Further, it was recommended that workers be allowed to participate in the management of the firm in which they worked (see Lutz and Lux 1979: 42–3).[10] Hobson was critical of excessive job specialisation for suppressing the creativity of individual workers; however, he believed that the division of labour could be used to achieve a noble end, namely the reduction of work time. As he wrote:

> It is desirable that work shall be highly specialised, but not that the energy of the worker shall be monopolised by this specialised work. Hence the need of protecting labour against excessive hours of labour and the 'driving' tendency of modern machine-production. The legitimate use of division of labour requires that a large margin of leisure and of energy be given to every worker for the free and healthy exercise and use of his other faculties. The farther division of labour is carried, the shorter should be the routine working day, the longer the time for other kinds of work and play. This is the 'true inwardness' of the agitation for shorter hours; it is not a plea for idleness, but for the healthy use of unspecialised faculties.
>
> (Hobson 1904: 217)

Like some other writers (e.g. Marx), Hobson saw an important role for machinery and technology in the extension of free time.[11] With greater time to do what they want, people would be able to realise and develop their faculties and ultimately enjoy fulfilling lives. Hobson thus looked forward to:

> a legitimate and most serviceable cooperation between machinery and human skill in the production of fine qualities of wealth, machinery more and more taking over the rough, coarser, routine groundwork, and leaving to human art the more delicate manipulation and finish which gives character and tone.
>
> (Hobson 1904: 224)

Overall, in his commitment to the enhancement of work quality, Hobson aimed to reach an outcome where those who worked could meet not just their essential biological needs, but also their higher level need for self-realisation (see Townshend 1990: 81–5; Lutz 1999: 93–4).

Veblen, in contrast to Hobson, seemed to imply that social progress could be achieved without any wholesale change in the organisation of work. What was required was to release modern industry from the grip of business enterprise. The ultimate aim was to create a 'Soviet of Engineers'.[12] Now, admittedly, Veblen's own views on reform were set out in vague terms (see Hodgson 2004: 221–4). However, one suspects that even if he had spent the time spelling out the kind of system he wished to see adopted in the future he would have still failed to reach a satisfactory outcome. The key problem was that Veblen underestimated the degradation and alienation of work evident under industrial capitalism. The costs of work in capitalist society were real, and were not simply determined by culture. What occurred to Hobson, but was elided by Veblen, was that there was a need to transform work, in order to meet the needs of people as producers. A society where work and workmanship were valued for their own ends, in short, needed a different kind of work organisation to the one that presently existed under capitalism. Veblen's hints at the superiority of a society run by engineers, in sum, were not helpful in the understanding of the necessary reforms to convert work into a meaningful and satisfying activity.

Post-war labour economics

With the contributions of Commons, Veblen, and others, institutional labour economics seemed poised to advance and prosper in the 1940s and 1950s. As it turned out, however, its influence waned in the post-war period, as neo-classical economists sought to remould labour economics (see Boyer and Smith 2001). Admittedly, there emerged a second generation of institutional labour economists that included writers such as John Dunlop, Clark Kerr, Richard Lester, and Lloyd Reynolds. These writers remained critical of neoclassical economics for its abstractness and lack of grounding in reality. Yet, in comparison with earlier institutional economists, there was a greater willingness to confront neoclassical economists on their own terms. Standard techniques of neoclassical economic theory, thus, were used to advance explanations of various labour issues. While labour economics in the immediate post-war period bore the imprint of the institutional school, it was much nearer to neoclassical economics than earlier contributions in the field. Indeed, looking back on their contribution, labour economists of the period such as Kerr (1988) have seen themselves more as 'neoclassical revisionists' than as 'neo-institutionalists', although in practice they achieved only limited success in revising neoclassical economics (see Boyer and Smith 2001: 205).

The decisive shift away from institutionalism and towards neoclassicism in labour economics took place after the mid-1950s. Key writers included George Stigler, H. Gregg Lewis, Gary Becker, and Jacob Mincer (see Boyer and Smith 2001: 208). These writers were concerned with the application of an analytical and formal method to the study of work and labour. From their perspective, neoclassical economics did not require any kind of modification or revision in its application to work and labour research: on the contrary it possessed all the necessary tools to build a rigorous and insightful labour economics. Characteristic of the fusion of labour economics and neoclassical economics was the theory of human capital associated with the work of Becker (1964). This theory helped to subsume the analysis of work and labour into the technical apparatus of neoclassical economics and, in doing so, stripped the concepts of work and labour of their social, historical, and institutional content.

There are several factors that led to the rise and eventual triumph of neoclassical labour economics after the mid-1950s. One factor was the increase in the availability of new data sources and the increase in the use of econometrics, developments that helped to shift labour economics in a quantitative direction (McNulty 1980: 191–2; Boyer and Smith 2001: 208). The turn to mathematics and econometrics in economics in the post-war period was an important contributory factor in the demise of institutionalism (along with other non-neoclassical approaches) in labour economics and economic analysis more generally. A second factor was the methodological critique promoted most notably by Milton Friedman (1953) that realism of assumptions was unimportant in the development of economic theory (see Boyer and Smith 2001: 207). For the institutional labour economists, neo-classical economic theory was problematic because it was based on unrealistic assumptions. Friedman's critique showed that this criticism was no longer valid and thus removed one obstacle to the encroachment of neoclassical economics into labour economics.

A third factor was the failure of institutional labour economists to offer a viable theoretical system that could trump the neoclassical paradigm. Neoclassical economists retained the upper hand in debate in being able to offer such a system and hence could dismiss the institutional labour economists for offering only a negative critique and for not providing any alternative economic theory. Becker and other neoclassical labour economists, from the mid-1950s onwards, provided the kind of systematic theoretical framework that was lacking in the institutional tradition in labour economics. Further, the reluctance of some institutional labour economists, most notably Commons, to break free from neoclassical economics left the door open to a revival of neoclassical theory in labour economics. While neoclassical explanations were merely 'incomplete' as opposed to fundamentally flawed, there was always the possibility for writers to extend neoclassical economics from within rather than from outside. This is exactly what the likes of Lewis, Becker, and Mincer succeeded in doing after the mid-1950s, effectively sidelining the contribution of institutional labour economics.

The resurgence of neoclassical economics in work and labour research had several consequences. In particular, it converted labour economics into a formal and technical sub-discipline and this led to it becoming isolated from industrial relations (see McNulty 1980: 199–200). In analytical terms, it resulted in a narrowing in the focus and range of labour economics. Labour supply, for example, was viewed merely as an example of rational choice, with individual workers seeking to allocate their time between work and leisure in the most efficient way possible. There was no sense in which workers were affected by the process and experience of work: quite to the contrary it was assumed that workers had stable and unchanging preferences for work and leisure. Further, while there was some interest in the process of training and skills acquisition, the internal relations of the workplace received scarcely any consideration. In the rush to devise mathematical models and to estimate regression equations, the focus on the situation of the worker within production was largely overlooked. What had been a key concern of early institutional labour economists – namely the improvement in work quality – was lost sight of, as labour economics became concerned with the behaviour of supposedly rational individual agents who were assumed by definition to be able to maximise utility.

Previously, as mentioned in Chapter 5, the view had come to develop in neoclassical economics that the labour supply decision could be treated as a simple trade-off between income and leisure. Effectively the study of labour supply was seen as a special case of consumer theory and was not afforded any separate consideration in economic theory. The resistance of institutional economists to this type of reasoning was one factor behind the emergence and spread of 'labour economics'. Thus, labour economics was seen to confront issues that were beyond the reach of neoclassical economics. However, the inauguration of neoclassical labour economics in the late 1950s and 1960s altered fundamentally the character of labour economics. It showed how the same devices used in the analysis of consumption and production could be applied widely in the analysis of work and labour. Such devices as utility and production functions, it was argued, had a general application and could be used to subsume labour economics into neoclassical economics.

The neoclassical approach to labour economics was seen to offer new opportunities for the development of theory and analysis. In practice, however, it reduced very substantially the explanatory power of labour economics by recasting it into the mould of neoclassical economic theory. The retreat from institutionalism meant that valuable detail on social relations in the labour market and in the workplace was lost from labour economics. The way in which labour economics was transformed in the late 1950s and 1960s ultimately made it appear as if the earlier institutional contribution to labour economics had never existed.

Conclusion

This chapter has documented the rise and fall of institutional labour economics. It was shown how labour economics as a sub-discipline in economics began life as a part of the American institutional tradition. The mainstream position in labour economics right up to the 1950s was imbued with the ideas and method of American institutional economics. From the mid-1950s onwards, however, neoclassical economics occupied labour economics and sidelined the institutional approach. The result of this was to delimit the field of labour economics.[13]

Labour economics, in its turn towards neoclassical economics, became infused with the methodologies of formalism and individualism. Model-building took priority over realistic analysis, and the increased emphasis on the application of mathematics and econometrics closed off opportunities for dialogue between labour economics and other areas of labour research, such as in industrial relations. In conceptual terms, there was a loss of focus on the role and importance of issues of power and conflict. There was also a move to see work in instrumental terms and not as an activity that also affects the capacity of workers to lead fulfilling lives. In these and other respects, neoclassical labour economics was inferior to institutional labour economics.

The chapter also discussed Veblen's analysis of work. Veblen dismissed the idea that people were naturally inclined to resist work and instead argued that work resistance was linked to the prevalence of a 'pecuniary culture' in society. Veblen clearly lamented this state of affairs and alluded to the desirability of moving to a different kind of society where the inherited 'instinct of workmanship' would be allowed to flourish. Yet, he made little attempt to spell out the kind of reforms that were required to convert work into a rewarding activity. Critically, by taking a benign view of modern industry, Veblen failed to observe the necessity for change in the organisation of work as a means to advance the quality of work life.

Veblen's approach did not have any impact on the economics of work and labour. His contribution, like that of other institutional economists, was ultimately eclipsed by the neoclassical paradigm. This was not because the neoclassical school could answer in a satisfactory way the questions raised by Veblen and the institutionalists. In fact, such questions were largely ignored. Instead, as we have seen above, neoclassical economics developed by excluding the contribution of institutional economists. The next chapter takes the discussion forward by considering the development of the mainstream economics literature on work and labour over the last thirty years.

7 Mainstream economics and the hidden abode of production

In the present instance, going back to the liver-pill circular, I had the symptoms, beyond all mistake, the chief among them being 'a general disinclination to work of any kind'.

(Jerome K. Jerome, *Three Men in a Boat* 1889)

Introduction

Research in labour economics, as shown in Chapter 6, became dominated by the technical and formal apparatus of neoclassical economics after the mid-1950s. Mainstream labour economics, in effect, was transformed into neoclassical labour economics. While the mainstream approach to labour economics has been challenged over more recent years, it has largely succeeded in deflecting criticism and indeed has actually widened its sphere of influence.[1] A notable development in mainstream economics since the 1970s has been the generation of theories based on the assumption of imperfect and asymmetric information. Such theories have become a prominent aspect of the analysis of work and labour in the mainstream (see Alchian and Demsetz 1972; Williamson 1975, 1985; Akerlof and Yellen 1986; Lazear 2000b). It has been argued that, in the absence of perfect information and hence also perfect monitoring, employers cannot rely on the employment contract to obtain the labour they require from the workers they hire. Rather it is assumed that action must be taken by employers to get their workforce to work hard.

In the past, as was outlined in Chapter 5, neoclassical economists assumed that workers were wholly indifferent towards the content of their work. It was implied that even if employers lacked the information to monitor workers they would not face any problem achieving their goals, so long as they paid workers wages that compensated them for the opportunity cost of work time. This view has been challenged in modern mainstream economics. Now, it is assumed that workers have interests in minimising their work effort. Workers, so the theory goes, are compulsive 'shirkers' and must be compelled to work. Accordingly, the workplace is seen as a place of conflict, with employers seeking to discipline workers by various rewards and sanctions.

The modern 'information-theoretic' economics has opened the way for mainstream economists to theorise the internal relations of the workplace. Where previously mainstream economists ignored the interactions between workers and employers, they have latterly come to consider such interactions with a new vigour and enthusiasm. The willingness of contemporary mainstream economists to deal with social relations at work, albeit as the outcome of informational imperfections, has helped to make the labour research of mainstream economics more familiar and also potentially more acceptable to other social scientists. In this respect, it has facilitated the process of 'economic imperialism' (see Fine 2002).

Another significant recent development in mainstream economics has been the emergence of research focused upon the analysis and measurement of human happiness (Oswald 1997; Frey and Stutzer 2002; Blanchflower and Oswald 2004; Layard 2005). The new 'economics of happiness', among other things, has entailed an extension in the subject matter of labour economics. It has addressed directly the qualitative aspects of work and their impact on worker well-being. Work is seen as important not just as a route to consumption but also as a potential source of intrinsic reward. In empirical research, attention has been paid to data on job satisfaction taken from nationally representative social surveys. These data have been used to measure and quantify workers' perceptions and experiences of work itself. Such research has created some common analytical ground between mainstream economics and the other social sciences.

The main aim of this chapter is to assess critically approaches that have looked to develop and extend the analysis of work in modern mainstream economics. In order to do this, the chapter will also offer an alternative conception of the nature and quality of work to that contained within mainstream economics, an alternative conception drawn from non-mainstream economics and from the other social sciences. The chapter begins with an examination and critique of the longstanding theory of compensating wage differentials. This theory purports to augment the simple income-leisure model of labour supply by considering the non-pecuniary elements of work. However, as argued below, it rests on an inadequate conception of the influence of work on human well-being. Against the subjective approach to well-being at work proposed by the theory of compensating wage differentials, an objective notion of well-being at work is developed, stressing the importance of human needs. The following two sections consider the moves made by modern mainstream economists to uncover the internal organisation of work. Such moves are found to be based on an incorrect conception of the employment relation. The emphasis on the problem of 'shirking' and 'opportunism' in the context of imperfect information conceals rather than illuminates the politics of production. To comprehend how the employment contract is enforced, it is important to consider the complex balance of conflict and consent in the workplace. The penultimate section appraises the contribution of the new 'economics of happiness' to the analysis of the quality of work. Among the chief faults with this approach is its failure to address the role and importance of human needs in the assessment of job quality. The final section offers some concluding remarks.

Compensating wage differentials

The theory of compensating wage differentials has been used by mainstream economists to account for the impact of the quality of work on the 'choices' that workers make between available job offers. This theory seeks to extend the conventional model of labour supply that reduces the worker's choice to a trade-off between income and leisure. In the latter model, as we have seen in Chapter 5, what the worker does during his or her working hours has no bearing at all on his or her utility. Work is undertaken to gain wages, and is not desired or opposed as an end in itself. In the theory of compensating wage differentials, by contrast, a variable capturing the worker's preferences for work is included in his or her utility function. Hence the direct costs and benefits of work are seen to influence the utility of the worker, in addition to the duration of work hours and the hourly wage rate. The degree to which individual workers value the non-monetary aspects of work, in turn, is assumed to affect the wages they are willing to accept in different jobs.

The idea that workers might be paid higher or lower wages to compensate for the intrinsic aspects of work dates back to Adam Smith (see Chapter 2). In mainstream economics, it has been developed and applied by writers such as Gary Becker (1965) and Sherwin Rosen (1974). A key point is that there are differences both in the characteristics of jobs and in the preferences of workers. On the one hand, it is recognised that some jobs have better conditions than others. For example, a job may offer the opportunity to work in a pleasant working environment and in the company of family and friends. Another job, by contrast, may be characterised by hard physical labour and may be undertaken in an unfriendly or hostile atmosphere. Workers, on the other hand, differ in what they want to get out of work: some are attracted to the intrinsic pleasures of the work itself, whereas others are mainly concerned with how much they can earn from work.

It is assumed that workers opt for jobs that best meet their preferences. Each individual worker's preferences are taken as given and are said to influence his or her 'reservation wage' for different jobs. The worker is suggested to 'reveal' his or her preferences through the willingness to accept or decline the wage offers of prospective employers. Assuming the labour market is competitive, the wages attached to different jobs are said to equalise the advantages and disadvantages across jobs, so that the marginal worker is as likely to choose one as another. Because workers differ in their preferences and because firms differ in their working conditions, a matching process is assumed to occur whereby workers with the strongest preferences for superior working conditions are allocated to firms with the most resources to offer such conditions. These circumstances thus ensure that the labour market reaches an efficient equilibrium that is beneficial to workers and firms alike (see Borjas 2000: Ch.6; Green 2006: 9–10).

Although an advance on the standard model of labour supply, the theory of compensating wage differentials displays a number of key weaknesses that are largely inherited from the standard model. An obvious shortcoming of this theory is that, in reality, many high-quality jobs tend to offer higher relative wages than low-quality jobs. There is little evidence that, in fact, workers can substitute higher income for less enjoyable work. Most workers, on the contrary, are forced to accept jobs on terms that are favourable to employers and thus face no guarantee that their preferences will be met by the jobs they do.[2]

Two further problems with the theory of compensating wage differentials can be highlighted. First, while there is a focus upon the preferences of workers for work, it is not explained how those preferences are formed and reformed. The idea that workers may acquire their preferences from the environment in which they live and work is not directly considered; rather it is as if workers are born with different preferences for work, one set being risk-lovers, another set risk-haters, one group workaholics, another group work-avoiders. Why workers should differ in their preferences for work is left unexplained. Certainly, no attention is given to the impact of working conditions on the motivation as well as commitment of workers to work. The whole question of the determination and variation of worker motivation and performance, indeed, is eschewed.

Second, the definition of job quality promoted by the theory of compensating wage differentials ultimately takes no account of human needs (see Green 2006: 10–12). Needs are to be distinguished from the desires or wants that people express through their decisions in the marketplace (see Lutz and Lux 1979: 14). A need is something that must be met for human life to be sustained and enhanced (see Kaufman 1999: 374–7; Lutz 1999: 127–32). In the work sphere, it can be argued that there are certain human needs that workers ought to be able to fulfil. These include the most basic human needs, such as the need for food, drink, and shelter. Within capitalist society, the fulfilment of these needs can be seen to depend on the wages that workers are able to obtain from paid work. From the perspective of human needs, there can be said to be some minimum level of wages that workers must receive to reach an adequate standard of living in society. Importantly, such a wage can be established without any direct reference to the subjective preferences of individual workers. Other needs can also be viewed as important. It can be argued that workers have a need to work in a safe environment, a need to exercise autonomy over work, and a need for secure employment. Whether or not workers are able to meet these needs will impact in significant ways on their well-being at work. The focus on human needs is absent from mainstream economics in general, and from the theory of compensating wage differentials in particular; however, it has been a key feature of debates in other disciplines, notably psychology. Abraham Maslow (1954), for example, famously proposed a 'hierarchy of needs', from basic biological needs, through safety and love, and on to esteem and self-actualisation (see Lutz and Lux 1979: 9–13). It can also be seen in Marxist theory with the view that work – understood as free creative activity – is part of the human 'species being' (see Chapter 4).

Francis Green (2006: 13–15) has proposed a needs-based approach to job quality which can be contrasted with that contained within the theory of compensating wage differentials. He draws upon and develops the valuation framework of the Nobel Laureate Amartya Sen. With Sen, it is argued that a person's well-being will depend on his or her 'capabilities', which defines the ability to pursue a set of 'functionings', that is, the ability to do or be something. A key proposition is that people value the freedom and opportunity to choose between available alternatives. Applying this idea to the work domain, Green (2006: 13) argues that workers will experience a higher quality of work life where they have the option to choose the tasks they perform than where they are required to perform a set number of tasks without any choice in the matter. Specifically, he defines a high-quality job as one that affords the worker a certain capability:

> the ability and the flexibility to perform a range of tasks (including the necessary sense of personal control), to draw on the comradeship of others working in cooperation, to choose from and pursue a range of agency goals, and to command an income that delivers high capability for consumption.
>
> (Green 2006: 14–15)

Here the definition of high-quality work is deliberately broadened to include both non-economic aspects (such as skill, discretion, and social relations) that have traditionally been the concern of researchers in sociology and psychology, and economic aspects that have been the centre of attention in neoclassical labour economics.

Green, developing the framework of Sen, argues that there cannot be any universally applicable approach to the quality of work life. The relative valuation of any one aspect of work quality will instead vary depending on circumstances. Hence it will be expected that the level of wages will be a much more important factor in situations where workers face poverty than where they enjoy a relatively high standard of living. Significantly, the choice of factors to be included is not an exact science; rather it is affected by 'underlying values and concerns' (Green 2006: 15). Green highlights skill, effort, personal discretion, wages, and risk as key indicators of job quality, consistent with his own aim to integrate ideas from economics as well as sociology and psychology. Thus, unlike in the theory of compensating wage differentials, the quality of work within Green's approach is not considered to be necessarily reflected in relative wages.

A problem with the approach of Green is that it leaves the issue of what constitutes 'good work' potentially ambiguous. Someone might easily object to the inclusion of one or more elements in any definition of job quality and thus could seek to propose an entirely new definition based on whatever factors he or she happens to see as important. Effectively, the question of job quality remains subjective to some degree. Instead, what is required is a conception of need that recognises the essential role of work in human life. Here one can draw insight from Marxist theory, one important facet of which is the idea that human nature has a basic need for creative activity. Human beings develop and realise their unique creative powers through productive activity. Work can be fulfilling if it allows for the development and realisation of the creative potential of workers, but is 'alienating' if it does not afford opportunities for creative activity and is imposed upon workers. From this perspective, it can be said objectively that work is, or can be, a source of fulfilment to workers, and that unfree, non-creative work represents the denial of a basic human need.[3]

The Marxist notion of alienation highlights the fact that under capitalism workers are forced to relinquish control over their creative activity and must work under the direction of employers, who decide when and how they work (a fact stressed also by some other authors in the history of ideas on work, as revealed in previous chapters). Workers, for example, may be forced to endure poor working conditions, suffer job dissatisfaction, and receive low wages, simply because there are no alternative jobs available. Thus, it is to be regarded as a product of the capitalist organisation of work, rather than of work per se, that work is often viewed as a means to an end and that workers are unable to directly realise their need for creativity. In all respects, the understanding of job quality in terms of alienation is antithetical to the logic of the mainstream concept of compensating wage differentials. Instead of being defined in terms of the market valuation of work, the quality of work is understood on the basis of the human need for creative activity. The lack of fulfilment of this need under capitalism can be seen as a key reason why work remains for many workers in modern society an unwanted necessity. Here the absence of 'good work' can be regarded as an objective reality of capitalism.

Overall, the theory of compensating wage differentials offers a fundamentally distorted understanding of the quality of work and its impact on worker well-being. The tendency is to see work quality as just another determinant of relative wages. In practice, however, there is no certainty that wages will adjust to compensate for the costs and benefits of work activities. The assumption that workers can maximise satisfaction or utility through choosing jobs that match their preferences, in short, is conceptually impoverished and factually unfounded. But how far have new theories that have emerged over recent years augmented the explanatory power of the economic analysis of work? This question will be addressed in the next section.

Opening up the black box

The last thirty years have seen a revival of interest among mainstream economists in the nature and organisation of work. Important perspectives include transaction costs economics, efficiency wage theory, and personnel economics. These perspectives have allowed mainstream economists to open up the lid of the 'black box' of production. Before the 1970s, most mainstream economists took for granted the fact that employers could write fully specified employment contracts and also enforce them at zero cost.[4] Effectively it was assumed that the employment contract was a solved economic as well as political problem. Mainstream economists have come to recognise since the 1970s, however, that complete and costless contracting is impossible, due to the presence of informational problems. It has been argued that employers have incentives to leave the employment contract open-ended to allow scope for adaptations in the use of labour, which arise from unexpected contingencies and events. Further, it has been suggested that employers cannot monitor all of the actions taken by workers: instead they must ensure that appropriate incentives ('carrots' and 'sticks') are in place so that workers work up to standard.

An important recent development is 'personnel economics', an approach associated with the mainstream labour economist, Edward Lazear. Personnel economics is 'defined as the application of microeconomic principles to human resources issues that are of concern to most businesses' (Lazear 2000b: 611). It signifies an attempt to theorise the way that work is organised and governed inside the firm. Lazear (2000b: 611) offers three reasons for the emergence of personnel economics. First, he recounts the problems that were faced in teaching traditional labour economics to non-economics audiences, especially in business schools. The boredom of business students with what labour economists could teach warranted a change of direction in research. Here Lazear speaks from experience, having himself moved from the economics department to the business school at Chicago University. Second, Lazear shows how in the past human resource management was unpalatable to mainstream economists: 'It was loose, unfocused, and *ad hoc*, and lacked the general rigorous framework to which economists were accustomed' (Lazear 2000b: 611). Elsewhere, Lazear is scathing about the contribution of researchers in the area of human resource management:

> Human resource executives are often regarded as the lowest form of managerial life. The same has been true of those academics who study human resources. There is a reason: historically, the field was loose talk. It was descriptive. It was *ad hoc*. It lacked positive prediction or reliable normative prescriptions.
>
> (Lazear 2000a: 119)

The alleged lack of rigour in the study of human resource management has been resolved by the application of the analytical framework of standard neoclassical microeconomics.

Third, Lazear argues that developments in mainstream economics, notably those in agency and contract theory, have opened the way for mainstream economists to tackle issues relating to the internal organisation of work that were previously regarded as outside their territory.

Personnel economics, along with the theories of transaction costs and efficiency wages, provide prominent examples of 'economic imperialism' (Lazear 2000a). These theories seek to extend the boundaries of mainstream economics by taking seriously the informational problems that face employers in negotiating and policing the employment contract. Lazear sees great potential for personnel economics to triumph over the subjects of industrial relations and human resource management. The future for the study of personnel thus is seen to lie with the building of formal models based on the concepts and techniques of mainstream economics.[5]

A common feature of this research is the portrayal of the employment relation as an archetypal 'principal–agent' problem: workers (as the 'agent') are assumed to be hired by employers (as the 'principal') to carry out actions on their behalf. The problem for employers is that workers possess discretion over their work. Because of imperfect information and thus incomplete monitoring, workers have the ability to take actions that are in conflict with those of their employer. Now, it would not matter that information is imperfect if workers could be relied upon to work hard on a voluntary basis. Assuming the interests of workers and employers are compatible, there would be no conflict over work, since employers would be able to rely on workers to further the interests of the firm. Harmony would prevail in production, in short, despite the presence of imperfect information.

However, it has come to be accepted within mainstream economics that workers wish to avoid the actual performance of work. Whereas previously it was assumed that the payment of compensating wages was sufficient to assure the compliance of workers in production, mainstream economists have latterly come to assume that workers are unwilling to expend any effort at all. 'Shirking' by workers is recognised to exist as a problem even after offsetting remunerations are granted.

Oliver Williamson (1985) exemplifies the modern approach to worker motivation in mainstream economic theory. As he sees it, all workers have an innate and irrepressible propensity to behave opportunistically. The term 'opportunism' is used by Williamson (1985: 47) to define any 'calculated effort to mislead, distort, disguise, obfuscate, or otherwise confuse'. The impression is given that workers will do whatever they can to avoid the responsibility and exertion of work. Transaction costs economics is not alone in painting all workers as idlers. In the efficiency wage model of Carl Shapiro and Joseph Stiglitz (1984), workers are assumed to 'shirk', that is, expend zero work effort, when not monitored by employers. The idea of effort avoidance also features in the seminal work of Armen Alchian and Harold Demsetz (1972). Rather than just pursue leisure outside work time, workers are said to also partake in 'on-the-job leisure'. Importantly, there is not thought to be any benefit in performing work for its own sake. Instead, work is viewed as an inherent bad that workers wish to resist at all costs.

It is now commonly believed in mainstream economics that employers face the task of eliciting effort from uncooperative workers. Employers are assumed to gain the compliance of workers through various means, including the use of threats of job loss and the implementation of internal labour markets. In all instances, the key objective of employers is to ensure that workers are deterred from acting in their own self-interest and instead are motivated to work hard. An important underlying idea is that the actions taken by employers to reduce opportunism will advance their own interests as well as those of their workforce.

Some modern commentators have celebrated the recent developments in mainstream labour economics. George Boyer and Robert Smith (2001: 218), for example, conclude that mainstream labour economics is now more 'realistic' than in the past, partly due to the new body of research on imperfect information, and is thus much closer in spirit and content to the approach of earlier institutional labour economists. To this extent, they argue that the longstanding criticisms made by institutional labour economists against the neoclassical analysis of work and labour are now no longer valid.[6] Others, however, are unconvinced that genuine progress has been made. They make the point that in spite of the developments in the mainstream literature the same methodological and conceptual principles remain as in older mainstream research. Writers such as Fine (2002) thus have pointed to the continued commitment to methodological individualism in the work of Lazear and other mainstream labour economists. As will be argued below, perspectives such as transaction costs economics and personnel economics face acute problems in dealing with important social phenomena in the workplace.

Production politics

A number of facets of modern mainstream economic theories of work can be seen as problematic. One problem is the failure to recognise that workers' preferences are affected and indeed changed by the circumstances under which they work. The assumption is made in the theories of transaction costs and efficiency wages that workers wish to expend as little effort as possible, regardless of the conditions and amenities of work. Opportunism, it seems, is a fundamental trait of human nature: human beings are born to dislike work and to love leisure or idleness. As we saw in Chapter 2, a similar view was taken by the mercantilists and the classical economists, who regarded work as something that workers would naturally prefer to avoid.

Williamson (1985: 2–3) has argued that opportunism is a characteristic of 'human nature as we know it'. While institutions may be adapted and changed in preventing opportunism, people themselves cannot be altered in any way. In the case of the work domain, it is assumed that workers will shirk, unless coerced to work by employers. Workers are seen as imprisoned by their own shirking proclivities and are regarded as incapable of acquiring any positive preference for work. In short, there has been no progress in the understanding of the social origins and transformation of workers' preferences. How and why workers gain their preferences for work remain important unanswered questions in mainstream economics.

Interestingly, Lazear has addressed the issue of exogenously given preferences in economic theory. He claims that while economists assume that people are 'lazy, dishonest and at odds with the goals of the managers', they only apply this assumption to 'behaviour on the margin. It is the marginal behaviour that is of interest to economists, and to personnel economists in particular, because the things that people want to do, do not require motivation' (Lazear 2000b: 614). Three comments can be made here. First, the impression is given by Lazear that workers' voluntary consent to work is something that arises in a spontaneous way. Hence, it appears that workers perform work out of some instinctive desire for work itself, that is, when not prompted to conform by the interventions of employers. This view is problematic in that it fails to consider the social organisation of consent, a point developed below. Second, the reasons why workers have the preferences they do are not confronted by Lazear. There is little indication of why workers shirk in some instances but not in others. Like most other mainstream economists, Lazear fails to consider the endogenous nature of preferences.

Third, the difference between the disutility of work as a marginal and an absolute concept has not been properly articulated in the mainstream economics literature. Indeed, in transaction costs economics and efficiency wage theory, it has been assumed that work is avoided from the first minute (indeed first second) of every hour that is worked. Lazear himself does not state clearly why work is resisted on the margin. He gives the example of an academic who is 'pushed to the point where the chosen task becomes a "bad" rather than a "good"' (Lazear 2000b: 614). But this begs the question of why the academic is made to experience work in this way. If it is simply a matter of the burden of work (e.g. teaching more than three-and-a-half courses per semester) then it would seem important to establish the ability of the individual to limit his or her work duties below a certain level, which brings in issues of power. Yet, such issues are slighted by Lazear; rather he assumes that employers base their decisions on 'efficiency' considerations such that their chosen actions yield outcomes which deliver mutual gains. In experiencing work as a 'bad', thus, workers are said to be compensated by employers in the form of higher wages: however, in reality, employees may be forced to suffer work as a disutility with no compensating wage increase, because of their lack of power to alter their present situation. It is simply unrealistic to argue that the work decision can be reduced to a situation of constrained optimisation in which workers are able to maximise utility.

The general criticism regarding exogenous preferences can be made more specific by drawing upon the objective conception of job quality and of capitalist work organisation set out in the critique of the theory of compensating wage differentials, above. As is effectively argued by Paul Edwards (1990), the employment relation under capitalism endogenously generates *both* conflict and consent within the workplace. Consider, first, the important sources of conflict in the workplace. It remains the case that the purpose of capitalist production is to meet the needs of employers, not those of society as a whole. Due to their monopoly ownership of the means of production, employers are able to force workers to sell their creative potential (labour power) for wages – the key point that was stressed above in the critique of the theory of compensating wage differentials. Accordingly, employers can dictate terms and conditions that are in their own interests but not necessarily those of the workers who they hire. When it comes to the organisation of work, employers seek to elicit the maximum amount of work from workers, not to maximise their welfare. However, these very bases of conflict imply important sources of consent within the workplace. Workers rely upon consent to secure continued job tenure, despite retaining interests in resisting their own subordination. Employers, while they have interests in controlling workers, are also concerned to release and harness the creativity of their workforce.

The precarious and potentially contradictory balance between conflict and consent in the workplace cannot be understood in terms of the concept of opportunism. There are two related conceptual flaws in the latter concept. First, conflict in the contemporary workplace is socially specific, not asocial: conflict does not derive from some natural human aversion to work labelled 'opportunism' that is universal across all workplaces and across all societies, but rather emanates from the specific structures of capitalism itself. Second, as explained in the previous paragraph, examination of these social structures reveals that, though conflict is an endemic feature of capitalist production, there remains an important role for consent in the workplace. Far from being born shirkers, workers often work assiduously, even where overt pressure from employers to comply is weak (see Edwards 1990: 45–8).

Burawoy (1979) provides an illustration of how consent to work is manufactured by workers in their everyday work lives. He has argued that even in the presence of harsh and oppressive working conditions workers may still be led to internalise the interests of their employer. Drawing on his own research, he has shown how consent is forged through the playing of a 'game' that workers devise to increase their pecuniary as well as non-pecuniary rewards from work. By manipulating established rules to achieve their own objectives regarding pay, levels of effort, the use of time, and so on, workers gain 'relative satisfaction' that enhances their experience of work. As Burawoy indicates, rules laid down by employers may be broken as part of the game of 'making out', if they are viewed as preventing workers from getting ahead in their work. Ironically, instead of being a threat to employers. 'shirking' by workers (understood here as rule breaking) may actually benefit them if it results in increased production (see Edwards 1990: 46). To further emphasise this point, it may be noted how effective a 'work-to-rule' tactic can be in disrupting production: rule-following and thus non-shirking by workers in this sense may be the least desirable option from an employer perspective (see also Hodgson 1999: 171).

Burawoy stresses more subtle consequences of game-playing activities in the workplace. From an ideological perspective, these activities help to coordinate the interests of workers and employers by legitimating the conditions and objectives of production. Workers' participation in the game thus involves consent to its basic rules and to the desirability of its outcomes, including most obviously the achievement of higher production (Burawoy 1985: 38). Using Marxist terminology, Burawoy sees the constitution of work as a game as having the unintended consequence of simultaneously obscuring and securing surplus value production (and hence also capitalist exploitation). Importantly, the game provides a means to secure the consent of workers to the goals of capitalism, without any direct coercion from capitalists themselves.

A key point of Burawoy's analysis is the suggestion that conflict in actual workplaces is not inevitable, but rather is organised in socially and culturally specific ways. Despite the fact that the interests of workers and employers are opposed at a fundamental level, the joint organisation of conflict and consent at the workplace implies diverse outcomes at a concrete level, contingent on circumstances. Labour research in modern mainstream economics misses both the deep-seated bases of conflict under capitalism and the possibilities for consent between workers and employers in the workplace (Edwards 1990: 59). This is no coincidence. The method within this research concentrates on individual optimising behaviour under conditions of imperfect information and fails to articulate and explain the social structures of capitalism that define the capital–labour relation. The reliance on an inherently individualistic methodology, too, stands in the way of an understanding of the social and cultural processes that operate in the workplace and that help to coordinate the interests of employers and workers.

Personnel economics emphasises the importance of rational maximising behaviour. By highlighting such behaviour, it is argued that personnel economists are able to strip away complexity and to focus on 'what is essential' (Lazear 2000b: 612). Yet, it is questionable whether the behaviour of workers and employers can be fully understood in terms of individual optimisation. Norms quite obviously are not pursued as a result of a rational estimation of the costs and benefits of the consequences of compliance and non-compliance but instead are supported by shared values and beliefs about how individuals *ought* to behave (Burawoy and Wright 1990: 252). The employment contract involves a high level of social interaction and is supported by norms and customs that are not reducible to the optimising decisions of supposedly rational individuals. Further, as argued above, the preferences and interests of workers can be seen as endogenous to the workplace and, though at a general level they will always display a complex mix of conflict and consent, their specific content will vary with the nature and conditions of work: they are not fixed in the way that is assumed in standard utility theory. Lazear (2000b: 612) dismisses the contribution of labour research outside mainstream economics for allegedly ignoring 'generalisation', when it offers potentially critically important institutional detail about the social organisation of conflict and consent at work.

In addition, it can be argued that modern economic theories of work organisation oversimplify and distort the process of labour management. A key concept that can be seen to be both oversimplified and distorted is that of 'effort' as used within both efficiency wage theory and personnel economics. While this concept is used frequently in both perspectives, and is presumed to be a key concern of management, it is not itself defined in any specific way. This leads to certain ambiguities. One problem arises in defining the benefits of leisure. If 'effort' refers to actual bodily exertion, then it would seem difficult to explain why workers gain utility from leisure activities (the word 'activities' is significant here, rather than inactivity or idleness) given that the latter will require workers to expend 'effort' (this problem is similar in kind to some of those raised in Chapter 5, in connection to the canonical labour supply model). Also, for many occupations, physical activity is a minor aspect of the work performed. Intellectual labour is an obvious case in point. Are we to believe that 'shirking' by workers includes resistance to mental as well as manual labour? The treatment of 'effort avoidance' as a universal human problem fails to grasp the complex and multifaceted nature of the concept of effort. The fact that effort includes not just physical activity but also other (qualitative) elements such as ingenuity and creativity makes it very difficult to think of effort as a quantity that can be represented in a formal model. Efficiency wage theorists, in particular, have attempted to model effort, without any regard to the nuances that are entailed in the definition of this concept (see Currie and Steedman 1993).

The theories of transaction costs and efficiency wages imply that employers have a clear-sighted vision of their management goals and how to achieve them. For example, it is argued in efficiency wage theory that employers can secure worker compliance by paying wages that exceed outside opportunities. There is no suggestion of any unintended consequences of such a policy approach. On the contrary, the use of wage premium, by causing equilibrium unemployment, is seen to offer a highly effective worker disciplinary device. Yet, it can be argued that in practice the policies adopted by employers have uncertain and potentially contradictory effects. Wage incentives that restrict the demand for labour and lead to unemployment, to take one case, may act to heighten the fear of job loss and to increase involuntary work effort; however, they may also be expected to lower work morale, and also to induce workers to take fewer risks in their work – in both these instances, the impact of equilibrium unemployment on productivity may be negative (see Kaufman 1999: 379–80).

There is also the notion that, by treating workers as shirkers and opportunists, employers may end up fostering these kinds of traits in their workforce (see Jacoby 1990: 334). Thus, given a negative view of the underlying character of workers, employers will be inclined to implement stricter systems of monitoring, and direct control. Such actions, however, may create resentment among workers and cause them to withdraw their cooperation. Using the terminology of principal–agent analysis, Frey (1993) has shown how workers will tend to reduce their voluntary effort if employers seek to monitor their actions closely:

> When, through intervention, the principals attribute a lower morale to the agents than they actually have, an implicit contract between principal and agent is unilaterally violated, and the agents reduce what they consider to be their 'excess morale' to the level attributed to them.
>
> (Frey 1993: 1530)

By exhibiting a lack of trust in their workforce, according to Frey, the actions of employers succeed only in 'crowding out' (effort-enhancing) work morale (see also Kaufman 1999: 381). Extrinsic incentives, in short, may have the unintended effect of driving out intrinsic incentives, with potentially negative repercussions for output and productivity in the firm.

Williamson has effectively ruled out the possibility for employer opportunism (see Dow 1987: 21; Edwards 1990: 42). He has claimed that employers operate within a so-called 'zone of acceptance' and do not act against the interests of their workforce. An underlying view is that workers create problems for employers and not the other way around. Williamson (1985: 261) is clear on this point, arguing that workers 'exploit' employers rather than the reverse. Opportunism allegedly gives employers a 'bad' reputation that impedes their ability to recruit new workers, and also leads incumbent workers to lower their work performance. According to Williamson, 'in circumstances ... where firms are continuously in the employment market and successor generations learn, efforts to exploit incumbent employees are myopic and will predictably elicit protective reactions' (Williamson 1985: 261). Employers thus will face incentives not to behave opportunistically.

This view is clearly open to challenge. If opportunism is truly a part of 'human nature as we know it', as Williamson assumes, then there is every reason to expect that employers will partake in opportunistic behaviour as often as workers. To suggest that opportunism is a 'worker problem' alone is to succumb to bias. Where efficiency gains occur in production, there is no necessary compulsion on employers to allocate some of these gains to workers. Indeed, for profit reasons, employers may be inclined to appropriate all of the gains for themselves. Efficiency-based explanations, in short, fail to appreciate the genuine conflict of interest in the workplace.

The language of 'opportunism' and 'shirking' used by modern mainstream economists has an ideological cast that tends to align more with the pre-conceptions of employers than workers. As argued by Warren Samuels: 'Pejorative emphasis on shirking merely but effectively, constitutes either taking the employer side or assuming that there is nothing further to be worked out, which in practice is typically simply inaccurate' (Samuels 1994: 1252). By casting all workers as 'shirkers', modern mainstream economics creates the illusion that the options for work reform are limited to the implementation of more effective systems of monitoring and the reduction of worker autonomy. Ultimately, workers are to accept the necessity and inevitability of hierarchies as well as unemployment in combating their own shirking proclivities. Such a view obviously favours the immediate interests of employers and militates against improvement in the quality of work.

To summarise, transaction costs economics, along with efficiency wage theory and personnel economics, are unable to adequately theorise the work process. Two important weaknesses in these theories can be emphasised (Edwards 1990: 59): first, the failure to recognise the specific origins of conflict over work under capitalism, and second, the neglect of the role of consent in the workplace. There is also ignorance of the complexity and uncertainty of the management process and of the impact of power relations upon the organisation of work.[7] The next section considers the contribution of the nascent economics literature to 'happiness', which offers a novel treatment of job quality.

The economics of happiness

Recent years have witnessed a move in mainstream economics to study the utility or happiness of individuals (see Frey and Stutzer 2002; Blanchflower and Oswald 2004; Graham 2005; Layard 2005). This new literature, collectively termed the 'economics of happiness', has posed a direct challenge to some well-established ideas in mainstream economic theory. In the past, mainstream economists assumed that utility was a purely subjective category that could not be directly measured. Now, in contrast, it is accepted by an increasing number of mainstream economists that utility is a scientifically measurable property of individuals (see Layard 2005). This argument is a spill over from a new approach within psychology ('positive' or 'hedonic' psychology) according to which well-being is a trait of individuals that may be evidenced by their brain states, as well as by sophisticated social surveys, and other techniques (see Kahneman *et al.* 1999). It is stated that utility or happiness can be directly quantified by social scientists through the use of various new data sources that aim to identify people's subjective evaluations of various activities, including work.

The standard definition of job quality in mainstream economics, as shown above, used to be centred on the consideration of relative wages. Workers, it was assumed, revealed their preferences for work by accepting the wages attached to particular jobs. Where jobs failed to meet their preferences, workers were argued to 'choose' not to work, and to opt for a life of leisure. Importantly, in this view, there was little direct concern with the feelings of workers for the nature and quality of work. Not only were such feelings viewed as subjective and hence non-measurable, but they were also seen to be fully reflected in the actions taken by workers in the labour market. The observed choices of workers thus were assumed to matter more than their reported levels of job satisfaction in the consideration of their well-being at work. As a result, mainstream economists tended to neglect data on work preferences (see Green 2006: 10–11).

The rise of the new economics of happiness has challenged the above approach. Among modern mainstream economists interest has grown in subjective measures of job satisfaction. On the one hand, reported job satisfaction has been used to predict labour market behaviour. A robust finding in the literature is that 'quits' are strongly related to reported levels of job satisfaction: workers who are least satisfied with their work have been found to be most likely to exit their jobs (Freeman 1978; Clark 2001). On the other hand, data on job satisfaction have been seen to offer a way to isolate and measure the utility and happiness that workers derive from work itself (e.g. Clark and Oswald 1996; Frey and Stutzer 2002).

A consideration of the history of economics reveals a deep irony in the recent move of mainstream economists to examine the issue of subjectively measured job quality. Neoclassical economists, as was shown in Chapter 5, were prompted to remove from their theories any reference to the quality of work, in part, because of a concern about the problems of quantifying and measuring the direct costs and benefits of work itself. The marginal disutility of labour was viewed as a metaphysical construct that had no place in the formal apparatus of economic science. What has changed to allow the utility and disutility derived from work to be reincorporated into mainstream economics? Two factors can be seen as important in explaining this shift. First, mainstream economists have reacted to changes in the availability of data. Nationally representative surveys on job satisfaction, unavailable to earlier researchers, are now seen to offer a way to gauge patterns and trends in the quality of work in advanced countries. Here the external push of mainstream economics is explained by the desire to undertake new empirical work. Second, mainstream economics has itself evolved over recent years. There has been some loosening in the commitment to core ideas and principles in mainstream economics. While there is still an abiding faith in utility theory, moves have been made to extend the reach of such theory, and consequently established nostrums have been challenged and indeed abandoned. In the case of the economics of happiness, there is now increasing recognition that interpersonal comparisons of preferences are possible and indeed necessary in the evaluation of individual well-being. Nonetheless, it is important not to overstate the recent developments in mainstream economics. Common aspects still unite the mainstream. In particular, there remains a strong commitment to the use and application of formal methods, including mathematics and econometrics. Thus, happiness researchers in economics still see the need to present their arguments in formal terms that are recognisable and acceptable to other mainstream economists.

The economics of happiness has extended the analysis of worker well-being in mainstream economics. To this extent, it has served a useful purpose. Further, it has created scope for dialogue between economics and other disciplines regarding issues of job quality that are currently prominent in policy debates. However, the economics of happiness approach to job quality contains several deep-seated flaws. Fundamentally, it does not challenge the basis of mainstream economics in individual optimising behaviour. The mainstream economic theories of work critiqued above could in general be considered fully compatible with the new economics of happiness. Hence the step back to utility and happiness made by the new economics of happiness does not offer an escape from the above-developed criticisms of these theories. Rather than challenge such theories, the new economics of happiness is intended only to challenge the mainstream approach to well-being, refocusing attention on experienced utility, as distinct from income. Further criticisms of the new economics of happiness can therefore be developed on the basis of the objective concept of well-being at work that was set out above.

First, the notion of human well-being as an eternally and qualitatively fixed entity, termed 'happiness', located in the heads of atomistic individuals, is fundamentally wrong. On the objective conception developed above, well-being can be seen to develop *qualitatively* as well as quantitatively in socially and culturally specific ways.[8] The well-being of workers varies qualitatively along multiple objective dimensions such as the creative content of work, pay prospects, the interest of work itself, relations with colleagues, position within organisational and class hierarchy, influence and discretion over work, and effort levels. It is important to recognise in this sense that how work is experienced by workers differs between jobs, workplaces, and societies. Such differences in the quality of work and their impact on worker well-being are not properly addressed – indeed are largely ignored – in the economics of happiness.

Second, as argued above, there is a need to consider the importance of objectively defined human needs in the evaluation of work quality. In this respect, two points can be seen as particularly important. In the first place, it must be acknowledged that beyond the subjective feelings of individual workers work ought to be able to satisfy certain basic human requirements. Work, hence, should not only offer access to an adequate level of income, but also provide the opportunity for creative activity. These requirements, importantly, offer an objective basis to evaluate the degree to which work is good or bad. The economics of happiness, with it roots in utility theory, omits the role of human needs. In the second place, there must be an awareness that as far as work under capitalism is concerned workers face difficulties in securing their needs in the jobs they perform for wages. As was argued above, the capitalist system requires that workers must sell their creative potential (labour power) for wages. For many workers, work is performed with limited discretion and without much creative content. Capitalist work in this crucial sense is marked by 'alienation'. This key point is missed in recent studies of 'happiness at work', just as it is in all previous mainstream economic theories. The new economics of happiness, no less than other mainstream theories, fails to see beyond the subjectively reported job satisfaction of individual workers, and thus fails to elucidate and explain the structural reasons for dissatisfaction with work that are built into the capitalist system itself.

In order to bring out the problems in the subjective approach to job quality found in the happiness literature, it is useful to draw on a particular concrete example. Consider the case of two workers, x and y, who report the same high level of satisfaction with work. Worker x has a low-paid job, in which he or she has little control over work. Worker y, by contrast, has a high-paid job, and is able to exercise a high degree of discretion over the work he or she does. It could be plausibly argued that worker x has low norms and expectations about work and that this explains his or her high *reported* job satisfaction. Worker y, by contrast, may have high norms and expectations, and may be satisfied with work because his or her norms and expectations have been met. (Indeed, evidence suggests that reported job satisfaction is higher at each end of the income distribution, giving a U-shape pattern – see Brown *et al.* 2007).

Now, from a utility point of view, both workers x and y would appear to be equally 'happy' with work. Importantly, there would be nothing to say that worker x is worse off than worker y, since both seem to be gaining an identical level of satisfaction or utility from work. Here one can discern the potential perversity of the utility approach to job quality. Hence an outcome of assuming that the two workers have the same quality jobs would be to recommend that the type of work undertaken by worker x should be encouraged. It would seem that one of the best routes to raise job quality is to encourage low-paid, low-influence jobs.

A different perspective, one sensitive to the needs of workers and of the objective differences in the quality of work, would argue that worker x, in spite of having the same reported job satisfaction, has an inferior level of well-being in comparison to worker y. The fact that worker x has few options to influence the work he or she does makes the quality of his or her work life much lower than that of worker y, who has significant discretion over his or her work. Objectively, the work of worker y is superior in qualitative terms to that of worker x. Although worker x may report high job satisfaction, this need not be taken as evidence that he or she is truly satisfied in his or her job, but rather may be seen to reflect his or her low norms and expectations. These low norms and expectations, in turn, can be viewed as being reinforced by the low quality of work that worker x is able to secure. As qualitative research has shown (see Walters 2005), the low paid in some instances may be seen to be 'satisficing' in their jobs, rather than fulfilling their inner-most desires. They can be viewed as 'making the best of a bad job', in the context of severe structural constraints that inhibit their attainment of truly rewarding work.

The view of job quality promoted by researchers connected to the economics of happiness, in summary, is fundamentally individualistic in nature, and in this sense does not break with previous economic orthodoxy. Thus, it is neglectful of the objective dimensions of work that give rise to important differences in the qualitative experience of work across jobs and also offers no account of the importance of human needs. Mainstream economics continues to obscure the limits to well-being at work imposed by the capitalist system. Yet, without measures to change the way that work is structured and organised, 'happiness at work' will remain illusory.

Conclusion

This chapter has focused attention on the conceptual as well as methodological underpinnings of some prominent aspects of the modern economics literature on work and labour. Starting with the theory of compensating wage differentials, it has been argued that mainstream economists have not adequately addressed the quality of work and its impact on the motivation and welfare of workers. The concept of compensating wage differentials effectively reduces the issue of job quality to a matter of wage determination and offers no real insight into the internal relations of the firm. The idea that this concept fills the gap in standard economic theory when it comes to the understanding of the quality of work and its relation to worker welfare can be seen as misguided.

Approaches such as transaction costs economics and personnel economics, on the other hand, do seek to explore social relations inside the workplace. These theories, however, are fatally weakened by a failure to consider the co-existence of conflict and consent in the workplace. The focus on 'shirking' and 'opportunism' by individual workers is a barrier to a full understanding of the true character of the social interactions between workers and employers. Finally, the new economics of happiness includes an attempt to identify and measure the well-being of workers. Yet, this approach fails to embed the concept of well-being in an understanding of the objective conditions of work as well as the particular qualitative aspects of jobs. More importantly, it fails to see how low job quality is endemic to the capitalist system, in part because it eschews an objective concept of human well-being that is based upon human need.

8   Conclusion

Fie upon this quiet life, I want work.

(William Shakespeare, *Henry IV, part I*)

No pain, no gain?

This book has identified a number of common and enduring themes in the mainstream economics literature on work and labour. These include the depiction of work as a means to consumption, rather than an end in itself. Whether one consults the writings of the mercantilists, the classical economists, or neoclassical economists, one is struck by the consistency with which work has been defined as something which people wish to avoid. Work has been characterised as a pain or disutility. It has been implied that it is a natural part of human nature to seek leisure over work. An underlying notion is that the ideal form of human society is one where consumption needs can be met in the absence of work. A life of leisure with unlimited consumption is supposedly what humans crave most of all.

As previous chapters have shown, opinion in mainstream economic thought about exactly why workers are averse to work has evolved over time. In early mercantilist thought, it was argued that the labourer was naturally idle and worked mainly from hunger. Such an argument was used to justify the maintenance of poverty for the labouring population (see Chapter 2). Later economists including Jevons, too, argued that the 'lower classes' were natural idlers and thus were sceptical about the case for higher living standards for those who worked to produce wealth (see Chapter 5). Indeed, the view that workers are essentially lazy and must be forced to work has resurfaced in a different form in modern mainstream economics. Approaches such as transaction costs economics and efficiency wage theory see the problem of work avoidance by individual workers as the root cause of hierarchy and unemployment in society (see Chapter 7). Workers, then, are seen to suffer a loss of control over the work process and joblessness, due to their own refusal to work in the manner required by employers. Within such approaches, there is little recognition that the system of work might be responsible for the hardships suffered by workers in their lives inside and outside work.[1]

Adam Smith and the classical economists, on the other hand, took the view that work was intrinsically irksome (see Chapter 2). Such a view tended to be applied indiscriminately, so that all forms of work were implied to cause discomfort to workers. In this sense, there was a failure to address directly the specific costs of work associated with the actual organisation of production under modern (capitalist) conditions. This can be seen as ironic in the case of Adam Smith, whose writings have been noted for their emphasis upon the degradation of work, due to the technical division of labour. In Smith's work the impression was given that productive activity was a source of 'toil and trouble' in all instances: there could be no opportunity for workers to experience rewarding work, since work was intrinsically painful. The endorsement of this view by subsequent generations of classical economists acted to deflect attention away from feasible reforms that could have aided in the improvement of the quality of work. Even apparently progressive writers such as J.S. Mill still fell back on the idea that work was painful toil and thus were unable to show clearly how work might be transformed into a positive activity in a future society.

Neoclassical economics, at least in its early manifestations, took into account the positive as well as negative aspects of work itself. Emphasis on the quality of work was apparent in the writings of both Jevons and Marshall. In Marshall's writings, in particular, direct attention was paid to the effects of work on the 'character' of those who undertook it. However, such insights were subsequently sidelined in neoclassical economics. Hence, as argued in Chapter 5, it came to be accepted by most neoclassical economists that work was a mere means to consumption. Work was assumed to be costly only because it took time away from leisure. The actual experience of work was not assumed to have any direct causal impact on workers' well-being. This approach, as was revealed in Chapter 5, evolved out of an acceptance of the opportunity cost framework that was originally formulated by Austrian economists in the late nineteenth century. It was also shown in that chapter how the establishment of this approach within neoclassical economics was driven by the recognition of the dangers of embracing job quality considerations. On the one hand, the focus on the opportunity cost of work time removed from neoclassical economics consideration of the alienation of work. On the other hand, the duration of work time and the level of wages provided a convenient way of measuring the cost and benefit of work, respectively. The use of these quantitative variables, thus, facilitated the formal representation of the work decision in terms of an income–leisure trade-off.

Institutional economics, for a time at least, challenged the neoclassical account of work. Indeed, in the first half of the twentieth century, it held a pre-eminent position in the field of labour economics (see Chapter 6). Institutional labour economics recognised the potential importance of work as an activity in its own right. Veblen, for example, took the view that work was important in the expression and realisation of the 'instinct of work-manship' that was possessed by human beings. Commons and other institutional economists criticised the lack of attention in neoclassical economics to the quality of work and expanded the range of influences on human welfare to include the conditions and experience of work itself. The institutional perspective on labour economics, however, declined in influence after the mid-1950s and was ultimately eclipsed by a reinvigorated neoclassical labour economics. As a result, it became more common for mainstream labour economists to treat work as an instrumental activity.

The last thirty years have witnessed moves to extend the analysis of work and labour in mainstream economics (see Chapter 7). Particular interest has been shown in the way that the employment contract is endogenously enforced under conditions of imperfect and asymmetric information. This research, however, contains several weaknesses. For example, it fails to say how the preferences of workers for work are determined and instead assumes (without adequate explanation) that workers have an innate desire to resist work. Against this view, it can be argued that the employment relation under capitalism involves a complex balance between conflict and consent. It is not helpful to reduce such a relation to the allegedly universal problem of 'shirking' by individual workers.

Problems can also be seen to confront contemporary research on job quality that forms part of the new 'economics of happiness'. A key weakness of this research, as argued in Chapter 7, is the lack of a needs-based definition of the quality of work (see also Green 2006). To say that workers report being satisfied with their jobs is not to conclude that these workers are necessarily fulfilled in their jobs. Proper account must be taken of the extent to which the jobs that workers do meet their need for creative activity and this can be seen to depend on the objective features of work in specific occupations and workplaces. Most researchers associated with the economics of happiness believe that the well-being of workers can be simply read-off from responses to social surveys. They do not consider that there may be an objective basis to the evaluation of job quality that focuses on the realisation of human needs, rather than on the satisfaction of individual preferences, as reported in social surveys.

Overall, despite attempts to advance its underlying conception of work, mainstream economics continues to lack an adequate theorisation of the role and importance of work in human life. Here, there are important lessons for those outside economics who are welcoming of 'economic imperialism'. It is true that in the acceptance of informational imperfections as well as subjective measures of happiness (including job quality) mainstream economists have been able to reach out to other subject areas in ways that were not possible in the past. In the other direction, with the retreat from post-modernism, some modern social scientists have become more interested in economic factors, creating a potentially more responsive audience to approaches such as the new information theoretic economics and the new economics of happiness (see Fine 2002: 195). However, the appearance of progress in mainstream economics is deceptive. Mainstream economists have only colonised new research areas where this has offered opportunities to apply their favoured methods (e.g. econometrics) and their established theories (e.g. utility theory). At the same time, the mainstream has continued to be incredibly intolerant of the ways of other subjects in the social sciences – note Lazear's (2000b) outright dismissal of human resource management as 'unscientific' and lacking in 'rigour' – and also has remained opposed to non-mainstream economics, even though the latter has a long history of tackling many of the issues (such as the nature and process of work) that have latterly been confronted by mainstream economists.

One consequence of 'economic imperialism' is that it creates new space for discussion between economics and the other social sciences about the analysis of the economy (see Fine 2002). It opens up opportunities to demonstrate the continuing relevance and significance of non-mainstream perspectives in economics. These opportunities must be seized by modern non-mainstream economists. One objective of this book is to argue that, in the context of the analysis of work in economics and the social sciences more generally, there is a need to revive interest in contributions within the tradition of political economy.

Work and creative activity

Mainstream economists have tradionally assumed that the monetary rewards from work time are the sole positive inducement to work and that 'happiness' can only be realised through consuming goods (including leisure). Indeed, in the real world, there are many workers who work only for the money and who long for the time when work is at an end. But this does not reflect anything about the essence of work itself. Rather it conveys the fact that people's jobs are uninteresting and toilsome. They take this form because of the way in which work is organised. Were changes to be made in the organisation of work, it remains possible that workers could experience their work differently.

In mainstream economics, human beings have been painted as compulsive leisure hedonists, who work only out of a desire for consumption. There has been a failure to consider the fact that people might have a need for work and thus that they might be driven to work, independently of any kind of material incentives. From a different perspective, it can be argued that human needs extend beyond the accumulation of consumption goods and incorporate the participation in creative activity, including in the work sphere. Work is not purely about gaining income, but rather can be seen as a potential source of creativity, a basis for skill acquisition, and an opportunity for self-actualisation. Far from seeking to avoid work, under certain circumstances, people may be attracted to it as a means to gain pleasure and satisfaction in their lives.

An important idea, well established in the Marxist and radical utopian literatures, is that humans are endowed with the ability to act in a creative manner. People are not passive creatures of consumption who want to idle away their time. Instead, they can be seen to work out of a need to realise and develop their creative thoughts.[2] The challenge and difficulty of work, rather than being a source of pain, can be satisfying in itself. Important social relations, too, are forged through work; hence people gain personal pride as well as social approval from supplying the goods and services that they and the rest of society need to live. Work in this sense can help to build a sense of community and solidarity between people. The contrast can be made here with consumption, which is primarily a private affair undertaken by isolated individuals.

Marx, as shown in Chapter 4, made the point that work had a specific form under capitalist production. For him, it was capitalism that had 'alie-nated' workers from the product and process of work. As argued by Sayers (2005: 615), Marx felt that the classical economists' view of work as an unwanted necessity was itself a symptom of the alienation evident under capitalism. Adam Smith and the classical economists had confused the alienated form of work present in capitalist society with the essence of work itself. Other nineteenth-century radical thinkers such as William Morris, as mentioned in Chapter 3, also argued that capitalist society had destroyed any intrinsic benefit in work. Marx, followed by Morris, believed in the possibility and necessity of making work into a satisfying activity. Marx argued that this goal could only be achieved by the transcendence of capitalism.

Approaches such as those of Marx urge us to look beyond the need to meet consumption requirements through work and to think about the possibilities for attaining a form of work that enhances the quality of life of those who perform it. Work, in short, need not be all drudgery and toil: quite to the contrary, it ought to be a satisfying and rewarding activity in its own right. The fact that so many people in society remain so dissatisfied with their work is a problem to be addressed through the transformation of work, rather than something to be accepted as a natural state of affairs.

The past, present, and future of work

The achievement of abundance in advanced capitalist economies was thought by several earlier writers (including some prominent economists) to bring forth the possibility for a great transformation in work. It was foreseen that the advance in technology and the constant increase in economic growth under capitalism would allow for a reduction in work time and an extension in 'free time'. J.M. Keynes was one author to envisage such a possibility (Keynes 1963).[3] Though accepting the view that work was in general irksome, Keynes looked forward to a future society when people would work only a few hours per week and ample leisure time would be available for all.

Keynes saw the potential for a great improvement in the quality of human life via the curtailment of work time, and he believed such an improvement could be achieved through the progress of technology under capitalism.[4]

But the much vaunted 'leisure society' has failed to materialise for most citizens of developed economies. In the period up to the 1970s, there were indeed some reductions in work time.[5] Yet, in a number of countries (including Britain and the United States), the trend towards shorter work time came to an end in the 1980s and 1990s (Schor 1993; Green 2006).[6] Other indicators of job quality worsened in several countries over the same period. For many workers in these countries, work became much more pressurised, less under their control, and less rewarding (Green 2006). Factors such as the relative demise of manufacturing industry and the spread of human resource management practices did little to arrest the decline in job quality. Paradoxically, however, living standards in most advanced economies continued to grow. The major exception was the United States, where real wages stagnated (see Green 2006: 123–4). Overall, in a period when richer nations grew much more affluent, many millions of workers in these nations became much less satisfied with their jobs.

The decline of job quality in an era of rapidly advancing technology and ever-increasing wealth requires some explanation. In terms of standard economic theory, this paradox can be explained in several ways. It is possible that workers have come to 'choose' lower-quality work because of an exogenous shift in their preferences. Either workers have become less concerned with the intrinsic qualities of work (for example, they have become more prepared to give up autonomy over their work), or they have acquired a stronger preference for income, with the effect that employers have looked to offer more low-quality jobs. Such an explanation is obviously fallible. The idea that workers can gain employment that fulfils their underlying preferences is based on the fallacy that the decision to work or not is discretionary. In reality, however, paid work is generally coerced rather than chosen. Further, the above explanation faces problems in accounting for the change in workers' preferences. It is not at all clear why workers who are 'free' in their choice of employment should come to choose higher income over more enjoyable work (see Wisman 1989: 94–5). Survey evidence, indeed, has consistently shown that workers place a relatively high value on the intrinsic rewards from work and are not solely motivated by the monetary aspects of it (e.g. Lane 1992; Clark 2005). It could be argued that consumerism has fuelled an indifference to work itself and a heightened desire for income. But this requires that consideration be given to the way that preferences are moulded and changed by the environment in which people live and work. This is exactly what is absent from mainstream economics that takes the preferences of individual workers as exogenous (see Cowling 2006). Finally, on a practical level, an explanation based on the effects of consumerism faces some difficulties accounting for the timing of the decline in job quality during the 1980s and 1990s (see Green 2006: 69).

Other explanations for the decrease in job quality are available in the literature. Green (2006) has focused on changes in technology and work organisation that have enhanced the ability of employers to monitor and enforce the pace of work. These changes, it is argued, have increased the intensity and stress of work, and have also reduced the discretion of workers over their work tasks. An alternative explanation provided by M. Goos and A. Manning (2007) is that technological changes have tended to reduce the number of 'middle'-quality jobs that are highly routine (hence can be easily computerised) leading to a polarisation of the labour market into 'good' jobs and 'bad' jobs. The findings of Goos and Manning contradict the view that Britain is becoming a 'knowledge economy', in which there is a system-wide improvement in the quality of work life (see Green 2006: 36). The work of Green and of Goos and Manning suggests that the causes of the growth in low-quality work are linked to the demand side of the labour market.

But, in some respects, the low quality of work in advanced capitalist nations is unsurprising. Capitalism has no tendency to increase the well-being of workers; rather it aims to increase profits for employers. Indeed, the drive to make profit conflicts with the pursuit of higher job quality. Hence, for example, employers have interests in raising work hours and intensifying work in order to increase the profitability of production. Avoiding measures to enrich work via the reform of work, too, reduces costs and helps to maintain the power of employers over the work process.

Yet, is it not the case that employers can gain more from their workforce by taking greater account of their interests in the design of work? Indeed, this argument has been commonly made in the human resource management literature. It is argued that greater participation by workers in the organisation of work can help to boost firm profitability. On the other hand, mechanisms of direct control have been assumed to reduce worker welfare and hence labour productivity. This argument, however, ignores the deep-seated nature of the conflict between workers and employers under capitalism. As Green has effectively argued:

> specific instances where firms have lost out through an obsession with control do not prove that *in general* the workplace is a 'win–win' game, where what is good for workers is always good for the firm. One has to hold to a very rosy ideology about capitalism to accept the story that all one needs is enlightened managers.
>
> (Green 2006: 167: emphasis in original)

While employers' decisions are swayed by considerations of the bottom line, there will remain major obstacles to better-quality work. It can be argued that, in the absence of a fundamental change in the nature and conditions of work, genuine and lasting progress in the quality of work will not be possible.

A further contrast can be made between the argument in this book and the position taken in modern debates regarding 'welfare to work' schemes. In

Britain and elsewhere, the view has been adopted by policy makers that work is the most effective way of combating economic as well as social problems in society. First, it is argued that those without work tend on average to be the poorest in society. Second, there is recognition that the unemployed suffer social exclusion as well as poor mental and physical health. Based on this, it is claimed that the unemployed should be made to take available jobs as a means to a better quality of life. It is not to be disputed that the economic and social costs of unemployment are high. The problem is that, in terms of welfare to work programmes, there has been little direct consideration of the quality (and also quantity) of available jobs. It can be questioned whether it is desirable to force workers into work, whatever its quality. Layard (2004), an architect of the New Deal programme adopted by the New Labour government in Britain, has argued that the unemployed should be required to take 'bad jobs', on the grounds that any job is better than no job. Such a view effectively condones and encourages the creation of low-quality, dead-end jobs. Any policy approach that aims to coerce people into work cannot be judged to be humane and accordingly is rejected in this book.

Neither work nor leisure

The emergence of capitalism can be seen as a major social development which led to a particular social form of work, wage-labour, becoming the predominant form, perceived and experienced by workers as an inevitable yet painful necessity. Faced with the need to sell their labour power for wages, workers have come to regard work as an instrumental activity. Yet, paradoxically, work remains for many workers in modern capitalist society a valued part of their lives. Workers participate in important social activities during the hours they work and also take pleasure and pride in doing a job well. But these benefits are achieved within a system that is, at root, inimical to the interests of those who work. The pursuit of profit under capitalism overrides any concern for the advance of working conditions and the curtailment of work time.

The great irony is that in modern affluent societies the technology exists to make work into a more fulfilling and rewarding activity (see Sayers 2005). Technology that is now used to create and prolong work could be used to counter drudgery and to extend free time. Many resources (human and natural) are currently wasted in ensuring that employers make a profit (see Perelman 2000). One can only imagine what society could achieve if it directed the energies and creativity of its people to realising real human needs and not increased profits.

A major objective of this book has been to show that work can be, and indeed should be, a source of fulfilment and pleasure. It has dispensed with the idea promoted by the majority of mainstream economists that work has no intrinsic quality and must be accepted as a means to income and consumption. It has been contended that much of the mainstream economics literature rests on a distorted and ultimately false view of human nature. In contrast to the approach adopted in mainstream economics, it can be argued that human beings have a need for creative activity and that this need ought to be fulfilled in the work that is undertaken to meet the material needs of society.

The distinction between work and leisure is, in reality, an artificial one. It is thanks to capitalism that people have no freedom over how they work and that they have freedom only in their leisure time. The leisure time of those who work in capitalist society, though, is frequently made less desirable because of the pressures to consume an ever greater volume of goods. With the problem of overwork and low job quality, many workers have neither the time nor the inclination to use their leisure time in creative ways.[7]

But the key goal should be to convert the time that is spent at work and at leisure into free creative activity and hence to move towards a situation where the distinction between work and leisure is blurred. This requires the use of technology to reduce the amount of unrewarding work that is needed to meet society's material needs and to increase the amount of free time during which people can undertake activities of their own choosing. It also necessitates that work be radically reorganised so that workers can take control over and develop their creative powers through the process of work.[8] The achievement of pleasurable work must become an objective of society. The alternative path is to accept the status quo, in which work is degraded and dehumanised by the profit imperative.

This book argues for a political economy of work that recognises both the specific costs of work under capitalism and the potential benefits of work under an alternative system of production. The focus on 'political economy' is deliberate. On the one hand, it signals a rejection of mainstream economics, in which work is portrayed as a means to obtain consumption goods and leisure time is viewed as a universal good. On the other hand, it establishes a commitment to develop perspectives outside the mainstream, such as in Marxian economics, where the alienation of the capitalist form of work is well-recognised and the need to elevate the quality of work life is seen as a key priority. A political economy approach to the study of work, thus, aims at the improvement of job quality by seeking to challenge and transcend the institutions and structures of capitalism.

The criticisms and ideas presented in this book, though capable of being developed and extended in the future, provide pointers towards a different way of thinking about and theorising the activity of work. In this way, it is intended that the contents of this book will encourage not only new theoretical discussion about the world of work, but also a more critical debate about the ways in which work could be undertaken in the future. Progress might then be made to convert work into a rewarding and satisfying activity rather than simply a source of 'toil and trouble'.

Notes

1 Introduction

1 The instrumental view of work is by no means exclusive to the economics literature (see Sayers 2005: 607–8). Rather it finds support in classical philosophy as well as in Christian thought. Early philosophers such as Plato and Aristotle, for example, regarded physical work as the lot of slaves and looked upon a 'life of reason' as the ideal human state. In the Bible, from a different perspective, work was portrayed as a 'curse' that was imposed on mankind in consequence of the original sin of Adam. See P. Anthony (1977) and K. Thomas (1999).

2 The different meanings of 'work' and 'labour' are discussed in Thomas (1999).

2 In the sweat of thy brow: concepts of work in pre-classical and classical economics

1 Apparently innocuous pastimes such as snuff-taking and tea-drinking were condemned for taking time away from work and for undermining the industriousness of the working poor (see Furniss 1920: 153–4; Hatcher 1998: 79–80; Firth 2002: 48).

2 Coats (1958: 36–8) refers to Jacob Vanderlint and Bishop Berkley as two writers in the pre-1750 period who were sympathetic to the plight of the labouring population.

3 Smith, in 1759, seemed to dispute whether poverty was a bad thing in itself. The poor might well be denied access to a comfortable means of existence, but they could be seen to be abundant in the things which gave 'real happiness':

> In what constitutes the real happiness of human life, they [the poor] are in no respect inferior to those who would seem so much above them. In ease of body and peace of mind, all the different ranks of life are nearly upon a level, and the beggar, who suns himself by the side of the highway, possesses that security which kings are fighting for.
>
> (Smith 1976a: 185)

That the poor were, in fact, 'happy' with their lot provided an obvious justification for not raising wages and for maintaining poverty. Smith's remark that 'the peace and order of society is of more importance than even the relief of the miserable' (Smith 1976a: 226) also sounds a less than liberal tone.

4 Smith's views on the human costs of the division of labour have been debated in the secondary literature (see West 1964, 1996; Rosenberg 1965).

5 Smith also suggested that state education would make the working class 'more decent and orderly' and 'less apt to be misled into any wanton or unnecessary

opposition to the measures of government' (Smith 1976b vol.2: 788). On social and political grounds, therefore, the state stood to gain from educating the masses.

6 Godwin's views on work and social reform are discussed in Chapter 3.
7 David Ricardo paid little direct attention to the issue of work motivation. He did, though, lend some support to the case for high wages by pointing to the potential benefits of increased consumption on the part of workers. Specifically, a rise in wages and hence in consumption provided a potential check to the tendency towards overpopulation. Hence he wrote that:

> The friends of humanity cannot but wish that in all countries the labouring classes should have a taste for comforts and enjoyments, and that they should be stimulated by all legal means in their exertions to procure them. There cannot be a better security against a superabundant population.
>
> (Ricardo 1955 vol.1: 100)

8 The working-class press complained about the middle-class bias as well as the abstractedness of classical political economy (see Webb 1955: 100).
9 Mill and Carlyle became friends in the early 1830s; however, they ceased all personal relations after the publication of Carlyle's controversial article in 1849.
10 Mill's views on Fourierism are discussed in Chapter 3.

3 Work contra the classical economists: pro-work sentiments in the late eighteenth and nineteenth centuries

1 Some of these authors were linked directly. For example, Carlyle's views on work influenced those of Ruskin and Morris (Hobson 1904: 305; Thompson 1976: 32; Knowles 2001: 127). Morris (1915d: 73), in turn, drew direct inspiration from the writings of Fourier (see Kinna 2000: 502–3).
2 All references to Fourier's work in the following discussion are taken from the edited collection of his work compiled by J. Beecher and R. Bienvenu (see Fourier 1983).
3 Fourier used his notion of the twelve basic passions to identify 810 different personality types among the general population (Fourier 1983: 39).
4 Fourier admitted that certain tasks might still remain irksome even in utopia (Fourier 1983: 52–3). He suggested that these tasks could be allocated to children between the ages of nine and fifteen, who were less picky about the work they did (Fourier 1983: 315–22).
5 Even in the paradise of the phalanx, people were still expected to rise at 3.30 a.m. and to work until 10 p.m. The working day was only punctuated by breaks for meals and by an hour's 'entertainment' in the evening (Fourier 1983: 276). The inhabitants of the phalanx (termed 'Harmonians'), Fourier reassured us, will 'sleep very well. Advanced hygiene along with varied work sessions will inure them against work fatigue. They will not wear themselves out during the day and they will need only a very small amount of sleep' (Fourier 1983: 277).
6 Fourier's proposals were put into practice in several European countries as well as in the USA, although none of these experiments were long-lived or successful (Fourier 1983: 65–6).
7 Marx (1972: 257) wrote that:

> It is self-evident that if labour-time is reduced to a normal length and, further-more, labour is no longer performed for someone else, but for myself, and, at the same time, the social contradictions between master and men, etc., being abolished, it acquires a quite different, a free character.

The editors of Fourier's selected writings are inaccurate in their claim that Marx saw work in the realm of necessity as a permanent curse (Fourier 1983: 71). In fact, Marx suggested that, with the transcendence of capitalism, workers would come to experience necessary work as a free creative activity (see Sayers 2003). This aspect of Marx's analysis of work is discussed further in Chapter 4.

8 The views of Fourier can be contrasted with those of his compatriot and fellow utopian socialist, Henri de Saint-Simon. Unlike Fourier, Saint-Simon believed in centralising power and was against extending the freedom to work. Further, in contrast to Fourier, Saint-Simon tended to agree with the classical economists that work was against human nature. Thus, he wrote in 1817 that: 'Man is lazy by nature. The man who works overcomes his laziness only because his needs have to be fulfilled, or through his desire for pleasure. He only works, therefore, according to his needs and desires' (Saint-Simon 1975: 158). Saint-Simon was not so convinced as Fourier that work could be converted into a pleasurable activity.

9 Carlyle's views on the ideal social system overlapped with those of Saint-Simon, who also advocated placing a cadre of experts in charge of society. Carlyle was appreciative of Saint-Simon's doctrines. Indeed, he went as far as to translate Saint-Simon's *Nouveau Christianisme* into English, but a plan to publish it was never realised (see Saint-Simon 1975: 60).

10 Whilst dismissing the commonly held view that Ruskin was opposed to all kinds of machinery, Hobson (1904: 213) accused 'him of being unduly swayed by "sentimental" considerations'. Thus, in Hobson's view, Ruskin underestimated the capacity of machinery to reduce work hours and to increase free time. Hobson's own views on work and work reform are explored in Chapter 6.

11 Hobson (1904) criticised Ruskin for suggesting that manual labour should be restricted to 'a specialised grade of servile beings'. 'Mr Ruskin's proposal', he claimed,

> would be a double wrong: first to these slaves by depriving them of their share of interesting and educative work, some of which is their due; secondly, to the other classes, by over-stimulation of nervous and mental powers through lack of a wholesome admixture of routine work.
>
> (Hobson 1904: 220)

12 After publishing a series of critical essays on political economy in the *Cornhill Magazine* in 1860, Ruskin was refused the opportunity to publish further work (see Hobson 1904: 42). Readers objected to the criticisms made by Ruskin and put pressure on the editor to censor his work (see Clark 1964: 264–5). It should be said that Ruskin did not endear himself to the classical economists: he portrayed Adam Smith as the 'Devil' and also described J.S. Mill as 'cretinous' and a 'type of flat-fish' (quoted in Henderson 2000: 34–5). Carlyle was equally contemptuous of classical political economy, calling it a 'pig philosophy' (see Persky 1990: 171).

13 Marx's ideas on socialism are discussed in greater detail in Chapter 4.

14 Morris's thoughts about possible reforms to the workplace were informed by his own experiences of running a factory at Merton Abbey, near London (see Kinna 2000: 504). This operated a host of policies aimed at enhancing the quality of work. Morris, though, was aware that progress in the conditions of work was limited by the capitalist profit imperative and that the ideal work environment would have to await the attainment of socialism.

15 There are, of course, other nineteenth-century 'utopian' writers that could have been considered in this chapter. These include the so-called 'Ricardian socialists', such as Robert Owen. Owen believed, like Ruskin and Morris, that modern industry had undermined work quality and he proposed a set of radical reforms to enhance the intrinsic rewards from work. Within his ideal society, Owen wrote that:

they [the working class] will all procure for themselves the necessaries and comforts of life in so short a time, and so easily and pleasantly, that the occupation will be experienced to be little more than a recreation, sufficient to keep them in best health and spirit for rational enjoyment of life.

(Owen 1991: 273)

Here, in common with the other writers considered in this chapter, Owen believed that it was important to create opportunities for workers to enjoy their work for its own ends.

4 The Marxian view of work

1 The terms 'work' and 'labour' were used interchangeably by Marx, and in the present chapter these two terms will be treated as synonymous.
2 Sean Sayers (2003) identifies the philosophical basis of Marx's pro-work views in the writings of Hegel. He points out that Marx maintained these views throughout his life, though without ever spelling out their roots in Hegel.
3 It is possible that Marx meant to be ironic in his statement of the typical day under communism, seeming as he does to focus on the pursuits of the archetypal 'country gentleman' (see Fine 1983: 224–5) and overlooking various pursuits (e.g. child care) that could be seen to form a part of everyday life in a future communist society. The key point for Marx, however, was that under communism people would not be restricted to any one occupation, but rather would be free to undertake a variety of different activities of their choosing.
4 This problem has resurfaced in modern mainstream economics, as we shall see in Chapter 7. Hence, in modern mainstream economics research on job quality, there is tendency to take at face value the responses of workers to social surveys, without any critical reflection on the objective conditions of work.

5 From pain cost to opportunity cost: the eclipse of the quality of work as a factor in economic theory

1 Jevons (1970: 189n) acknowledged that his own theory of labour overlapped with the earlier analysis of Hermann Heinrich Gossen. Nonetheless, perhaps the greatest influence on Jevons's thinking was the psychologist Richard Jennings. Jevons (1970: 190–1) took direct inspiration from Jennings's 'law of the variation of labour' in his model of the work decision (see White 1994b).
2 Jevons's theory of labour has not always been accurately represented in the secondary literature. For example, Kerton (1971) wrote that in Jevons's theory: 'Disutility increases at an increasing rate for two reasons: (1) the intrinsic irksomeness of work and (2) the rising opportunity cost of lost leisure' (Kerton 1971: 115n). This can be seen as wrong on two counts. First, Jevons did not regard work as intrinsically unrewarding: quite to the contrary he viewed work as a potential source of pleasure and utility. Second, Jevons did not explicitly present the opportunity cost of work time as a separate argument in his formulation of the work decision. The idea of opportunity cost was inserted by other neoclassical writers, as discussed further below.
3 Hobson (1926) criticised the relative neglect in Jevons's *Theory of Political Economy* of the human costs of production:

In this very book, indeed, Jevons made an elementary excursion into the intensity of labour, relating it to hours of labour, etc., and in his Preface he definitely states, 'In this Work I have attempted to treat Economy as a calculus of Pleasures and Pains'. Yet nowhere did he link up into a single calculus the pleasures and pains of the processes of production and consumption. No, 'The whole theory of the Economy' as he saw it, 'depends upon a correct theory of consumption'. In the last chapter of his *Theory*, 'The great problem of Economy, may, as it seems to me, be stated thus: *Given, a certain population, with various needs and powers of production, in possession of certain lands and other sources of materials; required, the mode of employing their labour so as to maximise the utility of the produce'*. It seems curious that he should have failed to add the words 'and so as to minimise the disutility of producing it'. Here was a real turning-point in economic theory. Had Jevons worked out his prefatory promise, the study might have been put upon a sound basis of utility conceived as human welfare; the utilities as well as the disutilities of production might have been put into the account, together with the disutilities which attend certain forms and portions of consumption.

(Hobson 1926: 91–2; emphasis in original)

Arguably, however, the major 'turning-point' came after Jevons with the adoption of the opportunity cost framework that failed to take account of the direct costs as well as benefits of work activities. Jevons, at least, recognised that work could be experienced directly as both pain and pleasure. This distinguishes his approach from other neoclassical economists, as will be shown below.

4 Note that J.S. Mill made much the same argument in response to the racist diatribe of Thomas Carlyle. Mill argued that the alleged laziness of the black population was actually the result of the lack of intrinsically rewarding work. Mill, unlike Jevons, asserted that the work resistance of black workers was endogenously determined and he rejected the allegation that the black population was naturally lazy (see Mill 1984b).

5 'Adequate motives may lead to and warrant overwork, but, if long continued, excessive labour reduces the strength and becomes insupportable; and the longer it continues the worse it is, the law being somewhat similar to that of periodic labour' (Jevons 1970: 193). Jevons, however, was sceptical that a shorter working day could be sustained without a fall in output and he remained opposed to legal restrictions on working time for adult male workers (see White 1994a: 438).

6 J. Schumpeter (1954: 917n) credited Green with coining the 'very felicitous' term 'opportunity cost'.

7 L. Derobert (2001, 2005) claims that Wicksteed was the originator of the canonical model of labour supply, in which leisure time is exchanged for income. This claim is challenged in Spencer (2003b, 2005b), where the origins of this model are traced to the work of earlier Austrian writers, such as Green (1894).

8 Marshall (1910: 348) said:

> We might as reasonably dispute whether it is the upper or the under blade of a pair of scissors that cuts a piece of paper, as whether value is governed by utility or cost of production. It is true that when one blade is held still, and the cutting is effected by moving the other, we may say with careless brevity that the cutting is done by the second; but the statement is not strictly accurate, and is to be excused only so long as it claims to be merely a popular and not a strictly scientific account of what happens.

9 In the *Principles*, Marshall (1910: 22) referred to 'the splendid teachings of Carlyle and Ruskin as to the right aims of human endeavour and the right uses of wealth'. The criticisms of Carlyle and Ruskin of economics would have been avoidable, Marshall contended, if it had been made clear in earlier economic discourse:

that 'money' or 'general purchasing power' or 'command over material wealth', is the centre around which economic science clusters, ... not because money or material wealth is regarded as the main aim of human effort, nor even as affording the main subject matter for the study of the economist, but because in this world of ours it is the one convenient means of measuring human motive on a large scale.

(Marshall 1910: 22)

The overlaps between the views of Marshall and those of Carlyle and Ruskin are discussed in W. Henderson (2000: 167–75).

10 Like Jevons, Marshall thought the responsiveness of labour supply to changes in wages would depend on the race and character of the workers concerned. Thus, he wrote that:

experience seems to show that the more ignorant and phlegmatic of races and of individuals, especially if they live in a southern clime, will stay at their work a shorter time, and will exert themselves less while at it, if the rate of pay rises so as to give them their accustomed enjoyments in return for less work than before. But those whose mental horizon is wider, and who have more firmness and elasticity of character, will work the harder and the longer the higher the rate of pay which is open to them; unless indeed they prefer to divert their activities to higher aims than work for material gain.

(Marshall 1910: 528)

Marshall's explanation of the relation between wages and the supply of labour, as argued by T. Parsons, combined different and competing arguments:

The behaviour of the 'more ignorant and phlegmatic races' is strongly reminiscent partly of hedonism, partly of instinct, but that of the more enlightened is due to a rising 'standard of life' involving the generation of new wants by new activities. That, and neither hedonism nor any instinctive greed, is Marshall's explanation of the tendency of modern men to do more rather than less work when their pay rises.

(Parsons 1931: 115)

Marshall, it seems, did not rule out the possibility that the development of activities would lead the 'more ignorant and phlegmatic races' to increase their labour supply in response to a rise in wages.

11 Marshall gained a firsthand knowledge of the plight of the working poor through the service he gave to the Royal Commission on Labour, which he joined in 1891 (Matthews 1990: 14–15).

12 According to Marshall: 'We all require for the purpose of health an hour or two daily of bodily exercise, during which the mind is at rest, and, in general, a few hours more of such work would not interfere materially with our true life' (Marshall 1966a: 110).

13 R. Bowman (2004: 507) writes that 'Marshall's analysis of the division of labour and technical change is, arguably, a watershed on the subject. It provides a basis for optimism not found in earlier writers.' Yet, Marshall was not the first writer to challenge Adam Smith's observations on the human costs of the division of labour. As was shown in Chapter 2, McCulloch had directly refuted this view some years previously (McCulloch 1849: 186).

14 Marshall, in fact, was sceptical about the wider use of mathematics in economics (see Levitt 1976: 436–8). Because of problems of interdependence, there was 'no room in economics for long trains of deductive reasoning' (Marshall 1910: 781).

The idea that economics was in some sense equivalent to the other established sciences was a delusion: 'economics cannot be compared with the exact physical sciences: for it deals with the ever changing and subtle forces of human nature' (Marshall 1910: 14).

15 T. Levitt (1976) suggests that the implications of Marshall's economic writings have not been fully understood and developed by later generations of economists:

> Given a certain turn of mind, one might conclude that Marshall thus achieved the opposite of his intentions. The precision and thoroughness of his formal analysis completely obliterated the insistences of his explicit policy conclusions. All that was remembered was the implicit message: *laissez faire*. Generations of admiring students selectively remember only the static models and well-phrased generalisations in which he himself seems to have had such limited faith.
>
> (Levitt 1976: 440; emphasis in original)

16 As Pagano (1985: 95) mentions, Walras's *Elements of Pure Economics* was inaccessible to many English-speaking economists up until 1954, when it was finally translated into English.
17 For a critical assessment of Robbins's model of labour supply, see Spencer (2005a).
18 The emergence and acceptance of the production function framework added to the impression that 'labour', like 'capital', was just another input into production and that the qualitative content of work was unimportant.

6 Institutional perspectives on work

1 Ely was not the only American economist to address labour problems in the 1880s. Henry Carter Adams and Richmond Mayo, amongst others, also made significant contributions (see McNulty 1980: 132–3).
2 The favourable view of unionism held by Ely in his 1886 book contradicted most standard economic theory that painted trade unions as monopolies. Indeed, Ely was strongly rebuked by other economists for his support of trade unions (see McNulty 1980: 141). The labour research carried out by institutional economists in the late nineteenth and early twentieth centuries, in general, was sympathetic toward unionism, whereas most economic theorists took a hostile view to the actions of trade unions, regarding them as an unnecessary fetter on a free labour market (see Kaufman 2000).
3 Hoxie studied under Veblen, but was led to criticise his view of the impact of the machine process on trade unions (McNulty 1973; Rutherford 1998; Hodgson 2004). Veblen's theory suggested that the close proximity of trade unionists to machine technology would lead them to acquire industrial (and non-capitalistic) habits of thought that would pose a direct challenge to the dominant 'pecuniary culture' in society (see below). Hoxie, however, discovered that the exact opposite was the case: trade unionists were mainly concerned with increasing the pecuniary rewards of their members (see Rutherford 1998: 474–5; Hodgson 2004: 220). Veblen's thesis on the relationship between unionism and the machine process thus needed to be revised. The loss of faith in Veblen's theory, it appears, had a profound negative effect on Hoxie's mental state (McNulty 1973). His personal distress was intensified by the less than favourable reception to his report on scientific management published in 1915. A particularly critical review of the report that appeared in the *American Economic Review* in June 1916 seems to have proved an important factor in Hoxie committing suicide in the same month (Nyland 1996: 1010–11).

4 The stress on 'instinct' is one important theme in Veblen's attack on the hedonistic account of human nature found in standard economic theory (see Veblen 1898a).

5 For a critical discussion of Veblen's account of man's cultural evolution, see K. Anderson (1933), C. Rojek (1995), and J. Wenzler (1998).

6 Veblen thought that people would still harbour interests in spending their leisure time in some useful way, 'as for instance in "social duties", and in quasi-artistic or quasi-scholarly accomplishments, in the care and decoration of the house, in sewing-circle activity or dress reform, in proficiency at dress, cards, yachting, golf, and various sports' (Veblen 1994: 58). These activities, whilst affording status to the individuals concerned, were ostensibly ceremonial in nature and were a poor imitation of industrial work.

7 Further criticisms of Veblen's analysis of work are provided by Hodgson (2004: 198–201).

8 These points about the nature of the employment relation are developed in Chapter 7.

9 C. Nyland (1996) has shown how Taylorism contained a number of progressive aspects such as the reduction in work time and the stabilisation of employment, and these aspects help to explain its appeal amongst some institutional writers. He also disputes whether Taylorism was itself the cause of deskilling in the US economy (see Nyland 1996: 988–9). But while Nyland is right to highlight the ambiguities in the theory and practice of Taylorism, he surely takes the argument too far in decoupling Taylorism from the tendency to skill erosion. A more balanced approach would recognise the part played by Taylorism in both creating and eroding skills in industrial capitalism. While the process of deskilling is complex and dependent on various contingencies, it can still be seen as an important tendency of the capitalist production process, in which the interests of capital and labour remain inherently opposed.

10 Hobson, however, was against worker-managed firms, suggesting that evidence proved them to be a failure:

> Experiments in the self-governing workshop make it evident that direct government by the workers in their capacity of producers is technically worse than government by the owners of capital. The selection and the remuneration of ability of management are always found defective, and the employees are often unwilling to submit to proper discipline, even when they have elected who shall exercise it.
>
> (Hobson 1914: 256)

Hobson continued to see a vital role for capitalist firms in the organisation of production in society and while he favoured some degree of social control of industry he remained opposed to socialism based on common ownership of the means of production (see Hobson 1914: 291).

11 At an economic level, Hobson believed that a reduction in work hours and work intensity would give a boost to labour productivity by releasing the creativity of workers: 'The strongest economic plea for a shorter and a lighter working-day is that it will liberate for invention and industrial progress the latent creative energy of countless workers that is stifled under the conditions of a long day's monotonous toil' (Hobson 1914: 51).

12 In contrast to Veblen, engineers have not proved a revolutionary force in capitalist society. Indeed, according to Layton (1962: 71), they have tended to uphold essentially conservative values, aiming 'to save the existing society, not destroy it; to avert a revolution, not to start one'.

13 The focus for much of this chapter has been on the nature and development of labour economics in America. This is understandable in view of the fact that

labour economics has its origins in American institutional economics, as discussed above. The history of labour economics in Britain remains to be fully analysed. Marshall, while often presented as an abstract and formal economist, offered a multidimensional analysis of work and labour issues that contained important institutional detail (see Chapter 5). Hicks (1932) obviously made a significant contribution from a neoclassical perspective, but other writers such as Kurt Rothschild (1954) and Henry Phelps Brown (1962) also require consideration. It is to be hoped that, in the future, the British contribution to labour economics will be more fully explored.

7 Mainstream economics and the hidden abode of production

1 In the 1970s, for example, American radical economists questioned the worth of neoclassical concepts such as human capital (e.g. Bowles and Gintis 1975). They argued that Marxian theory provided a better foundation for the study of work and labour than neoclassical economics (see Gintis 1976). From a different perspective, empirical analysis showed the importance of internal labour markets and cast doubt on the validity of the standard neoclassical assumption of a perfectly competitive labour market (e.g. Doeringer and Piore 1971). However, such challenges failed to alter in any fundamental way the core of mainstream labour economics. The challenge of American radical economics was largely ineffective. Since the 1980s, American radical economists have made inroads into the mainstream, but only by ditching much of the Marxian and radical content of their work (see Fine 1998, 2002; Spencer 2000b). On the other hand, while mainstream economists confronted the issue of internal labour markets, they did so by creating new theoretical models based on the standard concepts and methods of the mainstream paradigm (see Fine 1998: 157–74; Boyer and Smith 2001: 214).
2 Early institutional economists such as Commons were well aware that circumstances in the labour market were skewed in favour of employers and that workers were not guaranteed to be paid compensating wages (see Kaufman 2000).
3 Green (2006: 12, 151) mentions the Marxist tradition in his discussion of job quality and the above can be seen as a Marxist interpretation of the objective view of job quality that is proposed by Green.
4 It should be mentioned that Herbert Simon wrote on the indeterminacy of the employment contract back in the 1950s (see Simon 1951). However, he has been given little credit for his contribution in this area.
5 The popularity of personnel economics has grown in recent years. Two recent textbooks on the subject provide evidence of the growing interest in its core themes and ideas (see Garibaldi 2006; Neilson 2006).
6 The position taken in this chapter, developing the arguments in Chapter 6, is that, contra the stance of Boyer and Smith (2001), modern mainstream labour economists have not addressed (and have certainly not resolved) the criticisms made by earlier institutional economists (e.g. Commons, Veblen) against the neoclassical school.
7 These same criticisms can be levelled at the work of the American radical economists, Samuel Bowles and Herbert Gintis (1990), whose recent research on the capitalist labour process has been based on the concepts and method of mainstream economics (see Spencer 2000b).
8 The emphasis on the development of people (and hence their needs) through the activities they undertake, plus the focus on the concept of human needs, is common to a number of perspectives. These include the capabilities approach of Sen (1999). It is also an aspect of critical realism that is directly hostile towards the individualistic ontology of mainstream economics (see Lawson 2003). Further, in the Marxist tradition, stress is placed on the importance of work in the

development and realisation of human creative potential (see Chapter 4). Finally, contributions within 'humanistic economics' indicate the requirement for need fulfilment in the context of the organisation of work (see Lutz and Lux 1979; Lutz 1999).

8 Conclusion

1 Accusations that workers are lazy have remained popular amongst those in the world of politics and the media. In Britain, for example, the workshyness of the native population has recently been contrasted with the industriousness of migrant workers from Eastern Europe. A British government minister warned that the 'can work, won't work' minority who refuse to take jobs were at risk of losing benefits if they did not adopt a stronger work ethic (*Observer* 17 December 2006).

2 As we saw in Chapter 6, Veblen also recognised the potential positive attributes of work activity, but he was misled into believing that human work was instinctual, rather than creative.

3 There is an irony here in that Keynes's own analysis of the supply of labour was rooted in the concepts of the mainstream. For an elaboration of this point, see Spencer (2006).

4 In Keynes's vision of the ideal society of the future, people would be able:

> to return to some of the most sure and certain principles of religion and traditional virtue – that avarice is a vice, that the exaction of usury is a misdemeanour, and the love of money is detestable, that those walk most truly in the paths of virtue and sane wisdom who take least thought for the morrow. We shall once more value ends above means and prefer the good to the useful. We shall honour those who can teach us to pluck the hour and the day virtuously and well, the delightful people who are capable of taking direct enjoyment in things, the lilies of the field who toil not, neither do they spin.
>
> (Keynes 1963: 371–2)

For Keynes, in contrast to Marx, such an outcome was achievable within a reformed capitalism. See T. Winslow (2005) for a comparison of Keynes and Marx on the 'ideal social republic of the future'.

5 It is easily forgotten that capitalism created the problem of long working time (Schor 1993: 6–7). In the feudal structures preceding capitalism, people worked for fewer hours and they had longer hours of leisure (see Sahlins 1974). The expansion of capitalism in the eighteenth and early nineteenth centuries brought about a great increase in work time and caused a separation between 'work' and 'leisure' that was not so apparent in earlier times (Thomas 1964). Hence any reduction in work time during the twentieth century needs to be seen in the context of the peculiarly long working hours that featured a century or so before. Further, it should be noted that the curtailment of work time has been achieved in the teeth of opposition from employers. Generally, employers have preferred to use the advantages of industrial productivity to raise wages, rather than to cut work hours (see Philp 2001). Workers' demands for a shorter working day, on the other hand, have been partly driven by a desire for free time during which they can escape drudgery and undertake activities of their own choosing (see Cross 2005).

6 British workers tend to work much longer hours than their counterparts in other industrialised economies, with a quarter working more than forty-eight hours per week (Lee *et al.* 2007).

7 The endless striving for social status through consumption has turned leisure into a busy and frenetic pastime that can be equally as tiring and demanding as paid work (see Linder 1970; Cross 2005).
8 There is a large and diverse literature on democratic and cooperative forms of work organisation. See, for example, the various contributions in U. Pagano and R. Rowthorn (1996).

Bibliography

Akerlof, G. (1982) 'Labor Contracts as Partial Gift Exchange', *Quarterly Journal of Economics*, vol. 97, no. 4, pp.543–69.

Akerlof, G. and Yellen, J. (eds) (1986) *Efficiency Wage Models of the Labor Market*, Cambridge: Cambridge University Press.

Alchian, A. and Demsetz, H. (1972) 'Production, Information Costs, and Economic Organization', *American Economic Review*, vol. 62, pp.777–95.

Anderson, K. (1933) 'The Unity of Veblen's Theoretical System', *Quarterly Journal of Economics*, vol. 47, no. 4, pp.598–626.

Anthony, P. (1977) *The Ideology of Work*, London: Tavistock.

Armstrong, P. (1988) 'Labour and Monopoly Capital', in R. Hyman and W. Streeck (eds) *New Technology and Industrial Relations*, Oxford: Basil Blackwell, pp.143–60.

Baird, B. (1997) 'Necessity and the "Perverse" Supply of Labour in Pre-Classical British Political Economy', *History of Political Economy*, vol. 19, no. 3, pp.497–522.

Baum, B. (1999) 'J.S. Mill's Conception of Economic Freedom', *History of Political Thought*, vol. 20, no. 3, pp.494–530.

Becker, G. (1964) *Human Capital*, New York: Columbia University Press.

—— (1965) 'A Theory of the Allocation of Time', *Economic Journal*, vol. 75, pp.493–517.

Bentham, J. (1983) *Deontology, A Table of Springs of Action, and Article on Utilitarianism*, in A. Goldworth (ed.) *The Collected Works of Jeremy Bentham*, Oxford: Clarendon Press.

Blanchflower, D. and Oswald, A. (2004) 'Well-Being over Time in Britain and the USA', *Journal of Public Economics*, vol. 88, pp.1359–87.

Blaug, M. (1958a) *Ricardian Economics*, New Haven, CT: Yale University Press.

—— (1958b) 'The Classical Economists and the Factory Acts – A Re-Examination', *Quarterly Journal of Economics*, vol. 72, pp.211–26.

—— (1985) *Economic Theory in Retrospect*, 4th edn, Cambridge: Cambridge University Press.

Blum, S. (1925) *Labor Economics*, New York: Henry Holt.

Böhm-Bawerk, von E. (1891) *The Positive Theory of Capital*, trans. William A. Smart, London: Macmillan.

—— (1894a) 'The Ultimate Standard of Value', *Annals of the American Academy of Political and Social Science*, vol. 5, pp.149–208.

—— (1894b) 'One Word More on the Ultimate Standard of Value' *Economic Journal*, vol. 4, pp.719–24.

Borjas, G. (2000) *Labor Economics*, London: McGraw Hill.

Bowles, S. and Gintis, H. (1975) 'The Problem with Human Capital Theory – A Marxian Critique', *American Economic Review*, vol. 65, pp.74–82.

—— (1990) 'Contested Exchange: New Microfoundations for the Political Economy of Capitalism', *Politics and Society*, vol. 18, pp.165–222.

Bowman, R. (2004) 'Marshall: Just How Interested in Doing Good Was He?', *Journal of the History of Economic Thought*, vol. 24, pp.493–518.

Boyer, R. and Smith, R. (2001) 'The Development of the Neoclassical Tradition in Labor Economics', *Industrial and Labor Relations Review*, vol. 54, no. 2, pp.199–223.

Braverman, H. (1974) *Labor and Monopoly Capital*, New York: Monthly Review.

Breton, R. (2005) *Gospels and Grit: Work and Labour in Carlyle, Conrad and Orwell*, Toronto: University of Toronto Press.

Brown, A., Charlwood, A., Forde, C., and Spencer, D. (2007) 'Job Quality and the Economics of New Labour: A Critical Appraisal Using Subjective Survey Data', *Cambridge Journal of Economics*, vol. 31, no. 6, pp.941–71.

Buchanan, J.M. (1969) *Cost and Choice. An Inquiry into Economic Theory*, Chicago, IL: Markam.

Burawoy, M. (1979) *Manufacturing Consent: Changes in the Labor Process Under Monopoly Capitalism*, Chicago, IL: University of Chicago Press.

—— (1985) *The Politics of Production. Factory Regimes under Capitalism and Socialism*, London: Verso.

Burawoy, M. and Wright, E.O. (1990) 'Coercion and Consent in Contested Exchange', *Politics and Society*, vol. 18, pp.251–66.

Carlyle, T. (1843; centenary edn 1897) *Past and Present*, London: Chapman and Hall.

—— (1849) 'The Nigger Question', reprinted in *Thomas Carlyle: Critical and Miscellaneous Essays* (1899), vol. 4, London: Chapman and Hall, pp.348–83.

Child, J, (1693) *New Discourse of Trade*, London: n.p.

Claeys, G. (1987) 'Justice, Independence, and Industrial Democracy: The Development of John Stuart Mill's Views of Socialism', *Journal of Politics*, vol. 49, no. 1, pp.122–47.

Clark, A. (2001) 'What Really Matters in a Job? Hedonic Measurement Using Quit Data', *Labour Economics*, vol. 8, pp.223–42.

—— (2005) 'Your Money or Your Life: Changing Job Quality in OECD Countries', *British Journal of Industrial Relations*, vol. 43, no. 3, pp.377–400.

Clark, A. and Oswald, A. (1996) 'Satisfaction and Comparison Income', *Journal of Public Economics*, vol. 61, no. 3, pp.359–81.

Clark, K. (1964). *Ruskin Today*, London: John Murray.

Coats, A.W. (1958) 'Changing Attitudes to Labour in the Mid-Eighteenth Century', *Economic History Review*, vol. 11, no. 1, pp.35–51.

—— (1967) 'The Classical Economists and the Labourer', in E.L. Jones and G.E. Mingay (eds) *Land, Labour and Population in the Industrial Revolution*, London: Edward Arnold, pp.100–30.

Commons, J.R. (1919) *Industrial Goodwill*, New York: McGraw Hill.

—— (1934) *Myself*, New York: Macmillan.

Cowling, K. (2006) 'Prosperity, Depression and Modern Capitalism', *Kyklos*, vol. 59, no. 3, pp.369–81.

Cross, G. (2005) 'A Right to be Lazy? Busyness in Retrospective', *Social Research*, vol. 72, no. 2, pp.263–86.

Currie, M. and Steedman, I. (1993) 'Taking Effort Seriously', *Metroeconomica*, vol. 44, pp.134–45.

Defoe, D. (1704) *Giving Alms No Charity and Employing the Poor a Grievance to the Nation*, London: n.p.

Derobert, L. (2001) 'The Genesis of the Canonical Labor Supply Model', *Journal of the History of Economic Thought*, vol. 23, pp.197–215.

—— (2005) 'The Labor-less Labor Supply Model: A Reply to David A. Spencer', *Journal of the History of Economic Thought*, vol. 27, pp.101–3.

Dew, B. (2007) 'Political Economy and the Problem of the Plebs in Eighteenth Century Britain', *History Compass*, vol. 5, no. 4, pp.1214–35.

Doeringer, P. and Piore, M. (1971) *Internal Labor Markets and Manpower Analysis*, Lexington, MA: D.C. Heath.

Douglas, P. (1934) *The Theory of Wages*, New York: Macmillan.

Dow, G. (1987) 'The Function of Authority in Transaction Cost Economics', *Journal of Economic Behavior and Organization*, vol. 8, pp.13–38.

Edgeworth, F.Y. (1894a) 'Professor Böhm-Bawerk on the Ultimate Standard of Value', *Economic Journal*, vol. 4, no. 15, pp.518–21.

—— (1894b) 'One Word More on the Ultimate Standard of Value: Reply to Böhm-Bawerk' *Economic Journal*, vol. 4, no. 16, pp.724–25.

Edwards, P.K. (1990) 'The Politics of Conflict and Consent: How the Labor Contract Really Works', *Journal of Economic Behavior and Organization*, vol. 13, pp.41–61.

Ely, R.T. (1905) *The Labor Movement in America*, new edn, New York: Macmillan.

Engels, F. (1975) 'A Fragment of Fourier's On Trade', in *Marx and Engels Collected Works*, vol. 4, London: Lawrence and Wishart, pp.613–44.

—— (1993) *Socialism: Utopian and Scientific*, London: Bookmarks.

Fielding, H. (1751) *An Enquiry into the Causes of the Late Increase of Robbers*, Dublin: n.p.

Fine, B. (1983) 'Marx on Economic Relations under Socialism', in B. Matthews (ed.) *Marx: 100 Years On*, London: Lawrence Wishart, pp.221–56.

—— (1998) *Labour Market Theory: A Constructive Reassessment*, London: Routledge.

—— (2002) 'Economic Imperialism: A View from the Periphery', *Review of Radical Political Economics*, vol. 34, pp.187–201.

Firth, A. (2002) 'Moral Supervision and Autonomous Social Order: Wages and Consumption in 18th-Century Economic Thought', *History of Human Sciences*, vol. 15, no. 1, pp.39–57.

Forster, N. (1767) *Enquiry into the Causes of the Present High Price of Provisions*, London: n.p.

Fourier, C. (1983) *The Utopian Vision of Charles Fourier – Selected Texts on Work, Love, and Passionate Attraction*, trans. J. Beecher, ed. R. Bienvenu, Columbia: University of Missouri Press.

Freeman, R. (1978) 'Job Satisfaction as an Economic Variable', *American Economic Review*, vol. 68, pp.135–41.

Frey, B. (1993) 'Shirking or Work Morale? The Impact of Regulating', *European Economic Review*, vol. 37, pp.1523–32.

Frey, B. and Stutzer, A. (2002) *Happiness and Economics*, Princeton, NJ: Princeton University Press.

Friedman, M. (1953) *Essays in Positive Economics*, Chicago, IL: University of Chicago Press.

Fromm, E. (1961) *Marx's Concept of Man*, New York: Ungar.

Furniss, E. (1920) *The Position of the Labourer in a System of Nationalism*, New York: Houghton Mifflin.

Garibaldi, P. (2006) *Personnel Economics in Imperfect Labour Markets*, Oxford: Oxford University Press.

Gilbert, G. (1980) 'Economic Growth and the Poor in Malthus's *Essay on Population*', *History of Political Economy*, vol. 12, pp.83–96.

Gintis, H. (1976) 'The Nature of Labor Exchange and the Theory of Capitalist Production', *Review of Radical Political Economics*, vol. 8, pp.36–54.

Godwin, W. (1820) *Of Population, An Enquiry concerning the Power of Increase in the Numbers of Mankind: being an Answer to Mr. Malthus's Essay on that Subject*, London: Longman, Hurst, Rees, Orme and Brown.

—— (1946) *Enquiry concerning Political Justice and its Influence on Morals and Happiness*, ed. F.E.L Priestley, 3 vols, Toronto: University of Toronto Press.

Goos, M. and Manning, A. (2007) 'Lousy and Lovely Jobs: The Rising Polarization of Work in Britain', *Review of Economics and Statistics*, vol. 89, no. 1, pp.118–33.

Graham, C. (2005) 'The Economics of Happiness: Insights on Globalization from a Novel Approach', *World Economics*, vol. 6, no. 3, pp.41–55.

Green, D. (1894) 'Pain-Cost and Opportunity-Cost', *Quarterly Journal of Economics*, vol. 8, pp.218–29.

Green, F. (2006) *Demanding Work. The Paradox of Job Quality in the Affluent Society*, Princeton, NJ: Princeton University Press.

Hamilton, W. (1916) 'The Development of Hoxie's Economics', *Journal of Political Economy*, vol. 24, no. 10, pp.855–83.

Harrison, J. (1984) *The Common People*, London: Fontana.

Hatcher, J. (1998) 'Labour, Leisure and Economic Thought before the Nineteenth Century', *Past and Present*, no. 160, pp.64–115.

Heckscher, E.D. (1935) *Mercantilism*, trans. M. Shapiro, 2 vols, London: George Allen and Unwin.

Henderson, W. (2000). *John Ruskin's Political Economy*, London: Routledge.

Hicks, J. (1932) *The Theory of Wages*, London: Macmillan.

Hill, C. (1967) 'Pottage for Freeborn Englishmen: Attitudes to Wage-Labour in the Sixteenth and Seventeenth Centuries', in C.H. Feinstein (ed.) *Socialism, Capitalism, and Economic Growth*, Cambridge: Cambridge University Press, pp.338–50.

Hobson, J.A. (1904) *John Ruskin. Social Reformer*, 3rd edn, London: Nisbert.

—— (1914) *Work and Wealth: A Human Evaluation*, London: Macmillan.

—— (1926) *Free-Thought in the Social Sciences*, London: George Allen and Unwin.

Hodgson, G. (1999) *Economics and Utopia. Why the Learning Economy is not the End of History*, London: Routledge.

—— (2003) 'John R. Commons and the Foundations of Institutional Economics', *Journal of Economic Issues*, vol. 37, no. 3, pp.547–76.

—— (2004) *The Evolution of Institutional Economics*, London: Routledge.

Hoxie, R. (1920) *Trade Unionism in the United States*, New York: D. Appleton.

Hume, D. (1739–40) *A Treatise of Human Nature*, 3 vols, London: n.p.

—— (1752) *Political Discourses*, Edinburgh: n.p.

Hyman, R. (2006) 'Marxist Thought and the Analysis of Work', in M. Korczynski, R. Hodson, and P. Edwards (eds) *Social Theory at Work*, Oxford: Oxford University Press, pp.26–55.

Jacoby, S. (1990) 'The New Institutionalism: What can it Learn from the Old?', *Industrial Relations*, vol. 29, no. 2, pp.316–40.

Jevons, W.S. (1970) *The Theory of Political Economy*, intro. R. Collinson-Black, Harmondsworth: Penguin.

Kahneman, D., Diener, E., and Schwarz, N. (eds) (1999) *Well-Being: The Foundations of Hedonic Psychology*, New York: Russell Sage Foundation.

Kaufman, B. (1999) 'Expanding the Behavioral Foundations of Labor Economics', *Industrial and Labor Relations Review*, vol. 52, no. 3, pp.361–92.

—— (2000) 'The Early Institutonalists on Industrial Democracy and Union Democracy', *Journal of Labor Research*, vol. 21, no. 2, pp.189–209.

—— (2007) 'The Institutional Economics of John R. Commons: Complement and Substitute for Neoclassical Economic Theory', *Socio-Economic Review*, vol. 5, pp.3–45.

Kerr, C, (1988) 'The Neoclassical Revisionists in Labor Markets (1940–1960) – R.I. P.', in B. Kaufman (ed.) *How Labor Markets Work*, Lexington, MA: Lexington Books, pp.1–46.

Kerton, R. (1971) 'Hours of Work: Jevons' Labor Theory After 100 Years', *Industrial Relations*, vol. 10, pp.227–30.

Keynes, J.M. (1963) 'Economic Possibilities for Our Grandchildren', in *Essays in Persuasion*, London: Norton, pp.358–73.

Kinna, R. (2000) 'William Morris: Art, Work, and Leisure', *Journal of the History of Ideas*, vol. 41, pp.493–512.

Knight, F. (1921) *Risk, Uncertainty and Profit*, New York: Houghton Mifflin.

Knowles, R. (2001) 'Carlyle, Ruskin and Morris: Work across the "River of Fire"', *History of Economics Review*, vol. 34, pp.127–45.

Lane, R. (1992) 'Work as "Disutility" and Money as "Happiness": Cultural Origins of a Market Myth', *Journal of Socio-Economics*, vol. 21, pp.43–64.

Lawson, T. (2003) *Reorienting Economics*, London: Routledge.

Layard, R. (2004) 'Good Jobs and Bad Jobs', *Centre for Economic Performance Occasional Paper*, no. 19.

—— (2005) *Happiness: Lessons from a New Science*, London: Penguin.

Layard, R., Nickell, S., and Jackman, R. (1991) *Unemployment: Macroeconomic Performance and the Labour Market*, Oxford: Oxford University Press.

Layton, E. (1962) 'Veblen and the Engineers', *American Quarterly*, vol. 14, no. 1, pp.64–72.

Lazear, E. (2000a) 'Economic Imperialism', *Quarterly Journal of Economics*, vol. 115, no. 1, pp.99–146.

—— (2000b) 'The Future of Personnel Economics', *Economic Journal*, vol. 110, pp.611–39.

Lee, S., McCann, D., and Messenger, J.C. (2007) *Working Time around the World: Trends in Working Hours, Laws, and Policies in a Global Comparative Perspective*, London and Geneva: Routledge and ILO.

Levitt, T. (1976) 'Alfred Marshall: Victorian Relevance for Modern Economics', *Quarterly Journal of Economics*, vol. 91, pp.425–43.

Linder, S. (1970) *The Harried Leisure Class*, New York: Columbia University Press.

Lutz, M. (1999) *Economics for the Common Good. Two Centuries of Social Economic Thought in the Humanistic Tradition*, London: Routledge.

Lutz, M. and Lux, K. (1979) *The Challenge of Humanistic Economics*, Redwood City, CA: Benjamin/Cummings Publishing Company.

McCulloch, J.R. (1849) *The Principles of Political Economy*, 4th edn, Edinburgh: W. Blackwood.

McNulty, P. (1973) 'Hoxie's Economics in Retrospect: The Making and Unmaking of a Veblenian', *History of Political Economy*, vol. 5, pp.449–84.

—— (1980) *The Origins and Development of Labor Economics: A Chapter in the History of Social Thought*, Cambridge, MA: MIT Press.

Magnusson, L. (1994) *Mercantilism: The Shaping of an Economic Language*, London: Routledge.

Malthus, T.R. (1926) *An Essay on the Principle of Population*, London: Macmillan.

Marshall, A. (1910) *Principles of Economics*, 6th edn, London: Macmillan.

—— (1966a) 'The Future of the Working Classes', in A. Pigou (ed.) *Memorials of Alfred Marshall*, New York: Augustus Kelley, pp.101–18.

—— (1966b) 'Cooperation', in A. Pigou (ed.) *Memorials of Alfred Marshall*, New York: Augustus Kelley, pp.227–55.

—— (1966c) 'The Social Possibilities of Economic Chivalry', in A. Pigou (ed.) *Memorials of Alfred Marshall*, New York: Augustus Kelley, pp.323–46.

Marshall, M. (1998) 'Scottish Economic Thought and the High Wage Economy: Hume, Smith and McCulloch on Wages and Work Motivation', *Scottish Journal of Political Economy*, vol. 45, no. 3, pp.309–28.

Marx, K. (1968) 'Wage Labour and Capital', in *Marx/Engels. Selected Works in One Volume*, London: Lawrence and Wishart, pp.71–93.

—— (1969) *Theories of Surplus Value*, part 1, London: Lawrence and Wishart.

—— (1972) *Theories of Surplus Value*, part 3, London: Lawrence and Wishart.

—— (1973) *Grundrisse*, Harmondsworth: Penguin.

—— (1975a) 'Comments on James Mill', in *Marx and Engels: Collected Works*, vol. 3, London: Lawrence and Wishart, pp.211–28.

—— (1975b) *The Poverty of Philosophy*, Moscow: Progress Publishers.

—— (1976) *Capital*, vol. 1, trans. Ben Fowkes, London: Penguin.

—— (1977) *Economic and Philosophic Manuscripts*, London: Lawrence and Wishart.

—— (1978) 'Critique of the Gotha Plan', in R. Tucker (ed.) *The Marx–Engels Reader*, 2nd edn, New York: Norton, pp.523–41.

—— (1992) *Capital*, vol. 3, London: Penguin.

Marx, K and Engels, F. (1975) 'The Holy Family', in *Marx and Engels: Collected Works*, vol. 4, London: Lawrence and Wishart, pp.5–211.

—— (1976) *The German Ideology*, Moscow: Progress Publishers.

Maslow, A. (1954) *Motivation and Personality*, New York: Harper.

Matthews, R.C.O. (1990) 'Marshall and the Labour Market', in J. Whitaker (ed.) *Centenary Essays on Alfred Marshall*, Cambridge: Cambridge University Press, pp.14–43.

Mazur Thomson, E. (1999) 'Thorstein Veblen at the University of Chicago and the Socialization of Aesthetics', *Design Issues*, vol. 15, no. 1, pp.3–15.

Medearis, J. (2005) 'Labor, Democracy, Utility, and Mill's Critique of Private Property', *American Journal of Political Science*, vol. 49, no. 1, pp.135–49.

Mill, J.S. (1965) *Principles of Political Economy with some of their Applications to Social Philosophy*, in J. Robson (ed.) *Collected Works of John Stuart Mill*, vols 2 and 3, Toronto: University of Toronto Press.

—— (1984a) 'The Negro Question', in J. Robson (ed.) *Collected Works of John Stuart Mill: Essays on Equality, Law and Education*, vol. 11, Toronto: University of Toronto Press, pp.85–95.

—— (1984b) 'The Slave Power', in J. Robson (ed.) *Collected Works of John Stuart Mill: Essays on Equality, Law and Education*, vol. 11, Toronto: University of Toronto Press, pp.144–64.

Morris, W. (1915a) 'Art under Plutocracy', in *The Collected Works of William Morris*, vol. 23, London: Longmans Green, pp.164–91.
—— (1915b) 'Useful Work versus Useless Toil', in *The Collected Works of William Morris*, vol. 23, London: Longmans Green, pp.98–120.
—— (1915c) 'How We Live and How We Might Live', in *The Collected Works of William Morris*, vol. 23, London: Longmans Green, pp.3–26.
—— (1915d) 'The Hopes of Civilisation', in *The Collected Works of William Morris*, vol. 23, London: Longmans Green, pp.59–80.
—— (1915e) 'How I became a Socialist', in *The Collected Works of William Morris*, vol. 23, London: Longmans Green, pp.277–81.
Mortimer, T. (1772) *The Elements of Commerce, Politics and Finances*, London: n.p.
Mun, T. (1664) *English Treasure by Foreign Trade*, London: n.p.
Neilson, W. (2006) *Personnel Economics*, London: Prentice Hall.
Nyland, C. (1986) 'Capitalism and the History of Work-time Thought', *British Journal of Sociology*, vol. 37, no. 4, pp.513–34.
—— (1996) 'Taylorism, John R. Commons, and the Hoxie Report', *Journal of Economic Issues*, vol. 30, no. 4, pp.985–1016.
O'Brien, D.P. (1970) *J. R. McCulloch: A Study in Classical Economics*, London: Allen and Unwin.
O'Connor, J. (1961) 'Smith and Marshall on the Individual's Supply of Labour', *Industrial and Labor Relations Review*, vol. 14, pp.273–76.
Oswald, A. (1997) 'Happiness and Economic Performance', *Economic Journal*, vol. 107, pp.1815–31.
Owen, R. (1991) *A New View of Society and Other Writings*, London: Penguin.
Pagano, U. (1985) *Work and Welfare in Economic Theory*, Oxford: Blackwell.
Pagano, U. and Rowthorn, R. (eds) (1996) *Democracy and Efficiency in the Economic Enterprise*, London: Routledge.
Parsons, T. (1931) 'Wants and Activities in Marshall', *Quarterly Journal of Economics*, vol. 46, pp.101–40.
Perelman, M. (2000) *Transcending the Economy: On the Potential of Passionate Labor and the Wastes of the Market*, New York: St. Martin's Press.
Persky, J. (1990) 'A Dismal Romantic', *Journal of Economic Perspectives*, vol. 4, no. 4, pp.165–72.
Phelps Brown, H. (1962) *The Economics of Labor*, New Haven, CT: Yale University Press.
Philp, B. (2001) 'Marxism, Neoclassical Economics and the Length of the Working Day', *Review of Political Economy*, vol. 13, pp.27–39.
Postlethwayt, M. (1759) *Britain's Commercial Interest Explained and Improved*, London: n.p.
—— (1774) *The Universal Dictionary of Trade and Commerce*, 4th edn, London: n.p.
Ricardo, D. (1955) *Works of David Ricardo*, in P. Sraffa (ed.) *Principles of Political Economy and Taxation*, vol. 1, Cambridge: Cambridge University Press.
Robbins, L. (1930a) 'On a Certain Ambiguity in the Conception of Stationary Equilibrium', *Economic Journal*, vol. 40, pp.194–214.
—— (1930b) 'On the Elasticity of Demand for Income in Terms of Effort', *Economica*, vol. 10, pp.123–9.
—— (1932) *An Essay on the Nature and Significance of Economic Science*, London: Macmillan.
—— (1953) *The Theory of Economic Policy in English Classical Political Economy*, London: Macmillan.

Rojek, C. (1995) 'Veblen, Leisure and Human Need', *Leisure Studies*, vol. 14, no. 2, pp.73–86.

Rosen, S. (1974) 'Hedonic Prices and Implicit Markets: Product Differentiation in Pure Competition', *Journal of Political Economy*, vol. 82, pp.34–55.

Rosenberg, N. (1960) 'Some Institutional Aspects of the *Wealth of Nations*', *Journal of Political Economy*, vol. 68, no. 6, pp.557–70.

—— (1965) 'Adam Smith on the Division of Labour: Two Views or One?', *Economica*, vol. 32, pp.127–39.

Rothschild, K. (1954) *The Theory of Wages*, Oxford: Blackwell.

Rotwein, E. (ed.) (1955) *David Hume. Writings on Economics*, Edinburgh: Nelson.

Ruskin, J. (1904a) *Pre-Raphaelitism*, in E.T. Cook and A. Wedderburn (eds) *The Works of John Ruskin*, vol. 12, London: George Allen, pp.338–93.

—— (1904b) *The Stones of Venice*, vol. 2, in E.T. Cook and A. Wedderburn (eds) *The Works of John Ruskin*, vol. 10, London: George Allen, pp.3–439.

—— (1905) *Unto this last*, in E.T. Cook and A. Wedderburn (eds) *The Works of John Ruskin*, vol. 17, London: George Allen, pp.5–114.

Rutherford, M. (1998) 'Veblen's Evolutionary Programme: A Promise Unfulfilled', *Cambridge Journal of Economics*, vol. 22, no. 4, pp.463–77.

Sahlins, M. (1974) *Stone Age Economics*, London: Tavistock Publications.

Saint-Simon, H. (1975) *Henri Saint-Simon: Selected Writings on Science, Industry and Social Organisation*, trans. and ed. K. Taylor, London: Croom Helm.

Samuels, W. (1994) 'On "Shirking" and "Business Sabotage": A Note', *Journal of Economic Issues*, vol. 38, pp.1249–55.

Sayers, S. (2003) 'Creative Activity and Alienation in Hegel and Marx', *Historical Materialism*, vol. 11, no. 1, pp.107–28.

—— (2005) 'Why Work? Marxism and Human Nature', *Science and Society*, vol. 69, no. 4, pp.606–16.

Schor, J. (1993) *The Overworked American: The Unexpected Decline of Leisure*, New York: Basic Books.

Schumpeter, J. (1954) *History of Economic Analysis*, London: Allen and Unwin.

Sen, A. (1999) *Development as Freedom*, New York: Knopf.

Senior, N. (1837) *Letters on the Factory Act*, London: B. Fellowes.

Sennett, R. (2008) *The Craftsman*, London: Allen Lane.

Shapiro, C. and Stiglitz, J. (1984) 'Equilibrium Unemployment as a Worker Discipline Device', *American Economic Review*, vol. 74, pp.433–44.

Simon, H. (1951) 'A Formal Theory of the Employment Relationship', *Econometrica*, vol. 19, no. 3, pp.293–305.

Smith, A. (1976a) *The Theory of Moral Sentiments*, ed. D. Raphael and A. MacFie, Oxford: Clarendon Press.

—— (1976b) *An Inquiry into the Nature and Causes of the Wealth of Nations*, ed. R. H. Campbell and A.S. Skinner, 2 vols, Oxford: Clarendon Press.

Spear, J. (1984) *Dreams of an English Eden: Ruskin and His Tradition in Social Criticism*, New York: Columbia University Press.

Spencer, D.A. (2000a) 'Braverman and the Contribution of Labour Process Analysis to the Critique of Capitalist Production – Twenty- Five Years On', *Work Employment and Society*, vol. 14, no. 2, pp.223–43.

—— (2000b) 'The Demise of Radical Political Economics? An Essay on the Evolution of a Theory of Capitalist Production', *Cambridge Journal of Economics*, vol. 24, no. 5, pp.543–64.

—— (2002) 'Shirking the Issue? Efficiency Wages, Work Discipline, and Full Employment', *Review of Political Economy*, vol. 14, no. 3, pp.313–27.

—— (2003a) 'Love's Labour's Lost? The Disutility of Work and Work Avoidance in the Economic Analysis of Labour Supply', *Review of Social Economy*, vol. 61, no. 2, pp.235–60.

—— (2003b) 'The Labour-less Labour Supply Model in the Era Before Phillip Wicksteed', *Journal of the History of Economic Thought*, vol. 25, no. 4, pp.505–13.

—— (2004a) 'Deconstructing the Labour Supply Curve', *Metroeconomica*, vol. 55, no. 4, pp.442–58.

—— (2004b) 'From Pain Cost to Opportunity Cost: The Eclipse of the Quality of Work as a Factor in Economic Theory', *History of Political Economy*, vol. 36, no. 2, pp.387–401.

—— (2005a) 'A Question of Incentive? Lionel Robbins and Dennis H. Robertson on the Nature and Determinants of the Supply of Labour', *European Journal of the History of Economic Thought*, vol. 12, no. 2, pp.261–78.

—— (2005b) 'Rejoinder on Laurent Derobert's "The Labor-less Labor Supply Model: A Little Further"', *Journal of the History of Economic Thought*, vol. 27, pp.105–6.

—— (2006) 'Work for all those who want it? Why the Neoclassical Labour Supply Curve is an Inappropriate Foundation for the Theory of Employment and Unemployment', *Cambridge Journal of Economics*, vol. 30, no. 3, pp.459–72.

Thomas, K. (1964) 'Work and Leisure', *Past and Present*, no. 29, pp.50–66.

—— (1999) *The Oxford Book of Work*, Oxford: Oxford University Press.

Thompson, E.P. (1967) 'Time, Work-discipline, and Industrial Capitalism', *Past and Present*, no. 38, pp.56–97.

—— (1976) *William Morris: Romantic to Revolutionary*, New York: Pantheon.

Thornton, W. (1846) *Over-Population and Its Remedy*, London: n.p.

Tilman, R. (1999) 'The Frankfurt School and the Problem of Social Rationality in Thorstein Veblen', *History of the Human Sciences*, vol. 12, no. 1, pp.91–109.

Townshend, J. (1990) *J.A. Hobson*, Manchester: Manchester University Press.

Tucker, J. (1750) *A Brief Essay on the Advantages and Disadvantages which Respectively Attend France and Great Britain, with Regard to Trade*, 2nd edn, London: n.p.

Varul, M. (2006) 'Waste, Industry and Romantic Leisure: Veblen's Theory of Recognition', *European Journal of Social Theory*, vol. 9, pp.103–17.

Veblen, T. (1898a) 'Why Economics is not an Evolutionary Science?', *Quarterly Journal of Economics*, vol. 12, pp.373–426.

—— (1898b) 'The Instinct of Workmanship and the Irksomeness of Labor', *American Journal of Sociology*, vol. 4, pp.187–201.

—— (1902) 'Arts and Crafts', *Journal of Political Economy*, vol. 11, no. 11, pp.108–11.

—— (1904) *The Theory of the Business Enterprise*, New York: Schribner.

—— (1914) *The Instinct of Workmanship and the State of the Industrial Arts*, New York: MacMillan.

—— (1994) *The Theory of the Leisure Class*, New York: Dover.

Walras, L. (1977) *Element of Pure Economics, or The Theory of Social Wealth*, trans. W. Jaffé, Fairfield, NJ: Augustus M. Kelley.

Walters, S. (2005) 'Making the Best of a Bad Job? Female Part-Timers' Orientations and Attitudes to Work', *Gender, Work and Organization*, vol. 12, pp.193–216.

Webb, R.K. (1955) *The British Working Class Reader*, London: Allen and Unwin.

Wenzler, J. (1998) 'The Metaphysics of Business: Thorstein Veblen', *International Journal of Politics, Culture, and Society*, vol. 11, no. 4, pp.541–78.

West, E.G. (1964) 'Adam Smith's Two Views on the Division of Labour', *Economica*, vol. 31, no. 121, pp.23–32.

—— (1975) 'Adam Smith and Alienation: Wealth Increases, Man Decays?', in Andrew S. Skinner and Thomas Wilson (eds) *Essays on Adam Smith*, Oxford: Clarendon Press, pp.540–52.

—— (1996) 'Adam Smith on the Cultural Effects of Specialization: Splenetics versus Economics', *History of Political Economy*, vol. 28, no. 1, pp.81–105.

White, M. (1994a) 'Bridging the Natural and the Social: Science and Character in Jevons's Political Economy', *Economic Inquiry*, vol. 32, pp.429–44.

—— (1994b) 'The Moment of Richard Jennings: The Production of Jevons's Marginalist Economic Agent', in P. Mirowski (ed.) *Natural Images in Economic Thought: 'Markets Read in Tooth and Claw'*, Cambridge: Cambridge University Press, pp.197–230.

Wicksteed, P. (1910) *The Common Sense of Political Economy*, London: Macmillan.

Wieser, von F. (1892) 'The Theory of Value', *Annals of the American Academy of Political and Social Science*, vol. 3, pp.600–28.

Wiles, R.C. (1968) 'The Theory of Wages in Later English Mercantilism', *Economic History Review*, vol. 21, no. 1, pp.113–26.

Williamson, O. (1975) *Markets and Hierarchies*, New York: Free Press.

—— (1985) *The Economic Institutions of Capitalism*, New York: Free Press.

Winslow, T. (2005) 'Keynes's Economics: A Political Economy as Moral Science Approach to Macroeconomics and Macroeconomic Policy', paper presented at the *Research Network Alternative Macroeconomic Policies 9th Conference: Macroeconomics and Macroeconomic Policies – Alternatives to the Orthodoxy*, Berlin, 28–9 October 2005.

Wisman, J. (1989) 'Straightening out the Backward-bending Supply Curve of Labour: From Overt to Covert Compulsion and Beyond', *Review of Political Economy*, vol. 1, pp.94–112.

Young, A. (1771) *The Farmer's Tour through the East of England. Being the Register of a Journey through Various Counties of this Kingdom*, 4 vols, London: n.p.

Index

Adams, Henry Carter 147n
Alchian, Armen 121
alienation (Marxian theory) 5, 47,
  50–53, 66–67, 105, 118, 136, 140;
  Braverman's critique of mainstream
  view 61–62; ignored by economics of
  happiness theory 130
American institutional economics *see*
  institutional economics
American radical economics 67, 149n
Aristotle 141n
art, relation with work emphasised by
  Ruskin and Morris 41, 42, 43, 44
Arts and Crafts Movement 103–4
Austrian economists 5, 70, 71, 72,
  75–79, 92; role in eclipse of work in
  neoclassical economics 87–91;
  influence on Robbins 93

Baird, B. 18
Banfield, Thomas 81
Becker, Gary 109, 109–10, 110, 115
Bentham, Jeremy 22
Bible 23, 141n
Blaug, Mark 24, 25, 72
Blum, Solomon 95
Böhm-Bawerk, Eugen von 76, 77, 78
Bowles, Samuel 149n
Bowman, R. 146n
Boyer, George 121, 149n
Braverman, Harry 3; creative approach
  to Marx 60–63, 65, 67; criticism of
  Veblen 104
Breton, Robert 41
Britain: contribution to labour
  economics 149n; economy in
  eighteenth-century 14; recent
  comparisons between native and
  East European workers 150n;

welfare to work schemes 139;
  working hours 137
Brown, Henry Phelps 149n
Burawoy, Michael 65, 123–24
capital accumulation: in Braverman's
  analysis of labour process 61, 63; and
  mercantilist views on wages 11
capitalism: Carlyle's criticism regarding
  'cash-nexus' 40; and classical
  economists' labour theory 21;
  Commons's reformist view 97;
  employment relation under 123; J.S.
  Mill's critique 9, 27, 28, 29, 31; low
  job-quality as endemic to system 131,
  138; Marshall's confidence in 82, 84,
  85–86; Marxist critique of 47, 50,
  53–56, 69; Marx's concept of
  alienation under 50–53, 118, 130,
  136; Morris's critique of 44–46;
  priority of profit xviii, 138, 139;
  relationship with socialism 39, 47;
  social critics' view of detrimental
  effects 5, 32, 33, 36, 41–42, 46;
  Veblen's failure to see nature of work
  under 105, 105–6, 108; and Veblen's
  idea of pecuniary culture 101, 102,
  103; wage-labour system 130, 139

Carlyle, Thomas 1, 5, 32–33, 39–41, 79,
  143n; clash with J.S. Mill 26–27, 30,
  33, 40, 145n; influence on Marshall's
  views 145–46n; Morris's rejection of
  his idea of work 45; similarity of
  Ruskin's ideas to 41, 42, 43, 43–44,
  44
Cary, John 11
Chartism 24
Chicago University 19
Child, Josiah 12